# The Night Owl Sings

# The Night Owl Sings

## and Other Stories of Old Age

Judy McConnell

Boyle
&
Dalton

Book Design & Production:
Boyle & Dalton
www.BoyleandDalton.com

The locales and events in these stories serve as placeholders
from which to develop the plots. The ensuing material
is entirely fiction derived from imagination and exaggeration.

Hardback ISBN: 978-1-63337-779-0
Paperback ISBN: 978-1-63337-780-6
E-book ISBN: 978-1-63337-781-3

Printed in the United States of America
1 3 5 7 9 10 8 6 4 2

## Other books by Judy McConnell

*A Penny a Kiss: A Memoir*

*Just Keep Shooting: A Memoir*

*Dreamhouse: A Novel*

# Table of Contents

# Urgent Care

**AS SHE PULLED INTO THE DRIVEWAY,** Lila's pulse began to race. The yard was dancing with strings of colored lights around the windows, wind chimes ringing gaily, an artificial snowman with a long red scarf and bugle graced the front stoop. A glaring Christmas tree shone deep inside the front window. Warm sensations of years past flooded through her. She leapt from the car—not bad for an aging grandmother!—and walked eagerly up the charcoal pavers. On reaching the entry door, she turned the knob without knocking.

The minute she stepped into the house, she felt herself gripped by a flow of energy, the bustle of activity, the urgency of things to do. An electric mixer churned on one counter, low strains of sleigh bells in song streamed from a radio atop the refrigerator, a cupboard door was slammed shut, dishes rattled on the stove.

"Merry Christmas, Jayne!" Lila placed her jacket and overnight bag on the hallway bench.

"Hello dear, Merry Christmas! With you in a second."

Lila stood smiling, waiting to break in. "Can I help?"

The figure at the stove briskly stirring a sauté pant called over her shoulder, "No, I have everything under control, thanks." The kitchen sparkled. Even in the midst of apparent chaos, Jayne had everything running smoothly. Head of the advertising department at Swain Riggs, Lila could tell her daughter-in-law knew exactly what she was doing at all times. That included caring for Todd and their two children, cooking meals on her assigned day—she and Todd alternated duties—maintaining her share of the household, and co-hosting parties. They appeared to be a smoothly working pair, Jayne and Todd.

Lila felt superfluous. Her job was to be an accommodating guest and enjoy the activities as they presented themselves. It was understandable that Jayne wouldn't want to mess with parceling out cut-off jobs, having to explain, realign things. Lila would have preferred to pitch in, but she didn't argue. After all, she was family, no need to fuss, it was enough to know that she belonged, that she was an *insider.*

"It's so lovely here. You have done wonders with the house, Jayne." Lila, feeling warmth toward this important person in her family circle, thought it appropriate to pay compliments where compliments were due.

"Glad you like it," Jayne responded as she swirled the wooden spoon around and around. Clearly, the pot of vegetables needed her concentration. Jayne's small figure stood upright and commanding over the stove, her navy tights and long-sleeved striped sweater clean and fresh, every blonde hair on her head neatly combed into place.

Lila thought she'd go find Jeffer and Blake. She adored her grandchildren, and the fact that she'd seen less and less of them as they grew out of babyhood rendered her somewhat out of touch. Difficult to figure what they'd like, how to keep them engrossed.

"What can I do to amuse the children?" Lila stood at the doorway, uncertain.

"Whatever you like," Jayne replied, screwing the top on a garlic powder can and replacing it in the cupboard. She wiped her hands briskly on her crisp red-and-white checked apron. "I'm glad you're here, Lila. It's so good to see you." She turned with a broad smile.

Really, she was at heart a kind person, Lila thought. She might be elusive, always withdrew with a gracious smile as she buttoned up the kids and bustled them away. It was only natural for a wife to instinctively proceed to wrestle control from the lifelong caretaker she had replaced. Lila must make sure she didn't intrude—Todd had his own family now.

"Make yourself at home." Jayne pulled out a cutting board and began slicing potatoes and arranging them in a long crockery dish.

"Are your eyes any better, Jayne?"

"We'll see. I've an appointment with the optometrist next week."

"Oh, that's right by my house," Lila said. "Why don't you stop and see my new paintings? I have three new watercolors that I'm submitting to the art and design competition."

"I might have to work overtime that day, I'll have to see."

"Okay, fine." The grinding of the garbage disposal as Jayne swirled a sponge around the sink made further conversation impossible.

*Oh my gosh!* Lila realized she'd left Jeffer's birthday present in the car—better dash out and fetch it. She'd hide it until after the presents under the Christmas tree were opened tomorrow morning. Jeffer's birthday had been on December 15. She'd wanted to drive over with it on his birthday, but Jayne had advised her to drop the children's birthday presents in the mail. "Such a long drive for you. We'd love to see you, but with so much going on, planning is impossible until the last minute. I'm sure you know how it is."

Indeed yes, Lila got it, and she could visualize herself in Jayne and Todd's shoes. One has compassion for one's children, one understands, one forgives. That's what mothers do.

When Lila returned with the present under her arm and entered the sunken living room, it was empty. Where was everyone? Then she recalled: Todd had taken the kids to pick up Christmas pies at Honey & Rye, where during Christmas week they gave out free honey-bear cookies. Jayne had assured her they'd be back soon.

She sat on the piano bench and looked around the living room. Four gigantic, embroidered Christmas stockings hung from the granite fireplace in one corner. Facing the windows, a ten-foot-high spruce was coiled with strings of color, and miniature candy canes lined up like tin soldiers along the sweeping branches. Todd and Jayne had put love, labor, and money into this modern house set in the heart of the outer suburbs. A charming room decorated with cubist prints, modern oak and bronze shelving, and a soft beige wraparound couch. The Christmas tree lights blinking on and off added to the warmth of the room, a room that pulsed with human presence, radiating cheer and optimism.

She would spend the night. They would empty the stockings after dinner, but the presents would wait until tomorrow morning—Christmas day! She experienced a taste of heaven just being in the room, surrounded by the aroma of pine, cherry, and cinnamon. Here Lila felt secure and happy.

Her reveries were interrupted by a door slam, the clump of feet up the stairs. Todd burst into the living room, bare-necked, parka open, laughing. He rushed up, clasped her in a hug. "You look great, Mom. Let me get you an eggnog." Tall and energetic like his wife, the two of them could activate a room just by breathing. Jeffer and Blake scrambled in behind him, excitedly clutching bags of holiday treats, followed closely by Bruno, who wiggled between them, tail pumping.

Jeffer ran into the kitchen screaming, "Pie time, pie time!" but his mother swept the pastries away and tucked them safely on a shelf.

"After dinner. Go wash up."

Jeffer reappeared. "I guess I'll skip dinner."

"Come here and say hello to Grandma," Todd admonished. The two children flashed quick self-conscious smiles. Hello. Hello. Then eight-year-old Jeffer scampered out, little feet padding up the stairs to his room, shadowed by his little brother, Blake.

Todd disappeared into the basement to fetch spare bulbs for the miniature tree in the sunroom. He never stopped. Always busy, this family. Lila found few openings in which to wiggle her sparce presence.

Her last phone call to Todd to arrange for a New Year's dinner at

Lord Fletcher's sealed her apprehensions. "What do you mean, you're busy for the foreseeable future?"

Todd's voice, impatient: "Mom, you have to understand. I have an active family. We're tied to schedules and schoolwork. Things are super crazy at work. We have no time."

"But surely you can take off one night, any night…"

"You have to quit bugging me! We can't always spend time with you. Why can't you understand that we lead a busy life? Maybe you should get a life yourself and not expect Jayne and me to fill your needs."

She managed to curtail her disappointment. "Of course. I understand." *I understand*, her mantra. She couldn't know the challenges of their lives, which played out in happenings far beyond her single vision.

"I'll have to check the kids' schedules." Todd's voice had been laden with doubt. "Oops, here's Jayne. Got to run. Goodbye, Mother." Her cell phone went dark.

Drawing her thoughts back to the present, she snuck into the bedroom closet and slid Jeffer's birthday box onto a top shelf, determined to banish such memories. It was Christmas, and she was with her family, which was all that mattered.

Returning to the living room, she depressed a piano key, a second key, a third key—C, D, E—the notes vibrated through the empty living room like a bellbird call. A voice from the kitchen: Would she summon the boys for dinner?

She mounted the stairs and stepped hesitantly into the children's room, taking in the smell of fresh laundry and mineral oil. Jeffer, wearing a shirt with a horse on the front that read *TAKE YOUR LIFE BY THE REINS*, crouched by the bed. He was fingering through a splay of toy cars and miniature tin animals, his nose squeezed like a prune, the way it did when he was trying to puzzle something out. Blake was tipping a bubblegum machine this way and that, trying to dislodge its contents. Overhead, large yellow butterflies dangled from a pendant light. Lila stood for a moment, absorbing the sense of childhood and play and innocence that was tantalizingly familiar. So long ago, so out of reach.

Lila was proud of her grandchildren. Jeffer was such a beautiful child, with his crown of dark curls and bouncy laugh, so transparent, his thoughts and feelings always on the surface. And Blake so eager, so serious, looking around with his sweet smile. How she longed to grasp them in her arms!

Before she could speak, Jayne's voice shot up the stairs, "Dinner! Now!"

The table brimmed with steaming dishes and chatter. Between swallows of candied sweet potatoes, Jeffer remarked on everything that came into his head. His parents praised his singing, songs he learned from listening by the hour to Radio Heartland. He knew the words to the song "Playmate" by heart, all eight verses, but when Lila asked him to sing it, he claimed he was busy eating his dinner right then. Blake bent over his plate, absorbed in cutting every bit of fat off the slice of turkey leg.

After dinner, Lila, stuffed with pumpkin and banana cream pie—a sliver of each— strolled into the living room and leaned back in the oversized brocade chair. She could hear Todd and Jayne in the kitchen, dishes clanging, water running, scuffling, random voices. No, no room in the kitchen for help, thanks. The children scurried over to the bulge of brightly wrapped presents piled under the tree and began squeezing them eagerly.

"It won't be long," Lila told the boys. "When the dishes are done, you children can each empty your stockings and open one present."

"I can guess what's in all of them," Jeffer exclaimed as he poked one package after another, trying to determine which would be The One. Lila smiled at Blake as he seated himself on the padded stool, legs dangling above the floor.

"Grandma, why do you have brown spots on your face?" Legs kicked against the stool.

"I'm old. When you get old, it just happens."

"Can't you get rid of them?"

"No one has figured out a way to do that, honey." She laughed. "Come here, you little dickens." She reached out to hug him, but Blake peered at her shyly and then darted away and trundled down the steps to the garage.

Why was he so shy with her? She wished she knew him better, but one-on-ones with him were rare. Maybe there was good reason. Maybe Todd and Jayne worried about her driving at age seventy-eight; maybe Todd was concerned by her lack of parental skills; maybe Jayne resisted her ingrained dictatorial attitude as mother-of-old; maybe she found Lila unpliable—Lila found it hard to swallow her opinions. Could she bring dinner on her next visit? No, Jayne had everything under control. Busy taking care of things while Lila and Todd conversed on the cream sofas in the living room.

Although during their courtship Jayne had been sweet and deferential, once married, she ruled with steel competency. Nothing happened that didn't meet with Jayne's approval. Lila understood that each stage of one's lifespan required adaptation. She would adapt.

"In my day," she once explained to Todd, "children were given the support of discipline and authority. Families bonded in the outdoors. Now children are glued to their electronic devices. Experiences must be fast, explosive, exciting. As for taking on character-building chores, no more of that. They're praised to the sky for every step they take, declared winners of everything they do."

"You're probably right." Todd shrugged. "But that's the way things are today."

Noises in the hall brought her back to the present, and the family traipsed in and settled in front of the fireplace. They all watched as Todd lit the logs, which caught and spit up orange flames that warmed their faces. Unable to sit still another minute, the boys each jumped up and grabbed the stocking with their name on it and flung themselves on the carpet, while Bruno watched despondently from under the piano bench where he'd been banished to contain his excited antics. Squealing, Jeffer thrust his hand in the throat of the stocking and pulled out one by one: Santa knee-highs, a set of colored marbles for the fish tank, a gold whistle on a chain, four pairs of angora socks, and a Mickey Mouse watch—his hand reaching over and over down a bottomless hole. Blake dumped his loot in a pile between his legs, popping a cherry lollipop into his mouth.

Lila marveled as an entire department store emerged, the children squealing with excitement. She thought of the old days, when her stocking would have yielded yo-yos, jacks, hair clips, a fancy comb, a candy cane, an orange, a pair of socks. Definitely, she was antiquated!

Sitting back in the oversized chair, Lila succumbed to a warm glow—the mellow light of candles flickering on the shelf, the whiffs of evergreen and burning wood, the purring of the fire, and above all the sweet voices of Jeffer and Blake, opening, exclaiming, testing. Outside in the darkness, the quiet snow, the windless trees sleeping in pure stillness, peaceful in contrast to the vitality unreeling inside.

Lila experienced a melancholy surge of happiness. It felt as if all the sharing and fun and belonging threading through her entire life had been resurrected. She felt alive.

Bedtime.

"I'm too excited to sleep. I'll stay up all night and wait," Blake cried.

"But Santa won't come until you're asleep," Jeffer exclaimed, squeezing his face into a grimace.

"How about I tuck them in?" Lila suggested. "I can read to them. I brought a wonderful children's book, *Harry and Lulu*.

Jayne was kneeling on the floor, picking up scraps and stuffing them in a plastic garbage bag. "They're not used to others putting them to bed." Blake backed toward the stairs, looking skeptical. "Blake is very shy," she said. "Maybe not such a good idea."

Lila sought Todd's eye as he refastened the empty stockings on the mantelpiece, but he remained turned away.

"Good night, dears," she cried. The two boys waved over their shoulders at her as they bobbed up the stairs. She watched their little figures, Jeffer swinging his arms, Blake bouncing from step to step, the cowlick on the crown of his head sticking straight into the air. How lucky she was to have such grandchildren. How she missed them.

Lila picked up the glass of Irish cream Todd had given her and headed for the lower bedroom. She knew Todd and Jayne had to prepare for Santa's visit: last minute gifts, including a cookie plate with Santa's leftover crumbs and a bright red tricycle. She was determined not to be in the way, not to be a worry.

The stairway to the walkout level was steep. Lila descended one step at a time into a black pool of darkness, grasping the railing like a lifeline as she moved slowly into the bowels of the house. She'd better find the switch—where the devil was it? Reaching the bottom she swiped her hand along the wall and clicked on the overhead light, which gave out a dull glow as she moved slowly to the bedroom door. Groping her way inside, she felt the chair, the chest of drawers, the bed; finally she reached the table lamp, and the bedroom came to light. Leaving the door ajar she slowly draped her clothes over the armchair, pulled her nightgown from her overnight case and slipped it over her head. It seemed to take her a long time to get undressed, to brush her teeth, wash her face, go to the bathroom. Everything seemed to take longer now that she was seventy-eight, which she considered to be comfortably old. Eighty, just around the corner, was ancient.

As she sat on the bed, the space around her appeared to have shrunk. The low ceiling's black molding curved above in the shadows, and the square windowpane with rigid edges blocked the outside darkness like a steel door. Not a thing stirred in the yard or the encircling woods outside. She listened for living inside noises—groans from the furnace, flushing of water, openings or closings of doors—nothing. Dead still here in her cave. She took a series of deep breaths and assured herself that the house above her was alive and pulsing.

Sliding under the covers, she burrowed her cheek into the pillow. Her mind flashed to the family camping trips with Dan, before he left them without warning thirty-six years ago with his chesty young ingenue. They would sing together in the tent, Todd squeezed between them, "Shine on Harvest Moon." She hummed it now, feeling the warm pillow against her skin, the covers tucked around her shoulders. Between "June" and "July" she fell asleep.

**SHE AWOKE IN A STUPOR.** Where was she? When she opened the curtains, a spray of light hurled in and spread over the furniture, over the bed. Blinded, she crawled back under the covers. No clock, her watch on the bathroom counter. Heavy with sleep, she sank back into the pillow. *Wake up*, she murmured, then remembered—it was Christmas! My gosh. Blurred with sleep she rose, dressed more quickly than usual, and combed her hair. When she opened the door to the family room, the glaring light from a high sun gushed in, half blinding her. It must be late! She crossed and made her way slowly up the stairs. The house was strangely quiet. Bruno leapt up and trotted to meet her at the top, tail swishing, and she scratched his head, smiling at the red bell jingling at his collar.

The kitchen was empty. On to the living room: empty, the tree unplugged, ashes simmering in the fireplace, the room picked up, unoccupied. The windows had become living art, framing the snow scenes beyond—the yard carpeted with white mounds extending to the edge of the woods, branches drooping with snow powder, a forest of albino tree statues, impenetrable.

And then it struck her. It couldn't be. She stared at the bare red skirt flared around the base of the Christmas tree, a necklace of shiny velvet. The mound of presents was gone.

She hurried out to the garage. Todd's van, gone. She was alone in the house. Impossible. There was Bruno, looking up at her as if awaiting instructions. Her mind clicked into gear. Someone had been hurt, a dash to the hospital—but no, the place would have been left in the midst of something, not everything neatly in place like this. Searching, no note. No message on her iPhone. They had gone out for ice cream—no, nothing open on Christmas day. Possibly they had gone to visit one of Jayne's two siblings, whom they often visited on holidays.

How could she have slept so long? She wandered through the house, the kitchen spotless, still hinting of cornbread and roasted nuts, the living room still resonating with music and light, the bathroom with its odor of cherry aerosol. Remnants of interlinked lives.

She climbed to the bedrooms on the second floor. Deserted. She couldn't figure it; nothing made sense. The boys' room hummed with the residue of human presence, remains of cries and laughter. She looked around; there piled on a maple desk were the Christmas gifts stacked half-way up the wall. So they had opened their presents, had proceeded with Christmas without her!

It was unimaginable.

Her eyes lit on the nightstand: 1:00. Afternoon! How could that be? Why didn't they wake her? At Jeffer's last birthday she phoned that she'd be there in a jiffy, but when she arrived, they had already started the cere-mony. Todd made it clear that her needs were not a priority, that the kids came first. Of course they did, naturally.

If she had been abandoned like this, left in an empty house, there must have been circumstances beyond her knowledge. Something must have come up that morning for which there was a perfectly good explanation.

She looked around. The shelves held neatly stacked books; a sweat-shirt hung over the desk chair; a bulletin board with animal drawings, clippings, and some four-by-six photos. No sign of the spaceship piggy bank from Schwarz or the African lion pillow she'd purchased in Tanzania.

The living essence of family life that hung in every room of the house contained not a hint of her, Lila.

Of course, this wasn't her house; it held another family's tastes and dreams. She had let her expectations run away with her. Their family led a full life, and she was happy for that. They wouldn't have left this morning for no reason, had no doubt slipped out to see Jayne's beloved brother. She could understand.

And then she couldn't.

Not this time. Not like this.

The full impact of her aloneness hit her. She had to do something, but what? She took out her cell phone. No message. Wiped off the face of the earth.

A pain began to well up in the pit of her stomach. She'd been negated, eradicated by those she held dear. On Christmas day, the biggest holiday of the year, an entire day when she felt a sense of belonging, connected to ties that stretched back to the beginning. What was going on? Feeling faint, she sank onto the bed.

Casting her eyes out the bedroom window, she was confronted by the life-sized reindeer poised under the apple tree, reminiscent of Christmases past, full of acceptance and love, with conflicts drowned by joyfulness and song for a single day. All that crumbled, washed away. Cold shivers beat against her heart. The air had dried up, and she couldn't breathe. She stretched out on her back and waited for her mind to clear.

After some time she got up, walked down the hall, and peeked into the master bedroom. Clean and airy, presents stacked up on a cedar chest, bed freshly made. One thing stood out: She noticed the lid to the drop-lid desk was open, covered with a chrome letter holder, neatly stacked bills, and a container of pens. One of the drawers had a brass keyhole, a large iron key protruding from it. Curiosity drew her over. Todd, so secretive, this must be where he hid away—well, she couldn't imagine what. Impulsively, she pulled on the knob and the drawer opened.

The letter on top caught her eye. *Todd* written in large script—she recognized her own handwriting. With trembling fingers she grasped the envelope and withdrew a frayed letter, a letter she had written years ago, after Dan had gone.

It all came back to her. After an angry tirade from Dan, Todd would run off and hide in the swamp behind the hill, returning only the next morning after Dan had left for work. The screaming fights as Todd grew into adolescence, until the neighbor complained and Dan lowered his outbursts to a low, threatening pitch. The years when Todd hardly came home, running around with his teenage friends, uncommunicative, resistant.

On her own, it was up to her to take a stand. Her letter, trying to reach him. She read it trembling.

*Todd, you are behaving badly, and it has to stop. If you don't change your ways your life will go downhill, and things will end badly. You must keep me informed of your whereabouts. You must follow my house rules. I have neither the time nor the facility for this constant rebellion. If you want to continue to live under our family roof, you must learn to respect my authority as your parent.*

There was more.

Todd had complied with none of this, wanted to be left alone. After several years of nowhere jobs, collecting old tires, flipping hamburgers, and cleaning vats at a grain elevator, he enrolled at the university and managed to straighten himself around. Then marriage, children, and a gradual return to normalcy, and they became a family again. A family, she discovered, with a twist.

She collapsed on the bed, feeling the blood drain from her head, her hands cold against her chest. She stood accused. The extent of her past offenses blared through her, the strict, accusing admonitions frozen in time, unalterable.

Tears gathered on her cheeks as she faced her helplessness to redo the past. She subdued an urge to rip the letter out of existence and carefully slipped it back in the drawer.

She recalled the troubles young Todd had to face when left to his own devices as she pursued her legal career. She hadn't been there for him. He had become more and more elusive and defiant. Her increasing attempts to control, narrowing the rules, increasing the punishments, had not turned him around. Yet he had plunged ahead, floundered, and managed to turn out well, all on his own.

Downstairs the house felt empty, as if the air and its rich chemistry had been sucked away. A cup of coffee was in order. As she plugged in the Keurig brewer, she repressed an urge to call them. Maybe she should wait. She had made it a point, in her grandmother role, not to interfere or be a burden. She had forfeited her rights. But as she looked around at the emptiness, something surged within her. This was wrong. Things had gone too far. She had to act. It was time to take a stand.

She had to—to regroup, to break out where she could breathe. She was startled by something moist against her ankle, a soft nudge. Bending over, she grasped Bruno on each side of his muzzle and rubbed his head against her cheek. The German shepherd licked her face, tail swaying gently.

Good old Bruno! She felt his warmth flow through her. She went to the window and whipped open the drapes. The light, reflecting the snowy brightness outside, hurled through the window and washed over the room.

"It's you and me, Bruno!" She felt her strength gathering, and a flash of inspiration pulled her upright. "Okay, buddy, you and I are going to have an adventure. There's a bright new world out there. We're going for a walk."

As if he understood, Bruno leapt up, whimpering eagerly. Lila laughed. "Come." A command learned when she had taken the family dog to obedience school and was taught to use clear, curt commands: Come.

Stay. Sit. Down. Brief and effective. She tried it out on young Todd: Bed. Eat. Dress. Quiet. He did not find it cute.

She descended to the family room, Bruno's bouncy footsteps padding after her. Suddenly, quick as lightning, her foot flew in the air, her hand slipped from the rail, and she tumbled to the bottom and lay in a heap, feet twisted under her, a sharp pain coursing up the back of her head. After a few minutes, she slowly pulled herself up. Her head pounded, and turning, she located the culprit—the iron gate leading to the garage, fresh blood on the sharp edge.

She sucked in a deep breath, hoping to quell the dizzying rotation in her head. She shook her limbs. They seemed to be intact. The pain at the back of her skull was increasing; her fingers reached back and landed in a hot oozing wound. When she twisted her hand in front of her, it was smeared with blood. She felt again, her fingers probing a deep hole, bleeding profusely now.

Bruno watched as she pulled herself up, staggered to the bathroom and rifled through the medicine cabinet. Using a mirror, she gingerly stuffed the hole with cotton pads and secured it with strips of surgical tape. It will be fine for now, she thought, popping two Tylenol into her mouth. The pain beat against her skull. She would sit down on the bed for a few minutes. The skin was hot around her eyes, and she pressed them shut. Her breath fell into a quiet regularity. She drifted for several minutes into a meditative state empty of thought.

She moved her limbs gingerly. What to do? Blood had spilled over onto the bed, she had to get up and take care of it. The blood was making a mess, but by golly she was not going to worry about dirtying the fresh bedspread. She had to take care of herself. It was time to release the vise grip of the past and be true to her current existence. She needed to have her feet on the ground, to take control of things. With a sigh, she released her breath and felt the desperation and hopelessness drain slowly away. The past was solidified, done, unalterable. She couldn't let the mistakes she'd made determine her life. She would face up and get on with it.

She sat up and opened her eyes wide. They fell on a movement outside the window, the tail of a squirrel flickering over the powdery snow, snow that covered the yard with a blanket of white, gleaming with bright promise. The picture of freedom. She felt a pressing need to assert her independence. She could do this, carry on by herself; she would plunge in and be all right. She tucked her hair firmly behind her ears. The crunch in her head had diminished to a light throbbing. The hospital could wait. She had to get out, into the fresh air. She and Bruno would go outdoors and participate in the great winter production.

Going to the hallway where the coats were hanging, Lila tucked her wool cap tightly over her head, making sure the bandage was in place, and drew on her down parka and knee-high Sorel boots. Bruno brimmed with excitement as he waited impatiently for her to snap on the leash.

"Come on, buddy. Let's celebrate Christmas."

The pounding in her head had vanished, forgotten as they stepped out into a wonderland of whiteness. The snow-covered terrain lay glistening and untouched in the afternoon sun, cut only by a single set of tire tracks that led from the garage and out along the driveway before being swallowed by the contour of the land. The tree branches sagged peacefully under their snowy burden, the shed lay buried in white powder, and blankets of snow waved across the land to the west, pure, unblemished, a consummate December dreamland. Oxygen filled her lungs, bolstering her strength. She strode up the long gravel drive, breathing deeply. Bruno tugged ahead on the leash, bursting with energy.

When they reached the top of the hill, Lila began to tire. "We'd better go back before I wear out," she breathed, stopping. "Bruno, I know you're dying to get out and run. Okay, buddy, just this once before we go in." Jayne and Todd had warned her of Bruno's habit of running off, deaf to commands, requiring hours of trolling to locate. But the dog was prancing eagerly, and darn it, this was Christmas. To hell with it. Bruno needed his freedom too. She would take responsibility.

Pulling off a mitten, she bent down and unhooked the leash from his collar. With a yip of excitement, he flew off over the snow, bounding over mounds of powder up to his chin, jaws snapping mouthfuls of white fluff here and there. Once he paused to look back at her—Is this all right?—then bounded off in quick leaps, his prints creating fresh language of revelry in the white snow.

It would not do to let Bruno have all the fun! On impulse, she left the drive and high-stepped through the snow. She considered lying down and creating snow angels with her arms, but her head was beginning to throb again, and she feared she'd have trouble getting up. Still, she felt refreshed out there in the glory of winter. The cleansing snow covered the growth beneath her feet with a white gloss, highlighted the shadows between the tree branches, and curled a lightness around her toes, spurring her on, lifting her up, filling her lungs. The pain in her body didn't seem to matter. Each step she took extended a pattern in the field of unbroken snow. She looked behind her at the Rococo line of indentations she had created, as if improvised with an artistic brushstroke, and laughed.

Where was Bruno? She started forward, but his tracks disappeared into the woods, impossible to follow. She retraced her steps to the gravel drive and ambled toward the house, whistling and calling. When the dog did not appear, she brushed off a concrete bench by the side door with her mitten and sat down to wait. Her head was throbbing with a new insistence, he felt the sharp pain against her skull. She hurt. She would wait. That he would return, she had no doubt. A dog wants home and hearth. She would be patient, however long it took. Preferably before the children returned. There would be a search, with frantic phone calls and endless tramps through the snow. Her heart beat faster at the thought. But Bruno would show up; it was just a matter of time. She would stand her ground.

An hour passed. She forced herself to her feet and set out down the driveway, whistling and calling. The throbbing in her head was growing more insistent. Her ears buzzed; her whole body ached. Pulling her phone from her parka, she punched in Todd's number and waited as it transferred to voicemail. She spoke in a firm voice. "Todd, I'm hurt, and I need you to take me to urgent care. It's getting worse. Call me."

Just then she spied Bruno at the top of the hill, panting heavily, looking haughty, as if he had just rounded up a herd of wildebeest or chased off a wild leopard. Good boy!

Anticipating his reluctance to lose his freedom, she yelled his name and lay down flat in the snow. Sure enough, he soon came padding up and sniffed her ear, and she raised up and threw her arms around him, pressing his wet face against hers. Behind her a red stain of blood colored the snow. Numbed by cold and exhilaration, she became aware of the pain, remembered the hole in her head. She knew she had to take care of herself, as well as this scrappy dog.

She felt a sloppy tongue brush her cheek. "I love you, you naughty boy," she cried, wiping her face with the back of her mitten. Pulling herself up with difficulty, she snapped the leash on Bruno's collar.

"Let's go brush this snow off."

How energized she felt! She had no desire to go back inside the house to the close air and fabricated furnishings, the offshoot of a home where she had once held ascendency, those days long gone. Outdoors in the open things were different.

But she needed to collect her things. Inside the house was silent. It didn't take her long to dry off the dog, rubbing him vigorously with the towel edged in rosebuds hanging in the bathroom. Lila would take the towel home and wash it.

"How does that feel, buddy? Do you like being rubbed?" Bruno looked adoringly into her face.

She wiped the blood from her neck in front of the mirror, then stuffed fresh gauze in the still-moist wound. Bruno trotted into the hall, and she could hear the loud lapping as he drained his water dish. As she finished making the bed and stuffing her things into her overnight case, the dog poked his head in. She knelt down, took him in her arms, and squeezed him hard. Then she pulled on her coat and boots, picked up her case, and went out into the December sunshine. Immediately the crisp air roused a pink glow in her cheeks. The blue arc of the clear sky stretching above, the stark brightness of untouched snow stretching through the yard and over the hill, the crackling of creature sounds from the woods, the cries of a Canadian goose from the nearby wetlands: These brought a smile to her face.

There was one thing left to do before leaving. Going to Todd's desk, she pulled a piece of letter paper from the drawer and began to write. The words flowed easily. She knew what she wanted to say—how she had failed to protect Todd from his father's abuse, how she regretted her draconian running of the household. How she was so, so sorry. How she was doing everything in her power to be different.

She propped her letter against the desk lamp. There, her guilt exposed in black and white, stark reality staring her in the face, a tinge of relief entered her. It was not enough, but it was something.

The pain in her head could no longer be ignored. Todd had not returned her call; she would drive herself to the clinic. Coasting along the freeway she munched a powdered donut she'd stuffed in her pocket from a covered plate in the kitchen. It was crazy to worry about the children. They would call and explain. She could imagine several scenarios involving a reluctance to wake her and a desire to spare her the long stretch of present-opening and exuberant ooh-ing and ah-ing. Or a last-minute invitation to lunch at Jayne's brother's, and they would call her to join them. Or possibly an accident had sent them in panicked forgetfulness to the hospital.

There must have been a note. She had been unable to find it.

In reality, she could not know what had happened. Maybe they were doing what they had to. She no longer had to know. They would call. Or they wouldn't.

She needed help. That was clear.

She held the wheel with a tight grip. The freeway stretched straight ahead, and she followed it easily, settled in for the long journey back to her neighborhood. Mounds of fresh powder stretched alongside the freeway. The exit signs were half hidden in snow, leaving only a few letters decipherable. Cars streaked by, people joining loved ones for Christmas festivities.

Her mind sifted through the events of the past twenty-four hours. Why had Todd kept her horrid letter for all these years? Why was it right there in the drawer, on top? Had Todd shared it with Jayne—could that be why she was so distant?

But they were her beloved family, for better or worse. There could be no accounting; the truth lay hidden behind her ideas of them. The past would not change, but she could revise her perspective. For the first time, she felt up to the challenge. She had left no note at the house explaining her absence, contrary to her natural urge do everything right, to cross the t's and dot the i's so that no one would worry or be inconvenienced. The pain in her head propelled her in a different direction. It was becoming difficult to make out even the cars, with the snow flurries and grey dullness covering the road ahead of her. Pulling herself up so that she could see more clearly over the wheel, she focused her sights on the snow-sloshed road ahead.

The insistent throbbing in her head increased. Her entire skull was aching now. *You need to take care of this. You have a serious wound in your head.* Her fingers felt for the bandage, a cottony mass soaked with blood. Stitches would probably be required. She began to feel frightened. She must concentrate on the present. She knew exactly where to go. Urgent care was probably the only establishment in town open on Christmas day.

Switching on the radio, she sang along with the lyrics to "Winter Wonderland," her voice blending softly with that of the female vocalist. A favorite song since childhood, the scenes came alive, like the mounds of white glistening on the lawns, like the bells echoing from the nearby church, like the snow-topped cars parked along the curbs, bigger than life.

She drew the car into the clinic lot, past a large sign: *HEALTH MATTERS—WE CARE.*

At last.

# Uncle Basil

**WHEN UNCLE BASIL INVITED** his sister Florence and her daughter Rhyne to visit him in Maui, they started packing immediately. As co-owner of the local Greyhound Racetrack as well as county commissioner, he would get them choice seats in his box, wine and dine them at the Greyhound Club, and spread before them the hypnotic fragrances of Hawaii. Rhyne was glad to get away from New York and their luxurious apartment. Before she knew it, the three of them were seated on Uncle Basil's spacious balcony under a russet sunset, enjoying broiled lobster and artichokes ordered from the hotel dining room, surrounded by seductive ambrosial scents seeping from the garden below and the play of a soft ocean breeze.

After they had eaten their fill, Uncle Basil went inside and returned with a bottle of 1995 French Côte de Beaune Chardonnay—the best. "We must celebrate your arrival, nothing but champagne will do." With that, he poured the light-gold liquid into three stem glasses, passed out two with great dignity, and after swirling his glass, took a deep sip. "Tastes even better since I quit AA this morning," he said brightly. "Drink up, ladies."

Neither Rhyne nor Florence moved. He had earlier announced his intention to take the plunge, admit his excesses, to join AA—to no longer be pinned by the wicked prongs of alcohol.

Seeing their shocked looks, he hastened to explain. "I tried AA. When my turn came to tell my story, I complied. I confessed everything, pride be damned, and described the hardships and pressures I must deal with. I explained at great length that it would be impossible to uphold my position without the sociability of drinking, and when they finally told me to sit down and shut up, I left." With that he poured himself another glass. "I limit myself to two. That should do it."

"I don't think so, Uncle Basil," Rhyne said, her hands entwined in her lap. "You have to quit."

Uncle Basil jerked his head up. "Of course. But I have to begin somewhere."

Rhyne had a horror of alcohol. Her father Jonah had drunk himself into oblivion. The years of rage and abuse left Rhyne wounded and bitter. Upholding an airtight stance of soothing accommodation, Florence had managed to escape with minor wounds until her husband's death from a ruptured aneurysm. But now she said nothing. Neither of them dared confront Uncle Basil on his drinking.

Rhyne watched him take a swallow, his long fingers curled around the cup of his glass. His sparkling eyes, the same violet color as her own, smiled at them. She marveled at the powerful sway of his presence, with his gentlemanly, gregarious manner. Seduced by his worldly charm and amusing anecdotes, people ignored his scathing tongue. Parentless at age fifteen, Uncle Basil had created his own destiny, relying on his good looks, canny magnetism, and a suitcase full of luck. He quit Minnesota and ranged as far south as Jackson, Mississippi, where he spent nineteen years managing a posh golf club and working tirelessly as a Democratic Party leader, eventually becoming a democratic congressman. Those years burnished him with a coating of southern politesse that added to his alluring charm, although pity the fool unfortunate enough to cross his path.

"So, tell me, my girl, what is going on in the romance department?" Uncle Basil asked, wiping his brow with a white handkerchief. "Why hasn't some wayward fellow captured your heart?" For years he'd been teasing her about her boyfriends or lack thereof, chuckling at her embarrassment as she sat mute, staring at him.

"I'm fifty-two years old," she said, blushing. "My dating days are over." It irritated her that he seemed to think her happiness depended on this one thing. As if she were incomplete on her own. "You're still pretty," he kept saying, as if that gave him leave to tease her unmercifully. "If only you didn't go around looking like a washerwoman. You could at least comb your hair before you leave the house."

"Don't pester her," Florence said. "She's no spring chicken."

"Well, my dear, she's not getting any younger."

"All the more reason for her to stay home and act her age," Florence protested.

"You'd be better off if you got out more, Rhyne, instead of sitting around the house playing with those Rubik's cubes," Uncle Basil insisted.

Swallowing, Rhyne set her champagne glass on the table. "Why are we discussing this?"

"Never mind, my girl. There's someone out there for you," Uncle Basil said more kindly.

During a brief period in her youth, she flaunted her independence and changed her name legally to Rhyne. It wouldn't do to be Jane. Jane Aubrey. No! After several boys had broken through her reserve and then left her bed for a more desirable catch, she retreated into her family nest for good. She learned early on that if she did what she was told she could at least count on being tolerated. She didn't cause trouble. She was so accommodating and quiet that everyone liked her, but no one was interested in spending time with her.

"I'll introduce you to some of the eligibles I know," her uncle said, dipping a succulent lobster morsel into the butter sauce.

"Actually, there's a fellow, a coworker at the Arboretum." Rhyne's companions looked up in surprise. "Scottie's an assistant gardener, like I am. We eat our sandwiches together in the Japanese garden. He's asked me to take a trip with him to the Atlanta Botanical Garden," she said timidly.

"Bully!" her uncle exclaimed. "Good to see you getting out and about."

"We both love working with plants."

"So much the better."

"I turned him down."

"Well, I should think so," Florence cried. "Women in their older years must guard their dignity and not be taken advantage of."

Uncle Basil was of a different opinion. "Women your age don't get many chances. You must get out, take advantage of what this great world has to offer. You're like me—you love adventure or used to. What are you afraid of, girl?"

"You did exactly the right thing in refusing," Florence insisted. "What does she need with a man dangling her about? If a man his age is still single, there's a good reason."

Uncle Basil drained his glass of champagne. "That's my limit!" He turned to his sister. "Florence, you baby the girl too much. She's not as meek as you think. Yes, she's modest, but your desire to keep her home, near you, is not good for her. You should consider her needs."

Florence bristled. "My daughter's needs are well taken care of. Jonah left me well provided for, and I have my own inheritance. She'll be secure with me for life."

Rhyne stiffened. "I'm just fine. Do you hear me complaining?"

Uncle Basil, however, was on a roll. "You'd be very attractive, my girl, if you'd get that nose fixed. It precedes you by a quarter of an hour, to quote Cyrano. With your sweetness and compliance, you could easily get a man."

"Really, Basil." Florence set down her glass. "She can't help it if she's painfully shy." Rhyne once overheard her telling Basil how timid her daughter Rhyne was. Such a poor soul. Florence had expected her to flower, but the petals never opened. She guessed God made her that way.

Rhyne flinched. She always knew that her mother disdained the way she voiced no thoughts of her own, showed no initiative, just followed

26

meekly whatever anyone suggested. That Florence would have liked a daughter with more gumption, who *contributed*.

A tiny form flew in suddenly and landed on the balcony railing. Rhyne recognized a white-throated creeper, which turned its head this way and that, hopped a few inches closer, and looked directly at her. After uttering a few clear chirps, it flew off. *Wait for me*, she wanted to shout.

She missed Holly, the yellow cockatiel that had kept her company for so many years. Until the day her mother inadvertently left the apartment window open, and Holly swooped out, never to be seen again. Its mate died of grief a week later. Florence, after a brief mourning, accepted the loss, maybe because she abhorred the dirty mess and all the fussing. As she did anything that needed care or attention.

"You're quiet, but you're smart," her mother continued. "That should count for something."

Staring into her lap, Rhyne folded and refolded her cocktail napkin into a tiny square. Uncle Basil had no right to berate her. Since his wife died thirty years ago, he had been leading a freewheeling single life. According to Florence, Uncle Basil still chased the girls, which made Rhyne laugh—at age eighty-four, indeed. He denied it. "No more playing the wildcat," he'd told them. "I'm too old to take the bait."

Uncle Basil stood up and tapped his cane imperiously. "It's a beautiful evening. Let's walk along the beach."

There was no one like Uncle Basil. She often studied his portrait over the fireplace in their New York apartment, a photograph that dominated the living room—a handsome man in his prime, his long serpentine fingers resting on the back of a mahogany chair, tall and imposing in a plaid vest with brass buttons and an exaggerated sweep of yellow hair. She would feel his sharp eyes bear down on her as she hunkered on the couch, diminishing her with his presence.

*Isn't it about time you did something with your life?* his gaze implied. She had spent most of her fifty-two years in the spacious apartment overlooking a manicured park, where she lived a comfortable, non-threatening life with Florence—elaborate, comfortable, and empty. If only she could break out of the rut she was in.

When she was two months old, Florence and her husband Jonah had adopted her, and when Jonah died, Florence and Uncle Basil had taken her into their bosom. They were all she had. As much as she loved them, she felt a smoldering desire to know her real parents, to uncover who she was, what she was made of. And how she could lift herself out of the dead end she was facing.

**EVERYTHING HAD BEEN PREARRANGED** by Uncle Basil down to the last detail—the best choice on the restaurant menu, the proper shoes to wear on the trails, which papaya was ripe enough to eat. Nothing escaped his attention. "Tomorrow we're off to the caves," he reminded them the next evening. "My Lincoln has been cleaned and inspected." Florence and Rhyne exchanged looks. They had expected a hired driver; the idea of driving up the mountain with Uncle Basil behind the wheel was a nerve-wracking prospect. But Uncle Basil was not to be deterred. He'd been accident free for years, he told them, had just aced his recent driver's test. He claimed to be the epitome of caution, knew these roads like the back of his hands.

It appeared they had no choice.

The next morning, they piled in the Lincoln and headed along the Hana Highway toward the Haleakala mountains, Uncle Basil at the wheel, a map shop propped on the dashboard. Along the way they stopped to view the surfers ride the crashing waves at Lookout Ridge, figures skimming the surface with wild abandon, and to stroll along the rows of flaming flowers at the Haleakala Gardens, mesmerized by the scents of pikake, gardenia, and anthurium. As the Lincoln climbed up and up the narrow road, the azure ocean stretched out far below the steep banks of red and purple rock. Destination: the Wai'anapanapa Caves, carved over millenniums by volcanic movement, one of the most mysterious, treacherous, and erotic creations of nature, according to Uncle Basil.

"Exactly what do you mean by treacherous?" Florence wanted to know from the back seat. Rhyne was struck by the word *erotic*, a strange epithet for a cave. She experienced a novel feeling of stimulation. Something about heading into the dark mystery of an underground netherworld excited her.

"I mean wondrous and challenging. Like this." Uncle Basil, with a sweep of his arm, indicated the huge expanse of ocean, the sheer cliffs just feet from their wheels. "Not just the caves. All of it," he laughed, his voice rich as molasses. "Life. One must live. A little danger adds spark. Otherwise, there is no joy."

A sudden swerve as a green van whizzed by. "Damn fool!" Uncle Basil exploded. "You're supposed to honk going around these sharp curves," he exclaimed, not noticing that he had not done so himself. The two women, cowering in their seats, drew deep breaths and remained silent. The man would not be stopped.

The Lincoln swerved again as it rounded a sharp hairpin curve. "Have you taken that defensive driving class yet, Basil?" Florence inserted a mollifying tone into her voice. Usually she spoke to him forcefully, but Rhyne understood that with her brother behind the wheel, their lives in his hands, the last thing she wanted was to challenge him to greater excess.

He appeared oblivious. "I didn't complete the test. The first three directives were patsies: be alert, recognize your limitations, watch the other driver. Jumping Jehoshaphat, what could be more obvious! And I detest all the new-fangled technology built into the cars now, bells going off every time you turn around, actions initiated without your direction. You'll never get me into a driverless car. *I* determine where I'm going." He tugged at his tie for emphasis. "The instructor insinuated that one day the oldsters will have to quit driving." He shook his head and clamped his hands forcefully on the wheel. "I don't intend to quit driving. I can't operate without a car, that's all there is to it."

Mother and daughter exchanged alarmed glances. Rhyne recalled a few years back when Uncle Basil hit a jogger as she ran along the side of the road. Spooked by a cargo van, he swerved the car sharply and hit and the woman, who was nearly killed. When informed he failed the eye test and had to quit driving, he refused. "It wasn't my fault. She shouldn't have been on the road."

When they pulled into the parking lot, Florence breathed deeply. Solid land! They proceeded to the low white office building with WAI'ANAPANAPA CAVES posted above the entrance. Several tourists toting backpacks angled around a mounted telescope, and a couple shepherded two small redheads wearing helicopter hats through the main door. Rhyne spied the gaping hole of the cave entrance below, a black maw cut into the side of the mountain, breathing mystery. She felt a surge of anticipation.

"Fetch us some pamphlets," Uncle Basil said to Rhyne as they entered the building. "I'll get the tickets."

Rhyne looked around. "Where would they be?"

"You're such a helpless puss. If you'd stop reading all those esoteric books, my girl, you might learn something about life." Uncle Basil fastened his attention on the single customer waiting in line ahead of him.

His words hit Rhyne like needles. Here we go again, the scathing remarks. She determined to remain in the background for the rest of the afternoon, out of reach of her uncle's relentless digs.

As the lead customer turned away from the ticket window, a CLOSED sign was slapped on the counter. With a curse, Uncle Basil pounded on the glass. "These lovely people have come all the way from Minnesota! Curses, where has the clerk gone to?"

Rhyne felt her stomach tighten. She sensed an imminent scene, one of Uncle Basil's attacks on unsuspecting staff when things didn't go just so.

Just then a breezy young fellow in a chartreuse sweatshirt and torn jeans approached. "Jeremiah!" he called, leaning next to the window. It slid up a crack, the shade lifted, and a face appeared. "These people have been waiting a long time and need three tickets. No need to reopen." A pause: three tickets appeared under the window. "They know me here," he said, handing Uncle Basil the tickets. Without waiting for a response, he turned and strode off. Uncle Basil slipped a hundred-dollar bill through the window crack. "You're a handsome fellow. Keep the change."

As they followed a narrow path down to the cave, Rhyne observed a figure striding across the hill and recognized the chartreuse sweatshirt and pile of blonde hair. Something about him intrigued her, his air of confidence as he sauntered along the grassy slope, the broad curve of his shoulders, the free sway of his body. He carried what looked like a shepherd's staff. Abruptly he turned and disappeared between walls of volcanic rock.

At the cave entrance, a plaque described its formation thousands of years ago by the action of acid water eating through the limestone cliffs. Warning: be prepared for difficult narrow passages and slippery walking conditions. *Thousands of years*—to Rhyne, the prospect of dropping back in time, of entering a primordial world breathing ancient knowledge and hidden origins of existence, to lose oneself in a new sphere where anything was possible, was beguiling.

"Come on, Rhyne, don't just stand there, girl," her uncle called as he led the way down the path. Florence followed close behind, clutching her cane, the rubber-soled shoes she'd bought for the occasion crunching sharply on the gravel. Uncle Basil clearly enjoyed being the benevolent leader, the voice of knowledge. Having never had children—his youthful marriage to a wealthy Greek divorcee nearly twice his age had endured less than four months—his younger sister and niece inspired his parental side.

Uncle Basil stopped, dug into his canvas pouch, and pulled out a flashlight. "Did you bring your flashlight, ladies, as I advised?" Florence raised her arm, revealing a red and black led light. "Rhyne?"

"I didn't bring one," she admitted.

"Oh dear, she forgets everything," Florence exclaimed. "And Rhyne, your hair's a mess. Where's your comb? I don't know what I'm going to do with her."

Rhyne's throat tightened. She had left her flashlight on the bed at the last minute, thinking they didn't each need one, since the caves were bound to be lit. But she said nothing; no need to cause dissension.

As they entered the cave, Uncle Basil was in his usual jocular mood. "Are you ready to plunge into the lungs of hell?" Rhyne knew it amused him to shock his two acolytes, as he called them. "Take care, there are fractures in the bedrock that plunge into the earth—one misstep and you'll be swallowed up." He clicked his cane briskly on the gravel path.

The two women shot him reproachful looks but said nothing. Better to ignore the teasing, protests would only tempt him further.

"A friend of mine explored a cave in New Zealand with a group of aborigines and emerged with one foot missing. A boulder fell and caught him just above the ankle. They had to amputate."

"Just get on with it!" Florence cried, moving up behind her brother and striking her cane briskly on his calf.

Uncle Basil plunged into the darkness, the two women following. They moved along, straining to see as the sunlight behind them disappeared, leaving only a wan yellow swash of string lights along the base of the dirt floor.

"You girls have feet of iron," Uncle Basil said, looking over his shoulder.

"Walk faster," whispered Florence. "He can't abide slowpokes."

Rhyne hastened her steps. The smell of wet moss from the low ceiling intensified as they advanced silently into the depths of the cave. The metallic odor of ozone radiated from the walls, diluting the air that seemed to grow thinner and thinner. Florence sucked in her breath as if afraid she'd run out.

The steps slanted downward, outlined vaguely by the dim string lighting. Uncle Basil stopped, pocketed his flashlight, shifted his cane to one hand and grasped the railing with the other. "Are you ladies still kicking?" His voice sounded thin, as if absorbed by the dank earthiness.

"Yes, Basil," Florence said. "If only I could see better…"

"Hang on to the railing."

They descended cautiously. The ceiling was in total darkness, except for an occasional overhead bulb that cast a few grainy shadows on the sidewalls.

"I can't see." Florence slowed, searching with her foot for a secure place on each step. "Maybe we'd better go back."

"My adorable sister, we haven't reached our destination." They continued on. The musk scent of moist earth grew stronger. The path flattened, widened, curving between damp rock walls crusted with crawling amorphous earth layers that almost seemed alive. There were no breaks, no offshoots or open areas to stretch or catch your breath. Uncle Basil slowed to a crawling pace, announcing this crag in the rock, that irregularity in the angle of the path. Finally, he fell silent, breathing heavily. A single sound, the clap-clap of their shoes as they inched on, peering intently ahead, unable to see anything but the bare outline of matted rocks.

"I do believe we are leaving the civilized world as we know it," Uncle Basil said with levity, as if upholding his duty to raise their spirits.

"This is a popular tourist attraction," Rhyne said. "I'm surprised there's such poor lighting. We must have taken a wrong turn."

"I'd like to sit down," from Florence.

"We'll find you a nice bench under a palm tree," Uncle Basil said with a forced chuckle. "Damn fools should have provided rest spots for us old folks."

They finally reached a small circular area, more generously lit, from which several paths veered in different directions. No map or sign. Not a trace of other humans.

"Where is everyone?" Florence's voice sounded weak. "We saw plenty of people outside." Her voice expressed the need to connect with her species, to touch the real, everyday world.

Then Rhyne spied it, a sign with an arrow: *MAIN CAVE.* "Look!"

"Here we go!" Poking the metal sign with the tip of his cane, Uncle Basil harrumphed. Everyone breathed with relief.

They started forward eagerly, scanning flashlights in front of them. A sudden fluttering—Rhyne looked up to see a dark shape land on a crag above her—the little white-throated creeper! She extended her arm, but it was gone, into the whirlpool of her imagination. Off to parts unknown. If only she could lift off and follow it.

When she turned around, she found herself alone. Her companions had gone ahead; she heard their muffled voices not far off. An unbidden urge came over her, and before she realized what she was doing, she started down a path in another direction. Hurrying along the level passage, moving faster now, with no aim or thought, through the dim light until she heard a sound, the gurgle of water, and soon found herself in a large chamber holding a small shimmering pool. Not a soul. Flood lights covered the jagged walls of molten lava that mounted in rough irregular layers up to the ceiling and illuminated a craggy cathedral roof overhead. The subterranean odors of wet moss and decay reached her gently from every direction. She seemed to be in a theater of ancient growth, with the crusted earth holding microscopic secrets of the origins of the universe, the very meaning of life. She felt an incipient touch of reverence quicken her blood. And here, look here: a centipede! She leaned over. Along a crack in the wall a tiny yellow thing, moving, squiggling, ancient. She hovered her index finger over the mossy back, yearning to touch it, seeking an intimate knowledge, a unique connection. But she feared the creature might disintegrate at her touch.

As she stood upright, a feeling of freedom swept over her like a gigantic wave. She smiled to herself. Nothing could touch her down here in this subterranean lair, where nature ignored the realities of surface living. The pool shone darkly, reflecting ambient light on its surface, smooth except where drops from the ceiling created flickers of movement, like insects scooting over the surface. She breathed deeply, listening to the soft murmur of an underground stream.

A movement, barely perceptible, on the far side of the pool caught her eye; a shape broke away from the shadows and into the dim light. It moved slowly over the ground, she couldn't tell in which direction it was going or whether it was alive. As it grew larger, nearing, she recognized the chartreuse sweatshirt and shoulder-length yellow hair—the youth from the ticket office! He wore an assured expression, almost cocky she thought, but no, as he turned and looked at her across the pond his face was gentle, his soft brown eyes scanned the water, reaching across to her.

She stared at him in fascination.

"You must be lost. People don't usually make it this far," he said easily, his voice a close echo. He must have skirted the pond, for here he was beside her, looking directly at her, smiling.

Stunned, she shifted to reply, but no words emerged. This was unreal, this man-boy, materializing out here like a phantom from Neverland. He appeared at ease, as if he had wandered the caves all his life—or maybe she was lost in a dream.

"Don't be frightened. You're brave to come all the way here."

"I'm not at all frightened. It's so—so alive. I love it all."

He nodded and scanned the dark walls. "These caves are my home. I know all the chambers and the tunnels that connect them."

It struck her that being in this remote subterranean place felt like the most natural thing in the world. So did the inexplicable appearance of this stranger. For some reason, she felt at ease, as if he were an ally submerged in the cryptic mysteries of time.

"What are you doing here by yourself?"

"I seem to have wandered off. I was with my mother and uncle."

"You don't seem worried."

"I like being on my own—the caves come alive in a way they wouldn't if my relatives were here. Besides, I could never talk them into exploring this far. They don't think much of my judgment."

He picked up a wine-red stone, rolled it absently in his fingers. "You don't have to buy that." His words staggered her. His directness so casual, so innocently personal.

"During my attempts to find a place in the world I've always been supported by my mother and uncle. I'm used to being dependent. I'm obliging, I follow their guidance." She shrugged. "What alternative do I have?"

"Yet you broke away to come here."

"I am drawn to these caves. They don't lie. They know who you are."

He laughed. "You're a natural. I was raised here in the park, was allowed to do what I wanted, so I've become pretty independent. I can fell tall pines, lead mountain hikes, train search dogs, and teach classes in water safety. I quit college after three years to spend my life in nature where I belong, where I can wear my own shoes."

"Ah, to be comfortable in your own shoes! I've worn many pairs, and they have never taken me anywhere." Suddenly, moisture formed in Rhyne's eyes, a tear trickled down alongside her nose.

The lad sat down on a slab of rock and without a word she lowered herself beside him. The cool surface tingled against her buttocks.

"I saw you rubbing your fingers along the red rock formation back there. Did you know that when hot volcanic lava cools rapidly it retains this beautiful dark red color? There's no color like it," he said, turning toward her. "This cave tells the history of the Earth's evolution if you know how to read it." He had her total attention. "It holds many stories. Popo'alaea, wife of Chief Ka'akea, hid here to escape her husband's cruelty, but while his men were searching the caves they saw her reflection in the pool, captured her, and she was flung down a deep well to her death. Now, every spring, on the night of Ku, red shrimp enter and cover the cave floor with blood red, marking the anniversary of her death."

"Did your parents teach you these stories?"

"No. When I was ten, my parents were killed in a canoe accident in Kauai. I was brought up by my grandparents who live down the road. The staff here watched me grow up; they're like family. Now, at twenty-eight, I'm on my own. I love it here. I know these caves like the back of my hand. I lead tours here, as well as many other caves on the islands. The Hawaiian Institute of Genetic Engineering is sending me to Scotland to report on the Bone Caves that are rich with relics and fossils from millennia past.

She studied his face, expressive and gentle. His words, echoing against the steamy walls, seemed to be the most interesting thing she'd heard in her life.

He drew in his legs, regarding her. "My name is Olli, by the way."

She wet her lips. "I'm Jane." Why did she say that—what had come over her? For years she had been Rhyne, it suited her—or did it? She hadn't thought of her real name for years, but she seemed to have been stripped of all constraint. "Jane is my real name," she admitted. "I haven't used it forever."

Her companion looked sympathetic, as if he sensed her dilemma.

"I go by Rhyne. I made it up. I didn't want to be ordinary. I didn't want to be plain old Jane. I changed my name legally. It didn't really do the trick." Her attempt at reconfiguring the image of herself now appeared silly. She adjusted the strap of her knapsack. "I remained ordinary." Never had she told anyone that before. She felt her muscles relax, and a force welled deep inside her chest. Looking at him sideways, her laugh rang out over the water.

He smiled. "I don't believe you're ordinary," he said, "no matter what your name is. I read a lot in your face."

"Could I ask you a question?"

He nodded.

"Why do you wear your hair long, falling over your ears like that? Are you an artist or some sort of renegade?"

At this he laughed. "You might call me a maverick. I don't do well in so-called ordinary society. I much prefer the company of sheep that graze on the other side of the hill and the euphony of underground caves where I can hear the primordial stirrings of life. I love it here in the darkness tucked away from the flurry of every day."

"I understand what you mean! I've always fancied the darkness of my room in the quiet of the night, the midnight stars that flicker and talk to you in the black sky, and the shadowy movie theater before the screen comes on and you and the audience are one. There's a warm intimacy about darkness."

"Yes, that's it." He didn't look surprised at this confession, and she had the strange feeling that he knew her through and through. A warm sense of release invaded her body. Was any of this real? Was this friendly, unorthodox young man what he seemed, or did he materialize from the sentient depths of the underworld?

"You're not wearing a ring," the boy noted.

"Never married. I've lived with my mother for years. She runs the show."

"I see. Earlier I noticed you behind the others, lingering, as if you enjoyed a secret world all your own. Then when you took off like a sprite, I followed."

"I wanted to be on my own." She hesitated. "I'm not used to being alone. But I get lonely. Often, I feel I'd be better off on my own." There, her thoughts formulated and brought to life. She sensed she could tell him anything, as if they were on a desert island, devoid of regulations, where anything beyond the immediate was irrelevant. "I was adopted. I have no blood kin."

"I'm an orphan too, of sorts. My grandparents are old, always have been, and lead a doddering life of agreeable indifference. I've always been on my own. I fantasize about my parents, what they were like. So maybe I can figure out who I resemble."

They smiled at each other.

"Want to go for a dip? The pool's spring fed."

A crazy idea—down here in this preternatural underworld! To her own surprise, she nodded. She would surrender to the power of the dream where she could be herself, release her secrets, unacknowledged desires, all the things her restrained, contained, scrupulous, cautious little life curtailed. They stepped to the edge of the whale-shaped pool. Little islands of rock protruded the surface here and there, splotched with colors of deep purple and gold. The water lay calm, except on one side where underground rivulets seeped in with soft gurgles.

He dipped in his fingers. "It's warm." She had the impression that he would go into the water even if it were cold, that nothing bothered him, that there was nothing he couldn't handle. He removed his shoes and stepped into the edge of the pool. She stared at his soft sweatshirt curving gently down his back.

"I'm coming!" she cried, laughing, following his lead. She shut her eyes and absorbed the odor of musk from the walls, the feel of mist on her skin, the cradling of water around her feet. He moved forward, she followed as they waded up to their knees, stepping gingerly as the muck on the uneven surface of the floor oozed between their toes. When she puckered her mouth and groaned, Olli laughed at her squeamishness and took her hand. "I haven't done anything like this since I was twelve," she giggled. Her eyes were dancing; she felt like she'd been shot from a cannon and was flying into the unknown.

The water lapped around them as they moved, cool and invigorating. They tripped a few times, holding each other up, each time getting a little wetter. Rhyne stubbed her foot on something sharp and, oblivious to the pain, exclaimed, "Out of my way!" The water deepened, lapping smoothly around her hips, soaking into her; it felt pure and reassuring against her skin. "Let's see how far you can go," the boy exclaimed, and with a graceful movement ducked his full body under the water and emerged, shaking his dripping hair and grinning. Rhyne immediately followed, holding her breath as long as possible, hoping to worry him, but when she popped up he was already backing away, waiting for her to catch up.

Finally, they climbed out and Rhyne felt the wet drops tingling down her legs, her wet slacks pressing against her body. Her companion's jeans were also dripping. He looked pleased, wholly immersed in the moment. After some minutes, he started pulling off his clothes, slowly, first his jeans and his sweatshirt, laying out each item on the dry rock. His youthful body looked smooth, lean, energized.

"Do you want to remove your wet clothes?" he suggested matter-of-factly. "You must be cold."

"Not a bit cold." If so, she was too stimulated to feel discomfort, to feel anything but an overwhelming sensation of being alive for the first time in years.

Slowly, evenly, she let her neck scarf drop to the ground, unbuttoned her dripping slacks, and one by one each piece—slacks, shirt, bra, under-pants—piled beside her until she stood barefoot and naked on the hard earth. She didn't care. All she could feel was the play of air on her torso, brushing her breasts, her neck, curving around her thighs.

The boy moved closer, his nude body soft in the hazy light. "You feel free, I can tell. I suspected right away, at the ticket office, that you would take to the caverns the way I do. I've developed a sense, learned to read the people who come here." She could feel the warmth of his breath as he drew near. "You looked so subdued, following your companions like an obedient lamb, but your eyes were elsewhere, spinning a different world, and the way you looked at me so keenly—even from afar, I could tell there was something ethereal about you."

She said nothing, looking up at him without reserve. She had never heard herself defined in that way. What did he mean? Her mother called her unique, meaning different, bordering on weird. As for her uncle—he berated her hesitancy, her passive acceptance of whatever wafted in front of her, the epitome of a loser. Not a unique bone in her body.

The hypnotic scents of wet moss and mineral-infused water filled the cave. She thought she heard the shifting of life, maybe a worm or burrowing crustacean. In the pulsing earthy environment in which she found herself she could believe anything. The boy drew nearer. She couldn't take her eyes from him, every fiber of her being alert. Slowly, he pressed his body against hers, she could feel his warmth, impatiently, then his arms around her back, and a long kiss that sent hot shivers racing through her limbs.

"I thought you'd like that," he said softly. He kept holding her close, his chest pressed against hers. Then, glancing toward the path on the far side of the pool, "Now we'd better get dressed. Your people are surely looking for you." From afar, a rising cadence of voices, getting closer. With a gentle movement he dropped his arms, and they stood looking at each other, caught in the wonder of the moment.

She was beyond thought, but vaguely aware that not an ounce of shyness remained in her. Never had she felt so at ease, so sure of herself.

She drew her clothes back on. The thought of Uncle Basil and Florence had broken the spell, if that's what it was, and restored her to staid reality.

But it was a different reality. The air wasn't the same. She wasn't the same. The arched cave walls seemed to have expanded. Or maybe everything else had shrunk. She felt confident down there in the depths, removed from the bright sun that commanded order and propriety. Here she could catch up, prove herself, be something.

Voices approached, echoing along the stone walls. Olli switched on his flashlight. She had no words, but suspected that he already knew everything, that is to say enough.

Florence and Basil appeared out of the darkness, flashlights streaming in front of them. "We thought we heard voices!" Their faces looked sketchy, abstract under the variegated light flickering from different parts of the cave.

When Rhyne turned, Olli and his flashlight had disappeared.

"We were worried sick! Why did you wander off like that? You shouldn't have upset your uncle so. Look at those soaking wet clothes…" Florence stared at her daughter in confusion.

"I activated the magnetic induction wires to locate you," Uncle Basil said sternly. "They will be searching. We'd better get back."

"I'm sorry. I should have alerted you," Rhyne said, regretting their worry but not at all sorry she had followed her impulse. Luckily, they hadn't caught sight of the young man, and she had no intention of mentioning him. Although Uncle Basil did remark, as they clambered up the long tunnel to the surface, that Rhyne's face was flushed and that she carried herself with a strange air.

"You mustn't worry your Uncle Basil like that. He becomes irritable," Florence whispered to Rhyne. "We're dependent on him, you know."

"What do you mean?" Rhyne exclaimed. "We run our house, pay our bills, lead our own lives. Uncle Basil doesn't even manage his own household—he lives in a hotel."

"Oh, but your uncle takes us to amusing places and advises me on all sorts of things. I don't know what we'd do without his support."

It struck Rhyne that this was the most ridiculous thing she'd ever heard. Of course, her mother came from the fifties when men ruled; circulating in the larger world, their knowledge and experience were to be respected. But this attitude was passé, discounted—it was bunk.

"We want Uncle Basil in our lives because we love him, not because we need him, Mother," Rhyne said in a firm tone.

Her mother looked at her in surprise. "Well, of course," she said, clutching the railing with her free hand. "We'd better get back before my poor old legs give out." More loudly, "Lead on, Basil."

Back at the hotel, Rhyne stared out the screened window as Florence showered in the next room. Down below the pavers in the courtyard shone in the sunlight, the trellises burst with blue and orange and yellow flowers. Rhyne couldn't believe how beautiful and alive everything looked.

How had she ever indulged in such behavior? It had happened so naturally, so easily, as inevitable as sea lions romping in the ocean or rain falling from the sky. She had trusted this assured stranger completely and achieved the same sense of confidence as the time in school when she had been the sole student in the class to answer a question correctly. A mind of her own, they'd said. A stroke of luck, her mother called it.

That afternoon she had once again followed her instinct. A touch of excitement stirred in her. Change. What would it bring?

AS THE DAYS PASSED, Rhyne became filled with a sense of urgency. She was tired of coasting. Florence commanded emotional harmony that skirted dissension. Her stamp dominated the house, leaving little sign of Rhyne's presence. What had seemed comfortable and safe had become overbearing. What was she doing, at her age, living under her mother's wing?

It was time to make a move.

"What in the world do you want your own place for?" Florence cried in alarm. "You have everything you need right here, where you're happy."

"I'm not happy!" Rhyne searched for a rationale that would satisfy her mother. "Mother, a coworker has offered to share her home with me. I would be living close to work and have full house privileges. She wants me to join the neighborhood chess club. I used to love the game in college. It would be fun."

"You won't like such an arrangement. To live with someone you hardly know!"

Rhyne shifted on her chair and looked at the newspaper spread out on the table before her. "That's just one possibility. I'm also checking the ads for a place of my own."

"What would I do without you, darling?" Her voice was firm. "I need you. I'm an old lady in my eighties. I can't manage without your help." She took a bottle of lemon La Croix from the refrigerator and poured it into a glass of cracked ice that Rhyne handed her. "Who would keep me company?"

"I know, Mother." Already she was feeling ashamed. Her mother had seen that she wanted for nothing. She could not forget that. Rhyne owed her. Florence had no one else except Uncle Basil, four thousand miles away. How could she abandon Florence after everything she'd done for her? This apartment was comfortable, familiar, no need to assert herself or face the risks of a cold, impenetrable world where she had so far made no gains whatsoever.

Yet, this rationale was suspiciously one-sided. Most of what she did could be replaced by paid workers. She was not really needed. If she coasted through life as a martyr, it must be her own fault.

"You could easily hire someone to keep house, run errands, Mother."

"It sounds like you've made up your mind. Of course, if you're only going to think of yourself!" Florence stalked out, leaving her daughter bent over the newspaper ads swallowing a sore sense of guilt.

Uncle Basil called from Maui. "I don't agree with my hysterical sister. You should get out—uncage yourself. Out there where the world can mold you, teach you some lessons, sharpen your wits."

For years she had been comfortable here, had wanted for nothing. Except—it came to her in a flash—she had wanted for everything.

**RHYNE NOTICED SIGNS** of serious decline in her mother. Florence didn't know what day it was; the television controls were confusing; the clothes she wore didn't match; if a task proved troublesome, she gave up. Her house, always a pinnacle of good taste, every pin in order, began to look disordered. She no longer commanded. "Whatever you say, dear." Seeing her reduced figure sitting slumped on the couch in her baggy slacks as they watched television, she felt her mother slipping into the unknown.

When she left the stove burner on all night and was unable to find her way home from the store, Rhyne, in consultation with Uncle Basil, determined it was time to make a change. Before long, Florence was ensconced in an assisted living suite on the top floor of Cherrywood Terrace.

To Rhyne's astonishment, Florence took to the friendliness and convenience of the residence immediately. She soon became sought after for the bi-weekly bridge games and was invited to join dinner-table groups. "I can't keep up," she said, laughing. She showed off her new walker. "It has a padded seat, pockets, and a water bottle. I can go anywhere."

The night of the Christmas party, Florence joined a group gathered around the piano clutching song books. A woman with clipped white hair and a crimson boa around her neck was pounding the keys briskly. The recreation center was decorated with pine branches, colorful bows, strings of blinking lights, and frosted bulbs; an orange gleam from the fireplace flooded the room. Gray-haired women in shawls or red and green sweaters perched on couches, with a few men scattered here and there wearing green shirts or red vests, one in a Santa hat. The crowd increased as more people arrived and gazed around with expectant smiles, drifting through the room, chatting informally.

Florence adjusted her pink cashmere sweater spangled with white snowflakes and sugar canes and began clapping her hands in time to "Angels We Have Heard on High," singing out energetically.

When the last voice had faded, the pianist stood up. "As head of the holiday event committee, I'd like to welcome a newcomer to our residence, Mrs. Florence Aubrey. She lives on the twelfth floor. Let's make her feel welcome." A chorus of hi's, hello's, Merry Christmases.

"Merry Christmas, everyone. Isn't this fun? Aren't we all glad to be here!" Florence's tinkling laugh swept the crowd and she beamed with uncommon alacrity, the picture of gracious warmth. Rhyne, entering, spied her mother immediately as she stood brightly with one hand on the piano, the center of attention. She smiled. Florence looked like her old self with her hair blown into a silvery sweep around her ears, alert and fun-loving, the life of the party, uplifted by the music, the lights, the swarm of radiating faces. Rhyne felt a surge of pride. Her mother: There was no one like her.

"Go on Juliet, let's have another." People clapped gaily. The pianist flipped through the songbook and the mellow strains of "O Little Town of Bethlehem" rose across the room.

After several more carols, a stir came from the entranceway. A tall, imposing figure in a green plaid waistcoat, red silk tie, and taupe beret entered. His loud voice carried to every corner of the room. "Hello everyone! What a charming group! Can a lonely old man looking for some Christmas cheer join you?"

The room quieted. The pianist, a petite woman, grasped her walker and hobbled over to where Uncle Basil stood, his six-foot-three frame towering above others. "This is Mr. Basil van Linden," she announced. "He phoned and asked if he could join his sister, our new neighbor Florence, at our Christmas party. He came all the way from Maui. Welcome, Mr. van Linden. My name is Juliet."

He removed his beret, bowed formally, and cast his smile over the onlookers. Florence had a proud look on her face. She considered that her older brother commanded respect everywhere he went, with his flamboyant manner and the gentlemanly way he bowed to the ladies and drew laughter with his charming barbs.

At her place by the mantelpiece, Rhyne shot upright. He wasn't supposed to be here! Already his brazen entry stirred her apprehension. He would command the company. Was there no way to curb his remarks?

"I lived in Maui for two years," Juliet told him. "Are you the owner of the Maui Greyhound Racetrack by any chance?"

"The same."

"And you're a commentator on *Akaku News*?"

"At your service." Murmuring swept through the group—an important personage in their midst. How do you like our Midwest country, Mr. Van Linden?"

"Very nice for a provincial outlay. If it weren't for all those mosquitoes."

"We're honored to have you. Won't you join us at the piano?"

"Thank you kindly, madam. I don't sing unless I've had at least six glasses of potent Christmas whiskey."

"Only wine is served at our events, I'm afraid," Juliet told him.

Uncle Basil stroked his chin. "I must say, that's disappointing. I put on my best vest for the occasion. Never mind, I supply my own when necessary." He pulled a red leather flask from his jacket pocket, unscrewed the lid and took a long swig, Adam's apple jiggling in his long neck.

"Oh, my, we can't allow that," Juliet cried. No one said anything. The people standing by the punch bowl stared, little cups in their hands, looking as if they were awaiting an explosion.

Florence took his arm. "Basil, put that away and come to the piano. Show us your lovely baritone."

Rhyne grabbed her mother's sleeve. "What is he doing here?" The color had left Rhyne's face. "He had an appointment with the barber and some dry cleaning to take care of. We were supposed to meet later for dinner. He's going to cause a scene among these conservative people."

The pianist returned to her post and flipped the pages on the music rack. Two women scooted aside as Basil moved up to the piano. Someone handed him a songbook. Soon the notes of "Good King Wenceslas" fluttered through the room, Uncle Basil's sonorous voice leading the rest.

"You play delightfully, my dear lady," he said at the conclusion. "At least you would if you took a few more lessons. You missed the A-flat every time. And do have the piano tuned. It bellows like an old street organ." Seeing a shadow pass over Juliet's face, he added, "I only mention it because I'm sure people living in such a splendid residence deserve the best."

"It's very true the piano could use some attention," said a woman standing next to him, wearing a string of gold chain necklaces. She put her hand on Basil's arm. "We in Minnesota aren't used to such forthrightness."

"Never object to a good honest comment myself," Uncle Basil declared. "It shows lack of dissimulation."

The woman with the gold necklaces inserted her arm in his. "Come, take a look at this painting," she urged, navigating him across the room. "It was just hung yesterday. We are very proud of it." She looked up at him. "What do you think."

The large oil that hung over the mantelpiece displayed a slim birch branch and an enormous thimble floating on a pale blue background, meticulously rendered with stippling brush strokes. Uncle Basil surveyed it with narrowed eyes. The room grew hushed. Straightening his tie with index finger and thumb, he stepped back, leaned with one hand behind him on his lion-head cane, and drew his mouth into a wistful pucker.

"I've never seen a painting I didn't like," he said at last, "if I looked at it long enough." He twirled his cane into his other hand. "And I haven't looked at this one long enough."

"Come, come," said a lady in a reindeer sweater, "the artist has won many awards, including the Louise Nemeth Memorial Award."

"That may be so, my dear lady, but I have yet to discover a point to this painting. There is no relationship between the branch and the thimble, no interface with the colors. Such work should convey a feeling. I find none here." He turned with a courtly nod. "If I were you, I'd return this to the shop."

Before Uncle Basil could unwrap the cigar he now pulled from his vest pocket, his companion with the gold necklaces wrenched her arm from his and glared at him. "You may be ignorant of creative art, in fact you may be ignorant period, but I am the artist, and this painting has won honors…"

Basil broke in. "You ask for my opinion and then you reject it. I was unaware that you are only open to praise. Please accept my apologies."

The woman wouldn't have it. "I don't object to thoughtful criticism. But you don't know what you're talking about. You flaunt your ignorance with false authority and demonstrate a lack of manners. I have nothing more to say to you." She fixed him with a hard look.

"Ah, a woman with grit. Do let me take you to lunch tomorrow at the Carlton and we can discuss this further." But a group had formed around her, moving her off, and she didn't turn around.

Florence whispered in his ear, "I know you'll never change, Basil, but you really must learn to temper your opinions." His sister wore a stern expression.

"How was I to know she was the artist? The lady is touchy," Uncle Basil said. "Most love it—they like a man with force, who says it like it is."

"Well, never mind," Florence said.

"But we should mind!" blurted Rhyne.

Florence and Uncle Basil looked at her in surprise.

"Your friends in Maui accept your domination, you hold authority there, they know you. But these people don't find your contempt charming." Her voice had risen several notches. "You have insulted the residents, abused an artist, embarrassed Florence and me, and dampened the spirit of the Christmas party. You are *not* excused!"

Uncle Basil wiggled the cigar back and forth in his mouth. 'What have we here? It's not like you to create a scene in public. These good people will attest that I'm right."

"You're dreaming. Everyone is uncomfortable."

"Only because they're not used to frankness. But they know."

"Face it, Uncle Basil, you're out of line here. Look at the faces of the people around you. You'd better clean up your act."

"Harrumph," was his response.

"Come, Uncle, the guests want to get back to their celebration. Let's join Florence at the piano."

"I don't sing on a dry throat, my lass. I'll just settle myself here and listen."

Rhyne moved over and dropped into the chair next to him. "Are you going to behave, Uncle?"

"No fun in that. And you, my girl, are you enjoying yourself?" When she hesitated, he went on, "Have you found an apartment yet?"

"There's been too much to do, what with getting Florence moved and settled."

"You'd better get to it if you're serious about making something of your life."

"Uncle Basil, I have every intention—if only I could get work in a greenhouse or botanical center, challenging work that would make use of my degree in horticulture. The idea has lingered in the back of my head ever since I tended gardens on the Texas commune."

"So, get to it."

She sunk back into the chair. "It's not that easy," she sighed. "I'm too old."

"Nonsense. Attaining a dream never is. Unless you want it badly enough."

After a few more rounds of carols, Florence shuffled over, announced she was tired, and pulled Uncle Basil from his chair. "Ever since our return from Maui," she told him as they walked to the front door, "Rhyne has been strange. She asked for a raise at the Arboretum. And she's hired a weekly maid service to clean the apartment."

She wobbled slightly on the walker. Uncle Basil took her elbow. "Here, steady."

"She's got these crazy ideas. She's actually going to move to her own apartment." She tightened her hands on the walker handles.

"My good woman, she must make her own way. She's finally finding her voice. There's nothing you can do. I may be the butt in this instance, but I have to admit she reminds me of me." He patted the bulge in his back pocket. "Now if you'll excuse me, it's time to step outside for a refresher."

Rhyne, trailing behind, overheard the last remark and blinked. She like Uncle Basil? What an idea. But the thought made her smile.

**RHYNE ENTERED** her mother's hospital room to find her sitting up, looking pale in her pink fleece bathrobe. Florence turned her head, smiled drowsily, clicked off the television, and *Call the Midwife* disappeared from the screen.

"How are you, Mother? Are you still having trouble eating?" The symptoms of interstitial lung disease had been deepening, plans to return home after weeks of treatment abandoned.

"I'm fine, dear. How are you?" Florence said in a weak voice.

"I'm good."

The habitual comments ensued: The weather. *Cloudy.* The nurses. *Nice, so friendly.* Always the same conversation, the same replay as Florence's range of thought grew narrower and narrower. Her mind was slipping, sliding down a hill backwards, inch by inch. Rhyne sat on the chair across the room and searched for something to say.

"What would you like to talk about?" she asked her mother, anticipating the answer.

"Oh, anything."

"Guess what I did yesterday? I drove to the Mall of America and bought two cockatiels. They'll be good company when you return home."

Florence smiled blankly. She must have forgotten about the time she left the apartment window open and Holly, who had been a pet for ten years, wasted no time in flying out of it.

"I'll take care of the cage, Mother."

"That's nice, dear." Then, abruptly, "Don't you want to go say hello to Basil?"

"What? Where is he?"

51

"He's got a bed."

"Here? How? What's the matter with him?" But Florence couldn't remember and flapped her hands helplessly.

Rhyne called in the nurse. "Yes, just down the hall. He was brought in with advanced CHD. Number 398." Rhyne dashed out in disbelief. How could he be here? He'd only arrived four days ago from Maui, fit as a fiddle. Oh, maybe an occasional shortness of breath. Advanced coronary heart disease? It must be a mistake.

*Three-ninety-eight must be here.* She knocked. No response. Cracking open the door, she entered a darkened room and came to a halt. In the single strand of light streaming in between the window curtains, she made out the figure of a man in bed, hidden in shadow. "Uncle Basil?" she asked in a low voice.

"If you would switch on the light you'd find out," came the familiar voice. "That you, Rhyne?"

She walked to the window, swept open the curtains, and watched as the light waved over the room, revealing Uncle Basil tucked under a plaid blanket. He slowly pulled himself to a sitting position. "Come over here, girl, where I can see you," he commanded in a weak voice.

"So, what's the matter with you, Uncle? Did you come here to make trouble for the pretty nurses?" She sat down facing him.

He guffawed. "This morning I pinched the nurse as she was giving me my shot and told the candy striper she should dump her boyfriend for me."

"You shouldn't embarrass your caregivers."

"They love it! Come in here all the time fussing like hens. Can't get rid of them. Now sit yourself down and tell me about the romance in your life. You once mentioned a fellow at the Arboretum you liked. Fellow name of Scottie."

But before she could answer, his chin sunk into his chest, and he seemed to withdraw into himself.

Rhyne stared at the limp form on the bed. "Uncle Basil, your condition is serious. Shouldn't you return to the care of your regular physicians in Maui?"

"The medical care here is far superior. Besides—pull your chair closer—besides, I want to be here with you. Where I can see you. You're family; I want you to know that." He reached for her hand, squeezing it in his long fingers. "You and Florence are all I've got. There's no one in the world more special to me than you."

Rhyne felt her blood rise. What was he saying? This was unlike her unemotional, cocky uncle. His feeble voice, his drawn face, the tender way he looked at her, as if she were about to disappear. This man, whom she had revered from a distance, now as close as a breath of air. She stared down at the ruby ring he had given her for college graduation, her birthstone. He had given her so much over the years: extravagant gifts, foreign vacations, a generous college fund. Had entertained them with his ingenuity, wit, originality, and charm. Suddenly she wanted to take him in her arms.

"My girl, I need you to do me a favor. Go over to the cupboard and fetch the bottle of Jack Daniels stashed behind the towels." He attempted to raise his voice, but his words were hardly more than a whisper.

"You can't have liquor while on medication. Or in here at all."

"A sip won't do any harm. Be a lamb for your—for your uncle."

Rhyne jumped to her feet as a rush of adrenaline beat against her forehead. "No, Uncle." She strode angrily to the cupboard, grabbed the liquor bottle, and driven by blind instinct, marched to the sink and hit the bottle several times against the edge until it cracked in half. "You won't be drinking this," she exclaimed, standing back. Glass fragments flew into the sink, along the counter. Slowly a flood of dark liquid swirled down the drain. Rhyne lowered the half-bottle to the adjoining table, carefully avoiding its jaw-like edges. "No more nonsense. You must take care of yourself. And if you won't, I will."

"I've been drinking whiskey for fifty years, and I'm not going to stop now."

"With your heart, you are off booze. As long as I'm around." She pressed the red call button.

At his silence, she turned to find him looking abashed. "If you'll come often and see me…" he muttered.

The nurses brimmed with apologies, didn't know how the liquor had gotten by them, they would keep a close watch. Did she need anything? She did not. She'd never felt so vital, so in charge of herself.

"I'll return this evening," she promised, kissing him on the cheek.

As she strode back to Florence's room, Rhyne found herself smiling. He was undoubtedly sick, but nothing held him down for long. She would be there beside him, as long as it took.

TWO DAYS LATER Rhyne walked in to find her mother's wasted body stretched out on the bed, head floating on the pillow, her wafer-thin hands lying loose on the covers, looking small and vulnerable.

"What do you need, Mother?"

"Water, please." Florence coughed deep in her throat, a harsh drowning sound. Rhyne filled the glass on the table from the pitcher and handed it to her mother, who took several small sips. Then, her allotment of energy gone, her head drooped, and she sank into a wheezy sleep.

Rhyne carefully took one of her mother's hands in her own strong ones. There was no good way to break the news. It would be a shock, more than the feeble figure in the bed could bear. But an hour later her mother's eyes flickered open with a burst of energy, and she looked at Rhyne with an intelligent gleam, and a soft smile spread over the emaciated face. Rhyne decided the time had come. How long the reprieve would last was unpredictable.

"I have to tell you to be prepared, Mother. It's Basil. He's been sick, and longer than we've known." Florence's eyes rested on her gently.

"Basil—his heart—he died this morning." With effort, Rhyne kept her voice from shaking. Grieving could wait. This required stamina. "His heart. It just stopped."

Slowly Florence shook her head and, lifting one thin hand, placed it on her daughter's sleeve. "I've known for a long time that Basil was very sick. He was guarded about his health, his image and all that. No one must know, he planned to recover. If not, he wanted to confide in you before the end robbed him of the chance. But he waited too long, and now it's too late."

"Too late? What do you mean?" Rhyne felt a tight clutch in her stomach. Her mother didn't appear stunned by the news that this invincible man had succumbed, no longer existed on this earth, the power, the dash, the towering presence gone forever. Rather she seemed preoccupied by something else, and judging by her evasiveness, it was of an ominous nature.

"Now I have something to tell *you*. There's something...you should know..."

"What?"

Florence twisted a strand of hair brushing her face.

"Just say it."

Sucking in a deep breath, Florence drew her lips together. "You should know the truth. I just couldn't..." She stopped, looked at Rhyne with pleading eyes.

"I don't know how to tell you. Oh, I knew this day would come. You won't like it. But Basil insisted you should know the truth after he was gone. He was afraid for you to know before, that you would feel, well, abandoned, less valued by him." She paused, coughed into a tissue scrunched in her left hand. "Our lives were so good, why risk ruining things. That's what I thought. I just didn't have the courage to turn your life upside down.

Rhyne stood up. "I can take it, Mother."

"Dear, we loved you so! You were not abandoned in an orphanage, as you were told. You are—your mother was a French ballerina without family—" Florence's face was composed now, and she went on. "The ballerina died, and Basil—well, as Democratic National Committee chair, prominent in his community, news of a mistress and child would have cost him dearly." She breathed in a little gasp of air.

It hit Rhyne like a whip snapping across the room. Her brain struggled to sort the words into place. *Uncle Basil!* A sham, it had been a sham, she'd been deceived. She wasn't a poor soul, rescued from the orphanage by warm-hearted protectors to whom she owed eternal gratitude. Her whole life fake, she'd searched a lifetime for an identity, and they had possessed it all along, buried under false guard. Rhyne's brain whirled, ready to explode.

"You both lied! How could you"—she drew in several deep breaths— "pretend to be my mother...?" Florence was looking at her dejectedly. "You should have told me."

"I couldn't. Basil couldn't picture himself as a father. It was better the way it was." The words fluttered out low and pathetic.

"It would have made a huge difference." She looked straight at her mother. "I spent all those years avoiding Jonah's abuse. I felt guilty because I couldn't grieve his death, the death of my father. I always secretly desired a different father, one who would love and protect. And now that I've found him, he is gone.

"How could you?" she repeated, leaning over and clutching the railing of the bed.

Florence's cheeks were bright, flushed with a reservoir of energy drawn from the depths of her being. "Rhyne, sit down," she urged, patting the bed. "Your uncle couldn't bear for the world to know the truth. He couldn't bring you up. He wanted a normal family life for you with two parents, Jonah and me. But I see now we should have told you."

So, Basil had not been a devoted uncle, escorting them on occasional trips and excursions, using them as a surrogate family he could summon when needed before returning to his expansive, self-absorbed life. He had abandoned his father role. How could she ever forgive him?

Still, he had cared for them in his own way. Maybe it was all he was able to offer. She had loved him, after all, despite his crushing cynicism. Maybe he had given her the best of himself.

Florence sucked in her breath, speaking slowly. "I owe Basil everything. Basil took care of me while our parents traveled the world. He was my support. Together we endured our father's temper and our mother's coldness. I owe him everything. I owe him you. I took his child as my own, and we became a family, a solid family. It seemed a perfect arrangement."

It was almost too much to absorb. Rhyne's eyes moved to the medicine shelf across the room displaying several tubes of lipstick, which until recently her mother never went without, and next to them a framed photo of Florence at the golf club dressed in a swede jacket and wearing pearl button earrings, looking fresh and beautiful. So familiar. So distancing. Maybe she couldn't relate to her mother's elegance, but her force and appeal couldn't be denied. Now that Rhyne no longer sought more.

"You're everything to me. Always have been. I'm sorry…" whispered Florence. She reached out a limp hand, it hung weakly above the covers. Rhyne reached out and felt the fragility of the tiny fingers, the skin like tissue paper, and slowly her anger began to dissolve into a pool of sadness. Her mother sank down in the pillows, her face turned ghostly white, her mouth drawn, her breathing slow. Her brief rally seemed to have depleted her, spent her last ounce of will.

Basil her father, dead, gone. Florence would soon join him. She was losing them, her family, who had always been there, could always be counted on, the only people in the world she loved. It was time to orchestrate her own life, to define her own happiness. How could she ever sort it out?

Florence opened her eyes. They formed a question. "I never did understand you," she murmured. "But I loved you." She closed her eyes, her head sunk into the pillow. Rhyne held the voice in her memory, rich and musical, that had surrounded her for so long, that held years of care and non-care and misunderstanding and love. The shrunken figure outlined under the blanket, the white hair thin and limp around her cheeks, had fallen into an unconscious slumber.

She was on her own now, infused with new blood. All her life she drifted in the wake of Florence and Uncle Basil, had buried her own preferences and settled. Henceforth she would be her own person.

Whatever came, she was up to it. She would make it work.

**THE FIGURE OF UNCLE BASIL** above the fireplace loomed over Rhyne as she lay curled on the couch sipping her Sprite, rehashing the events of the six months since his death. He looked different; the portrait held subtle characteristics she hadn't noticed before. The same dominating elegance could be seen, the same patriarchal air. But the portrait had softened, taken on a gleam that suggested a buried vulnerability. She noticed for the first time a hint of melancholy in the soft blue eyes. The stretch of lines on his brow had loosened, the steely pose suggesting fortitude and struggle now reflected the hard strokes of a makeshift life. She detected conflicting traits of warmheartedness and severity, of love and distaste, of zeal and pessimism.

"Well, Basil, what have you got to say for yourself?" she said aloud. During his last days he claimed to have reformed, that his cutting wit had marked its last victim.

"What a shame," he'd said, "that wisdom overtakes us after the fact, when the experience is over, and it is too late to act differently so we don't end up hating ourselves."

Rising, she moved to the window and drew open the curtains, passing the embossed silver birdcage hanging clean and shiny that Florence had always fancied, without the cockatiels that is, without the mess. Two yellow and white birds faced each other, chirping back and forth randomly.

She had an instinct to let them go, to give them the freedom to fly, to soar. Their little world in the cage might offer safety, but drifting on the free air they could move unstifled and feel what it's like to be alive.

But she would care for them and keep them happy in their little world. And she would be free. "Remember last year when Scottie, my coworker at the Raptor Center, invited me to a hike in the Colorado Rockies and I turned him down? Guess what?" she said aloud to the man in the portrait, "I have just asked him to join me on a guided bird-watching trip to the Everglades. He agreed at once."

Scenes from her early youth circled through Rhyne's mind—the climb on Mount McKinley; the stay at a Texas commune where she helped birth a calf, blood running down her arms; the move to Tampa with a college roommate to write, and her news story on criminal activity on the Tampa waterfront. She'd broken out, explored the vast unknown, but when things slowed, she had folded her wings and darted back to Florence, where she fell into a routine of certainty and comfort that tightened over the years. And then the mystical experience in the bowels of the Maui cave, hearing the subterranean voices reaching effortlessly to far off galaxies, to some far place bigger than them all, a breath of release had reached her.

And then the death of Uncle Basil. No sooner had she acquired a father than she lost him, but his legacy was burned into her. His attentions, his gifts, his subtle guiding motions—her father had been there all along.

She still had all those years.

She looked up at the portrait. Approval shone in the bright eyes. Her gaze turned to the stacks of cardboard boxes piled up in the front hall, the horticulture prints from her bedroom wrapped and taped, furniture marked for the movers with tape. The birdcage and the portrait of Uncle Basil she would carry in her car to the new apartment, a one-bedroom located not far from the theater district. She looked forward to a job interview at Bailey Nurseries, an extensive facility that she had toured on her own and would give her last farthing to work for. She handed over her skimpy resume nervously, her age, the empty work years glaring on the page. But one interviewer had already shown approval for her innovative ideas and unfailing enthusiasm. There was bound to be a fit out there somewhere.

Outside snow was falling. The temperature had dropped below zero, and the wind whistled around the windows as if seeking entry. Bushes swelled with white blossoms of snow, and beyond the lake was veiled by thick white flakes. She slid open the balcony door, exposing the wild beyond. The wind found her immediately, and she closed her eyes as the snowflakes smacked her face, invigorating her cheeks, blowing and howling until she was thoroughly alive in every pore.

# Bring Me Little Cupcake, Darlie

**I HAVE A FOOD PROBLEM.** So does my friend. It's my friend I want to talk about.

After a forty-year friendship, Darlie and I stepped into retirement in tandem, ready to face a new life of freedom and exploration. Since my husband Roger died, I have answered to no one and become quite absorbed in my own drawing and watercolor-painting production. No more high school art students pressing for waivers and negotiating grades, although I will miss the interchange of ideas with those who get that learning is a goal in itself, with its own rewards.

It's a bright July morning when Darlene zips up to the house, her leather-cushioned Oldsmobile stacked to the brim. It's our first trip together without husbands—Darlene's Smithy is evidently off on a hike in the mountains with his buddies. I'm full of excitement.

"Good morning, Allison," she waves from the car window. At one time Darlie was judged exceptionally pretty, with her creamy white skin, soft as down, and deep blue eyes. In the old days, before she grew from size 10 to 18, male hopefuls would show up in the school break room to get her coffee. When we were together at the University of Minnesota she won a Miss Grain Belt contest and rode around the football field waving gaily to the noisy crowd, red hair blazing in the sun, and was listed in the school's *Varsity* magazine as The Friendliest Girl in the dorm. But that was forty-five years ago. Over time her flesh has spread, the shape of her body loosened. But she remains lively and bright. My best friend.

After stuffing my suitcase in the trunk, I get in the car. There are bags of chips and Oreos stuffed between the divided front seats. Immediately I am wary, anticipating the challenges I will face during the twelve days of our boat cruise down the Illinois River. Plenty of food, the dreaded health-destroyers that I so strenuously avoid, will be out in full force, the sweets and cakes drifting seductively in front of my nose. Mounds of buffet dishes at every meal, midnight snacks, unrelenting treats and energizers, with food accosting me from all sides day and night, unregulated, with no concern for health or safety—how will I ever live through it?

Darlie talked me into this cruise, overcame my doubts about being stuck on a boat smothered with lavish buffets, constant eating day and night. But what the heck—I'd been cooped up too long, there would be hikes through the canyons—go for it.

"Hey there, Coco." I turn to the American Eskimo dog in the back seat. Although I'm fond enough of dogs, I shudder at seeing this white fluffy bundle brushed and ribboned and ten pounds overweight, crammed among suitcases, diet Pepsi six-packs, and a mound of boxes piled in the back seat. You'd think we were setting out on a circus tour in which Coco is the star, surrounded with treats, stuffed rats that squeak, rawhide bones, rubber balls, colorful braided leather collars, and four-legged raincoats of varying weights. Coco glances at me, a sweet, friendly expression on her soft face. Relaxing a frown, I swing around to face the front. Get back on track here. We're on vacation; one is not allowed to fret on vacation.

Darlie starts the engine, turns the air conditioner to high, and roars down the road toward the freeway, on our way to the outlying Minnesota countryside.

"Darlie, we're free, free!" I exclaim, throwing my arms in the air. The sky soars beyond the windows, a clear cornflower blue brimming with bright morning light. We chatter and joke excitedly as we glide, air conditioner blowing, through our residential neighborhood, past shopping malls and sprawled office buildings bordering Minneapolis. After reaching I-94 toward Hudson, we cruise through lush rolling Wisconsin countryside scattered with distant houses and cattle grazing in wide-open grasslands. A delicious escape from routine and the dash and clutter of the city—including travel time, two whole weeks!

"How will Smithy manage if he returns from his trip before you're back?" I ask.

"Oh." Pause. "He'll be all right." I glance at my friend enthroned in the driver's seat, propped with cushions, her hands clasped firmly on the wheel, head straight ahead, red hair hanging softly along her full neck. She wears oversized red sunglasses, and a Byzantine cross hangs in the neckline of her billowy polyester blouse.

Why is she being so vague about Smithy? I get the impression she's hiding something. I know her husband has an unquenchable wanderlust, loves travel, seeing foreign places; he's not one to sit home while we cavort on an intimate river boat. But I decide to let it go, to respect her silence, to ignore the messy car and thick musty dog smell drifting up to the front seat. *Accommodation*—that's the watchword, the secret of a successful trip.

Still, I sense a problem. Darlene and I take diametrically opposite approaches to food. I've always been slim and athletic, and I like it that way. So when age started to bulge my body, puffing out my belly, dulling my reflexes and weakening my organs, I rebelled. Health became my obsession. No more junk food—only fresh, unadulterated nourishment allowed into my mouth, a counter to the pitiful shifts age thrusts on the body as it heads slowly toward inevitable cessation. The secret, of course, is to avoid temptation. I ban sweets from the house and eat only fresh produce and dishes that are healthful. The ship may go down, but I intend to be the last passenger to disembark.

I fear my religiously sustained diet is in imminent danger and steel myself to withstand the temptations ahead. The secret is to resist that first bite, the first warm, delightful taste of sugar on the tongue that glides easily down your throat and sends waves of exotic energy throughout your entire body. Because once I succumb, all is lost; the craving takes over. Once, I stashed a bag of Lindt truffles in a freezing cold garage in a move toward moderation. Without success—the bag was empty by lunchtime.

Abstinence is required.

Darlie, on the other hand, admits no such problem. She eats whatever she desires, unconcerned about weight, as if the way one looks, feels, and moves is unimportant. I simply don't understand. It's not that she tries to exercise restraint but gives in. She doesn't care.

This is not a subject for discussion between us. One word from me about the enlivening effects of health, and she bristles, whereupon I become mute. An unspoken friendship pact.

Darlie threads the Oldsmobile up and over the sprawling land of Wisconsin, revealing panoramas of rich green pasture curving toward the rolling hills, pocketed with crackerbox farmhouses and further up, the thick spread of forest. We chatter about the incompetency of the travel agent who first booked us on the wrong tour; the difficulty of finding a cruise that allowed dogs, since Darlie will not budge without Coco; the history of early French settlement in the state of Illinois; and the probability of finding card partners on the boat.

"We'd better start looking for a lunch place," Darlie says after a while, pulling her cell phone from the overstuffed black bag at her feet and handing it to me.

"We just had breakfast." I'm in too good a mood to be annoyed. Food will be a target at which all Darlie's efforts are aimed—might as well get used to it.

"Do you have something else to do?"

I take the phone and dutifully begin to Google.

"Find a place that offers desserts as part of the meal package," she urges. I'd just as soon get a sandwich at a Grab and Go, but say nothing. Darlie took charge of the trip arrangements from the start, and I defer to her well-tuned management skills. Lean back and enjoy the ride; I can do that.

"First we have to stop at the next gas station for Coco to do her thing and get a caffeine pickup for the driver," Darlie says. This will be one of the frequent stops for a cafe latte and pastries that Darlene requires to stay alert and which will keep the car continually flushed with the odor of rich vanilla creams, sugar, burnt cinnamon, melted chocolate—warm, alluring, demanding. All the way to Peoria.

I soon discover that the freewheeling manner in which Darlene satisfies her love of sweets she extends to good-natured Coco. She pulls out a foil bag that reeks of dog biscuits and reaches a handful to Coco in the back seat. The dog leaps forward and clamps her two front paws on the tray between Darlie and me. Inches from my ear I hear chomping, swallowing, then expectant silence. "Still hungry, darling?" The arm reaches back again, more chomping. My throat clutches. I watch anxiously as saliva forms and hangs from her muzzle, a few inches from my sleeve.

According to the vet—I recall the visit—Coco is dangerously overweight, a fact that flies over Darlene's head and out the car window. As we speed along Interstate 90, Darlene continually coaxes the dog with beef-flavored treats. Even when Coco twists away, a look of pleading in her eyes, Darlene insists until the poor beast gives up and obligingly accepts another mouthful. I bite my lip hard. How can my friend be so blind, without a clue as to what Coco wants or a thought of what's good for her? It reminds me of the manner in which ortolan songbirds in France are force-fed grain and brandy until they can't stand and served as a rare delicacy at top Michelin restaurants. I steel myself to silence, vowing never to let escape the words that throb in my head: stop, stop, stop!

Later we lunch at a roadside restaurant, complete with two side dishes and chocolate turtle pie, with an extra piece slipped into a napkin for Coco.

THE *SPIRIT OF PEORIA* will be our home base on the Illinois River for the next twelve days. The paddle wheel's white hull has been freshly painted, and I spot padded chaises and small umbrella tables on the open decks—the perfect setting to relax and cruise languidly through the crested hills and forests of Illinois. The scent of duckweed and river water permeates the air. This vacation is going to be fun! Airy, amicable, and worry-free.

We line up at the gate, buzzing with excitement. Darlene stands next to me in a floppy white straw hat and oversized sunglasses, looking freshly scrubbed. A free-flowing violet tunic hangs loosely over her hips, and a large, flowered scarf hides the contours of her neck. Her face, in contrast to the plumpness of her body, preserves a great deal of the dainty, well-defined features of youth. Coco stands patiently at her side, tail curled over her back, a fountain of streaming white. I look around at the other forty-odd tour members shifting and chatting quietly in the heat, waiting for the gate to open. Most wear brimmed hats against the sun, their shoulders dripping with cameras, backpacks, and canvas sun bags with *SPIRIT OF PEORIA* emblazoned on them in purple letters.

At last the boarding bell sounds, and the group shuffles up the wooden ramp. A steward leads us to our cabin, advising us to appear in the upper deck lounge in one hour, when the tour director wearing a red bandana will review the *Spirit of Peoria* itinerary. Coco immediately settles on one of the twin beds, burrowing into the pillow. I ignore this.

"Rather tight," I observe. I look around at the set of built-in drawers, a pull-down shelf, and two narrow beds connected by a nightstand, leaving just enough space to maneuver. There is also a small bathroom with sparkling blue bath tiles and a corner shower hung with a blue-and-white checkered curtain.

"It's tight, but that's to be expected in a small boat like this," I say, determined to concentrate on the positive and curtail my tendency to pinpoint the downside of every occasion. Beyond the porthole the blue-green surface of the river glistens in the afternoon sun. This is what it's all about! Fresh air and sunshine as we glide through the water and trek through the neighboring hills. I feel the thrill of pending adventure. Then I detect the odor of warm cinnamon and swing around to see Darlie stuffing a bulging paper bag into the bottom drawer of the bureau.

"I got these at the bakery back at the dock. We'll need snacks." Darlene, seeing me watching, smiles self-consciously, warily. I never see the bag again. I imagine hordes of foodstuffs stashed between the pile of shoes in her suitcase, or in a jewelry box, or even behind the pillows. I manage to hold my tongue, submerging my dismay at my honest, forthright friend's subterfuge. She hides her surreptitious eating from me as if I couldn't understand, and I must admit she might be right—I find her eating habits nothing short of deplorable.

**THAT EVENING DARLIE AND I** choose a table in the dining room by the window. Waiters in red vests and passengers in fresh-looking shirts and colorful slacks bustle back and forth among the long tables. From now on, we will be provided with buffets overflowing with entrées three times a day. Potato salad, standing rib roast, deep-fried chicken, lobster mac and cheese, French toast, creamed corn, deli sandwiches, fettuccine Alfredo, pasta salad wraps, pancakes, wet-cured ham, boysenberry syrup, every type of dessert imaginable laid out on tables along one wall—ALL YOU CAN EAT.

I pile my plate with a dab of every dish I can fit in, with the intention of returning to fill up on my favorites, but by the time I have tasted them all I'm full. Like most skinny people, I don't have a large appetite, yet my capacity for consuming sweets is limitless. One taste of a sugary confection and my whole system cries for more, while my mind yells, *Stop!* I'm convinced that sugar, like alcohol, has the power to get into your system and twist the healthy habits you have safely built up into insidious patterns, sabotaging your most sincere intentions.

"What's wrong with eating candy now and then?" Darlie wants to know. She doesn't comprehend how refined sugar can over-stimulate, preventing sleep and making you feel tense and even crazy.

"Oh, I don't know," I say carefully. "Sugar can lead to diabetes, Alzheimer's disease, cancer, heart disease, memory deficiency."

But Darlie is busy sawing at a ham shank. "That's when its consumption is overdone. Get with it woman, we're on vacation."

Of course, she's right. Exceptions don't count. Although I manage to avoid the ravages of sugar by not allowing sweets in my home and avoiding treat-based socials—nothing tempting within a mile—I can't resist the waft of fulfillment right before my eyes. Already I'm eyeing the dessert table across the room, the lineup of crème brûlée, chocolate mousse, warm apple crisp, raspberry nut cheesecake, cups of fried ice cream swirled with caramel. It occurs to me, if I wait until the diners have left and the waiters are preoccupied, I can sneak a few extra pieces of cake and chocolate tarts from the tray. Thoughts of maintaining my figure and fighting the toxic effects of sugar dissolve in the prospect of luscious tidbits entering my mouth.

Across from us, a thin woman with sallow cheeks sits stiffly erect as if about to conduct a Sousa march. Dressed in a dark brown linen suit with gold buttons, her brown hair tucked under a hair net, she primly plucks a bite of beet salad with her fork. Mrs. Heller, an accounts payable specialist from Connecticut, is traveling, she tells us, with her twelve-year-old nephew, an unpredictable fellow who doesn't tell her where he is going, just shows up at the meal table or surprises her at the cocktail bar bearing some outrageous toy weapon he got who knows when, who knows where. His parents, after settling him safely on board with his aunt, set out for a tour of the Indonesian islands. Mrs. Heller had no idea what she was getting into; she came on the cruise to *relax* not duel with this headstrong youth. Soon the nephew, Vaughn, a scrawny boy with *You Know What I'm Saying?* inscribed on his t-shirt, sits down next to her and wordlessly digs into a plateful of barbecued ribs and three kinds of potatoes smothered with sweet molasses.

Next to him a large woman in a polyester blouse covered with dolphins talks rapidly between mouthfuls, explaining that this is her fifth cruise with the same agency, different rivers, of course, and she can't recommend the accommodations and service highly enough. She tells us she always loses weight on these trips, that although she eats more, she walks her derriere off on the tours and is obliged to climb steep staircases and goes home healthier than she came. Viewing her ample flesh, I distrust her claim but refrain from seeking details. Darlie is more effusive; this is someone she can relate to. She flashes Mrs. Neff a bright smile and invites her to join us on deck for a game of cards. Mrs. Neff thrusts out her hand. "Oh, you must call me Hilda. So glad to meet you. Now tell me all about yourselves."

Hilda Neff quickly becomes a favorite at the table, noted for her generosity and kind remarks. She regales us with stories of the mysterious Orient and the three months she spent tending sheep in the Austrian Alps as a young student on an exchange program. I notice her eating habits immediately. She eats as much as Darlie, with one difference: She heaps her plate full on her first trip to the buffet, whereas Darlie fetches dainty portions, which she replenishes several times during the meal with just another spoonful.

Me, I eat until I'm full—less chance to fill up on dessert. Nevertheless, I fetch four dishes from the dessert table since it is necessary to sample each to select the best. I end up devouring them all. The air from the window is too soft, the lull of the boat too intoxicating, the aroma of the chocolate cream cake too powerful. The devil be damned, I'll eat what I want.

My plan to snitch a few more desserts comes to naught when the last tray is whisked away before the dining room has emptied.

It's only later in the cabin, stomach heavy, feeling sluggish throughout my body, that I am overcome with regret. My pathetic lack of control glares before me. Heaving myself uncomfortably on the bed, shame sets in. Once again, I've been gorging, although it goes against everything I believe. What is the matter with me?

EACH DAY BRINGS US to another landing, and I perk up. Another chance to explore the outcrops and cliffs spread along the shore. "Darlie, you missed a wonderful walk this morning. The canyons in Starved Rock were breathtaking," I say as we lie flopped out on the upper deck like two manatees, sun spilling down on us from a cloudless blue sky. The table between our chaise lounges holds tubes of sunscreen, a Louise Penny novel, and a *New Yorker* magazine.

"Let me know when you can get there by trolley."

"Come on, Darlie, you bought those expensive new walking shoes. Join us tomorrow morning. You'll have a good time. It would be good for you and healthy."

"I wish you'd stop worrying about my health. I'm in great shape. I take good care of myself."

We say no more. No need to go further with this, not when the sun is warm and the drifting air from the river sends intoxicating scents of earth and damp vegetation across our faces. I observe the scenery floating by, the scattered houses dotting the shore, narrow dirt roads that disappear toward dark-hued ridges rising in the distance. Next to us, fellow tour members in straw hats and sunglasses and noses coated with white cream recline in deck chairs, talking softly or reading magazines. Darlene lies beside me, eyes closed, sunk in blissful lethargy.

AS I PEER FROM UNDER MY HAT, a strange figure appears shuffling along the deck, a small man somewhere in his thirties. I see that one leg is shorter than the other, and he limps along with the aid of an African cane carved in cheetah and giraffe patterns. He appears no taller than a child, barely five feet. Sun rays shine on his bald head, and he moves steadily forward as if he hadn't a care in the world. When he notices me watching him, he catches my eye, smiles, nods, and passes by. His cane tap-taps as if he's announcing his presence or marking a lively rhythm in his head. He stops at the railing and looks out calmly over the serene expanse of water. Something about his independent demeanor suggests that he is on the trip alone, and a premonition tells me that I will be seeing more of him.

Sure enough, that evening after dinner I chance upon him in the recreation room. He's at a table with two elderly women in red bucket hats. Seated in a leather straight-backed chair, he looks bigger, his broad shoulders and a torso covered by a lavender t-shirt, his sinewy arms resting at his side. He looks up at me and smiles. "Join us in a game of hearts?" he asks, fanning out his fistful of cards with a neat twist of the wrist.

"I can't, thanks. I'm looking for Darlie. Have you seen her? She's wearing a baby blue tunic and purple scarf." I suck the word obese under my tongue, although it would have identified her in an instant.

"Yes," the little man responds. "I saw her in the corridor heading toward the cabins. She was carrying a piece of cake in a napkin."

I'm not surprised. Darlene has been displaying deceptive behavior. She mimics the eating habits of a thin person—appears to eat little, nibbles daintily at meals and leaves uneaten food on her plate, limiting herself to half a dessert (the other half, I note, goes into her purse). She never fails to refuse the cream croissants and Twix bars offered on deck by strolling waiters, claiming lack of appetite. I notice, as we share meals and spend hours in each other's company, that Darlene consumes less than I do. There is no way she can maintain her current weight with the meager supply of food that visibly enters her mouth. I suspect she makes secret visits to the snack shop during her fresh-air strolls around the deck with Coco.

I suppress my qualms at this parade of deception. Better focus on her bright conversation, fun-loving laugh, and intriguing ideas for new adventures. It's doubtful that my long-term friend, colleague, and strong supporter over the years could be guided toward a healthy lifestyle by any method at my command, and I abandon all thoughts of turning her into a better, more attractive, and need I say happier, longer-lived person.

**WHEN I RETURN TO THE CABIN** to freshen up for the evening concert, there is no sign of Darlene. After donning a white blouse and linen slacks, I climb the stairway to the recreation room. Passengers freshly cleaned and coiffed are arriving; the rows of folding chairs fill up rapidly. On stage, a crew member is giving the microphones a last check while the musicians tune their instruments. I find two seats in the third row, and soon I see Darlene enter from a far door, blue tunic billowing. As she attempts to squeeze into the chair next to mine, a steward steps forward.

"Madame, let me get you a larger chair."

"No need. This one is fine." With a graceful swirl, she lowers herself into the seat. The woman in the adjoining chair pulls aside with a brisk gesture, while Darlie leans back serenely, smooths her skirt, and tilts her head toward the stage.

After a high-pitched introduction by the master of ceremonies, the musicians raise their instruments, and the spotlight swings to center stage. Willie, billed as the lead singer, struts on stage in a black-and-gold vest and purple polka-dot scarf. He spins his acoustic guitar, adjusts his shoulders, strums a quick riff, and launches into a rousing "I Walk the Line," fingers flying over the strings. His voice fills the room as he sways and pumps to the beat of the drummer. He looks directly at the audience, eyes scanning faces as if addressing each one individually.

"I so love Johnny Cash!" Darlene breathes as the song dies out, as if transfixed. After the applause, the singer lifts his head, adjusts the guitar, and the strains of "Georgia on My Mind" fill the room. Now he stands tall and serious, delivering the words with slow and intimate immediacy. Darlie tilts her head forward, enraptured. I notice a flush cover her face as Willie swings his eyes over the audience and fastens them directly on her. Maybe he's drawn by her rapt attention, or maybe he's one of those performers who likes to select an attentive target, a recipient whose clear rapture deepens their own feelings. *A song of you/Comes as sweet and clear/As moonlight through the pines.* His voice sweeps sweet and clear as moonlight over us, and Darlie sways her shoulders to the beat, smiling dreamily.

Seeing the look on my friend's face, I lean over and whisper, "Does this make you want to dance? I vaguely recall you and Roger were into ballroom years ago."

"Glory to heaven, those days are long past! I'll be drawn and quartered before I'll attempt that again." She gathers her skirt around her protectively. "But they were amazing," she adds in a low voice.

The bass guitar player steps into the spotlight and strums the next tune, shoulders hunched, head swaying. The spotlight swings over to the keyboard, and the notes soar up and down the scales as the keyboardist performs his solo. Then the lights lower, and Willie resumes his spot, enfolding the microphone in his hands, sings.

> *Bring me little lovin', Sally*
> *Bring me little lovin' now*
> *I know you're not a giveaway lover*
> *I'm beggin' for it anyhow.*

His eyes sweep the audience with intensity, resting several times on Darlie. On the last refrain he picks up the tempo, his throaty voice arching dramatically.

After two more songs, to which she listens with ardent attention, Darlie stands up. "I have to attend to Coco." With a heave she rises and walks off.

It's the turn of the banjo player. He sets a fast country beat and, with the entire band singing, waves to the audience to join them—"Come on, you all know this one! 'Good Night Irene.'"

As the song concludes, a blue-clad woman flies into the far end of the room, waving her arms and yelling. "The steward, where's the steward?" The music stops abruptly; all heads turn.

I leap from my chair. It's Darlie. "What's the matter?"

"Coco! She's hurt. For God's sake, hurry!"

Darlene clumps down two narrow staircases to the boiler deck, blue tunic flowing, along a long corridor, with three stewards and me following close behind. Inside a dark room, next to a row of drying machines, there is a vent pipe attached to a wall, and from the floor opening protrudes a clump of white fur that I recognize immediately. Sharp whines are issuing from inside the pipe. The little man with the limp has somehow arrived before us and stands patting the dog's furry rump reassuringly. Coco appears to be caught in a lock-tight grip, but after her fur is doused with water and her haunches twisted this way and that, along with gentle tugs, she emerges at last, limp, bleeding, and wide-eyed.

Darlene clutches the dog in her arms, covers its face with kisses. "Look, she's crying! Oh, poor baby, my beauty!" More of this as we make our way to our cabin, where Darlene turns on the shower and shampoos out the dirt and blood as the dog looks up at her with beaming devotion. After rubbing the thick fur with a towel and drying the ends with a hair dryer, she tucks Coco under the covers in her twin bed and stuffs a few truffles in her mouth.

I confess my sympathy for all this distress is lacking. The dog has not been seriously injured. Darlie maintains an indulgent latitude with Coco, as nothing seems to be off limits. She sleeps and eats wherever she wants and follows her mistress everywhere, even into a toilet stall and a restricted hospital room. Coco pilfers crumbs from the meal table. She hides under Darlie's seat at a movie theater. Now the sight of the wet animal burrowed between the clean white sheets, head sunk into the pillow, sends my nerves jangling. Next the dog will be sitting in her own chair at dinner!

"I wonder how Coco got down to the lower level?" I ask, calming my voice. "It's against the rules to allow dogs free run of the ship."

"Hooey! What do I care for their silly rules? Coco needs exercise. She's well-behaved. For heaven's sake, she only ran off for a few minutes."

Darlene plucks a jar of cream from the nightstand, slathers lotion over her hands and rubs them together.

"Are you aware that if Coco weren't so overweight, she wouldn't have gotten stuck?" But Darlie is leaning into the mirror, surveying a large freckle on her cheek.

I give up. Coco is a good-tempered, friendly dog who has been pampered into a waddling, overweight beggar. And I can't stand the animal. Until now I've never found a dog I didn't like. Even a friend's defensive growler or aloof terrier ends up sitting cozily in my lap. But over the last few days I have been repulsed at the sight of this dog drooling at my elbow as I eat, jumping on the sheets with dirty feet, whining for treats, with the strong smell of dog food and saliva everywhere. I glare at the creature that is now soaking the covers in the next bed.

*Rules have a purpose. If you'd followed them, poor Coco wouldn't have gotten into trouble,* I want to say. Instead I grab a *National Geographic* and skim furiously through the pages.

**THE FOLLOWING DAY,** after a hearty lunch, Darlie and I recline on the top deck. The river at our side flows lackadaisically downstream, and the sun spreads over us, warm and relaxing. I'm deep into my John Grisham novel. The evil attorney is about to undercut the chief witness with secret data obtained from a Taiwanese stoolie when I hear a scream pierce the air a few chairs away. I turn to see our tablemate Mrs. Heller twisted in her seat, clutching a trembling arm to her side. Curious passengers turn to stare as she utters another shriek.

"Get that animal away from me!" the woman cries, sliding to one side of her chair. Then, in a rage, she hoists herself up, lifts her elbow and thrusts it into the flank of the dog sitting in the chair next to her.

"Leave Coco alone!" The scream comes from Darlene, who scrambles up, grabs the dog, and presses it against her chest. "What are you doing to her?"

"Her? What that animal's doing to me!" At the sight of her tormenter out of reach in Darlene's arms, the woman quiets down. "I was writing a letter to my poor husband, bless his soul, laid up with a broken back, fell off a bull in the county rodeo, at his age—never mind that, look at this!" She raises an arm, which is covered with wet scum. "Argh, it's sticking to my skin. Your beastly dog has been eating my cookies and has drooled all over my arm and ruined my new Liz Claiborne blouse." Pulling a blue tissue from her sleeve, she dabs at her arm.

"She was just being friendly. She loves everyone." Darlie rubs her cheek against Coco's ear. "It will wash out. What's the big deal? Look, you've scared the poor thing." Coco fastens her master with an inquiring look, eyes wide, tail moving hesitantly. "It's all right, babykins." She rubs her hand vigorously along the dog's back. "My poor precious, Mommy's here."

Mrs. Heller fixes Darlie with a look of steel. She harrumphs, clucks her tongue. "That dog is disgusting!"

"She's hungry." Darlene's cheeks are flaring. "You've been eating those ginger snaps she adores. Coco's on a strict diet, you shouldn't be eating sweets around her." Darlene snaps a leash on Coco. "Bring your blouse to cabin 33, I'll wash it out," she snaps and shuffles off.

The little man with the short leg has been leaning against the deck railing watching the scene with a studied air. A pea-green bucket hat protects his bald head from the bright sun. "Dogs will be dogs," he says sympathetically, limping over to me with amazing dexterity. He plants his cane solidly under him. "Mrs. Heller must be blind. The dog has been eyeing the cookies for quite some time, following every mouthful. Mrs. Heller should have taken precautions. My name is Gabriel, by the way."

"Hello. I'm Allison." Right off I like his air of musing intelligence.

"I noticed you and your friend immediately. You're opposites. You're thin and she's large; you're always on the move, while I see your friend prefers to be sedentary. I'm no psychologist, mind you, but from what I've overheard I would say that, as the extrovert, she runs the show, while you, the introvert, drift happily in dreamland. Mutt and Jeff. I find such dichotomy intriguing. I always wonder what draws people with opposing traits…"

I break in, preferring not to be analyzed by this stranger. "You're quite perceptive. But there's a lot more to it than meets the eye," I say agreeably. I decide to take him for a colorful character, presumptuous but evidently a close observer of human nature. No doubt his disabilities have served to sharpen his understanding of human frailty.

"I noticed you as well." I stop, afraid he would think I was referring to his limp. "You seem to be everywhere and know a lot. We'll have to get better acquainted." Something about the ingenuous candor of this fellow intrigues me. I reach beside the chaise for my polka-dot beach bag. "Right now, I'd better see if Darlene needs me."

That evening I arrive at dinner to find the little man seated at our table. "Hello, again," I say, sitting next to him.

"Your usual dinner companion is seated at another table. I've taken her place," he explains, looking at me with keen alertness.

"Lose some, gain some," I remark. "I'd say the gain was on this end." I laugh, feeling suddenly flippant. His appearance is stimulating, something about him suggests a depth of wisdom and a keen ability to make things happen. I like his way of stating things directly, as they are, without gloss or pretense. I determine to know more about him. Gabriel nods to Darlene and the other seven diners and launches into a general discourse on the pros and cons of the various river boats that tour the Illinois River. He loves the river cruises, the passing history, being on the water, and meeting new people, every one of whom he finds fascinating. Several of us linger with him after dinner, exchanging stories over a last cup of coffee. Gabriel becomes a regular at our table, and I find myself listening for the tap of his cane.

THE NEXT MORNING I find Gabriel on the lower deck, and we lean side by side against the rail and watch in silence as the world opens a new day.

Slowly, the emerging sun brightens the sky with splashes of light, bringing the river and drowsing landscape into view. We talk sporadically of this and that. There's not a subject Gabriel hasn't dissected; he throws his full attention into every detail. He describes his accident, his subsequent life on the outskirts of society, making friends everywhere, holding on to none. He listens intently to my worries about Darlie and the double life I lead as loyal friend on one hand and exasperated critic on the other.

"I'm having a hard time accepting my friend's relationship to food," I tell him. "I don't want to be a traitor so I hide my feelings. I hate being judgmental, and also hate being hypocritical."

"You shouldn't have to front for her, buried as she is in secrecy," he tells me. "She's a generous, kind person with an unhealthy lifestyle. She deserves to hear the truth."

**AFTER A FRESHEN-UP IN THE CABIN,** I wander on deck to find Darlie and Hilda Neff, our gregarious tablemate, relaxing under an umbrella and discussing the upcoming Latin dance contest, staged by a well-known impresario. Having taken an immediate liking to each other, the two spend afternoons on the deck together, refusing to leave the safety of the boat, ever since the guide talked them into taking a horseback trek to view one of the eighteen canyons in the area. He assured them that there would be no walking and that special treats would be provided after the ride. Just their cup of tea. After being hauled onto the backs of what they were assured were the gentlest of horses, they ascended the steep hills in what they claimed was a ride from hell. During the entire three hours, they bounced along over the rocks, snatching their blouses from the claws of overhung branches, were hissed at by a long-tailed weasel, thrown this way and that by stumbling horses who released foul-smelling lumps every five minutes. One even rubbed a snotty nostril along Hilda's arm. Thighs aching, glutes sore, they staggered back to the boat for tea and petit fours. Not for all the gold in Fort Knox will they be persuaded to venture again into the wild, unfriendly hills. In future they will stick to short ambles near the dock. Or better yet, remain on board, where there is plenty of opportunity to walk the decks should they be so inclined.

Since then the two women have become inseparable. Hilda offers me a sample from her ready box of pecan turtles, and I take one—only one— and savor the taste of caramel melting under my tongue, press the nuts between my teeth, rub my lips together, not swallowing until the last minute. Then I settle on a nearby chaise and open my book. Whiffs of chocolate drift over from the box on the table a few feet away, but the presence of others keeps me from indulging further. The realization fills me with guilt—my obsession with sweets dominates everywhere I go, while I hide my weakness under cover of being slim and healthy. Who am I fooling?

"Good afternoon, ladies." A steward in a crimson jacket weaves through the tables on the upper deck, tray lifted in front of him. He halts in front of our table. I eye the plate of rich bars sprinkled with powdered sugar that spreads the sultry aroma of fudge over our chairs.

"Freshly made walnut brownies, compliments of the chef. How about you, Mrs. Neff?" He lowers the tray, and she scoops several square pieces into her napkin, nodding thanks.

Like Darlie, Hilda Neff lives for desserts. "I don't understand the meaning of the saying 'You can't have your cake and eat it, too,'" she says, biting into the rich chocolate. "What else can you do with cake?"

"No, thank you," Darlene says when the steward turns to her, waving him away breezily. "I don't indulge." By now I'm used to her subterfuges and the way she acts like the daintiest eater on the planet. I stiffen in protest but say nothing.

"Oh, you must try one, my dear," Mrs. Neff exclaims. "They're made with freshly ground cocoa from Brazil. And still warm."

"No, no, I'm really full," Darlene says, straightening the nylon scarf around her neck. "This iced tea is enough for me." She takes a slow sip and peruses the distance with a nonchalant air.

Hilda would have none of it. "Now honey, try one. You're too persnickety. We must learn to accept ourselves—life is short. If it's your weight, I'm here to tell you that you are *not* fat. I know fat when I see it."

I sit up as if I'd been stung. The forbidden word!

"I can tell by looking at you, why you're robust and healthy, the way a woman should be. And young; I'm not fooled by those strands of grey in your hair. My dear, we women must stop trying to imitate the fashion models and admire ourselves as the pleasing, full-fleshed, lovely beings we are." She takes another bite of the brownie, and a look of contentment passes over her face. "You can't get chocolate this good at home," she says, munching.

"Thank you," Darlene says in a monotone, attempting, I guess, to keep calm. She must be in a state of alarm. No one ever mentions her weight. It's been taboo during all our years of friendship. We don't discuss weight because, according to Darlene, there is nothing to discuss.

Hilda's description of Darlene is shocking. Robust and healthy—I don't think so, Hilda! Everyone knows obesity is a major factor in heart disease and stroke and can be dangerous for those with high blood pressure or type 2 diabetes—both of which Darlie has. She must know this, must realize her eating habits are destructive, otherwise why would she take pains to hide them? It's hard to understand why this former beauty queen would continue habits that could jeopardize her health and threaten her life.

"Thank you, Hilda. I don't eat those things." Darlie slides her fingers daintily along her sleeve.

"Well," Hilda says, "I see you are set in your ways. I must return to my cabin to shower. See you lovelies at dinner." She lifts her rotund body, grabs her handbag from the table, and ambles slowly to the stairwell, kaftan ballooning around her in the breeze.

As we resume sipping our iced tea, suddenly we hear a shrill "Oh, dear me!" Mrs. Neff's unmistakable soprano voice from the depths of the stairwell. A few seconds later, Gabriel shuffles over and addresses the questioning faces. "I saw her fall. The steward caught her just in time, and has taken her to her cabin," he says, planting his cane in front of him with a philosophical expression.

"Mrs. Neff should be more careful," he says evenly to Darlie and me. "People that heavy shouldn't be using these steep stairways. I've seen it before. She's unwilling to face reality, doesn't see herself as fat and therefore she doesn't take care of herself."

Darlie slaps her *Inner Dog World* magazine on her lap as if she'd been struck by a bolt of electricity and glares at the little man. The taboo word!

"The woman has every right to use the staircase," she exclaims. "She's strong and knows her way around. She's been on dozens of cruises and trekked in the Rockies and cared for her sick mother until the end. She's as strong as you and me!" Darlene's cheeks are flushed, her neck arched.

Gabriel regards her evenly. "Do you deny she is seriously overweight?" Although he speaks in a calm, reasonable tone, his opponent shows no such equanimity. My skin begins to tingle, as if a schoolmaster is looming over me with a ruler.

"What has that to do with it?" Darlene shouts, drawing her feet under the chair. "She's an honest, considerate lady, entirely independent. As I am. You want to clamp restrictions on us. Why don't you mind your own business?"

"It concerns me when people are out of touch with the truth and ignore the danger to their health."

"I'm a deacon in my church! My friends value me for my honesty. Honesty is my mantra."

"Is that so?" A frown creases the little man's forehead, but his voice is calm. "I've been watching you. I saw you stash long johns from the bakery in your doggie bag. And hide a five-pound box of Whitman chocolates under your jacket at the Taylor Loop gift shop,"

"That was a gift for the minister!"

Gabriel stretches out his arm, clutching the cane handle, and bends towards her with a look of determined concern. "My good lady, you'd better face it, you're *fat*."

I clamp my teeth together and turn to stare out at the river, dreading the next move while at the same time struck with an intense curiosity.

"What I am is none of your business!" Darlene screams. Her hands splay open, her eyes seem to spit flakes of lava. She attempts to rise, breathes heavily, falls back into the chair. By the solicitous look on Gabriel's face, I think he's about to capitulate, but her next words stop him. "I am *not* overweight!"

This is more than Gabriel can endure. "My poor soul! How much of the rest of your life is fake?"

"How dare you doubt my word? I eat healthy food and am strong and happy just the way I am, which is completely within the realm of normal."

"Think of Coco. The poor animal must be assisted onto a chair, while you keep force-feeding her because you believe the more you eat the happier you are. An owl in the glaring sun can see more than you can."

Darlene looks up at him with defiance, then turns her head away. He regards her, then his expression softens, he lowers his voice. "I'm an animal lover," he resumes more quietly, before she can respond. "I have three cats, two dogs, and a parrot. The way you overfeed that dog breaks my heart."

I detect a flash of hesitation on Darlie's face, a sliver of recognition as she struggles to come to terms with his words. "Yes, she should be on a diet. But we're on vacation!"

At their lowered voices, the rest of the passengers return to their sunbathing and reading. Gabriel moves closer. He speaks in a sympathetic voice, as if addressing a child. "Dogs are supposed to be taken to the animal relief room, but you allow your dog to poop in the pump room. It smells up the deck," he says.

"Coco hates the relief room, it's damp and it reeks. It's too much for her."

"My poor woman, that is nonsense. The relief room is at the opposite end of the boat, possibly too far for you to walk. I'm sure you could make other arrangements."

Darlene looks at him with steel eyes. "You say all this out of pure prejudice. You project problems onto others to distract from your own disability."

"I haven't the power to overcome my disability. You do."

Darlene snatches her magazine. "You need to stop spying. You need to get a life," she says.

Gabriel clutches his cane. "I have no close friends—cripples live with being ignored. I'm an observer. That's what I do."

Darlie sinks back in the chair, releasing the magazine on her lap. She closes her eyes, and I wonder at the unfamiliar expression of hopelessness on her face. Slowly, she reaches for her sunglasses, slips them on, and tilts her head back. "I don't have any either," she says unexpectedly. "Except Allie here." Gabriel and I are too stunned to speak. "All I've got is my food."

I've been following this exchange with rapt attention. Hearing my repressed thoughts voiced aloud suffuses me with overwhelming gratification. It is affirming to hear the sound of truth ringing out. As I hear Darlie's weakness aired aloud and see her slumped in her chair, I feel my resistance lower and something in me melts. All I can think of is how charming she looks sitting there in her ribboned straw hat, and of her fun-loving ways, her crazy ideas, her strong advocacy of me over the years, her loyal friendship. I reach out and touch her shoulder.

"I'm sorry..." Gabriel seats himself gingerly in a vacant chair and says no more. The murmur of low voices and the patter of passing steps buzz around the deck. Darlene is sunk in a well of thought. "Maybe I've said too much." Gabriel stands up. "But you should know these things," he says as he shuffles off, cane tapping rhythmically along the deck.

It is my turn to squirm. I recross my legs and study a silver streak of cloud floating above the bow. The fire in Darlie's unspoken denial and my adherence to live-and-let-live have long kept the subject of Darlie's weight buried. I learned to take it for granted—if she doesn't care why should I? But during this trip evidence of the bald truth has surfaced, impossible to ignore.

Now the taboo has been broken.

"Your take, Allison?" There is incredulity in her voice. She swings her legs and sits upright on the side of her chaise.

"Well…" I hesitate, sensing the danger zone between us. I can't get the words out attesting to her weight, certainly not the three-letter verboten word. How would it affect Darlie's feelings, affect our relationship? I hesitate to breach my unspoken vow of silence. Still, while I stand fully by my friend, I no longer want to misrepresent something I feel strongly about. "I don't know, Darlene. I can't say. It's not my place." I set my glass of sparkling water on the table. Drops of sweat cover my palms.

"Allison!"

I regard her. There is no rationale that can convince me that Gabriel's words are false. He has no reasonable motive for accusing her, other than a strong intolerance for deception and a New Yorker's manner of bluntly direct but amicable confrontation.

Clearly Darlene intends to push this to the end. I plunge in. "I don't want to judge you, but I won't lie. Darlie, your health is failing. Your physician warned that your weight undermines everything they're trying to do for you." It feels as if I'd been dipped into a pot of boiling water.

Darlene smooths a wrinkle in her skirt. Her voice is measured; in it I hear both defensiveness and restraint. "The trouble with you, Allison, is that you're skinny and don't know what it's like to worry about eating."

"Little do you know!" I fling out, stung. "You've no idea what I go through."

What she does not know, can't possibly comprehend, is the agony I experience around eating. Darlene's home is a peaceful tribute to comfort and enjoyment. Darlene does not fret, she just eats. But not me. Me, I engage in daily battles with sugar. Since the onslaught of arthritis has brought a halt to the tennis and marathon races that kept my weight down, I can no longer eat the sweets and heavy pastries I adore without paying a price. Each bite encourages the next; I eat more and more often until the space between meals shrinks and I can no longer get my skirt buttoned. Or sleep soundly. I have pledged to eat only foods like Mediterranean salads and fresh fruit. But against orders and without my knowledge, my hand reaches out and slips delectables into my mouth. In a furious effort to exert control, I have turned my home into a hotbed of self-trickery: I hide cowboy bark in my panty drawer and pastries in the freezer, prolonging the time it takes to get them into my stomach. I leave desserts purchased for company locked in the trunk of my car and bury the key in the backyard. But it's no good. I awake in the middle of the night and fetch the goodies that seem to be blinking red lights in their hidden corner. All this produces a mad seesaw of thwarting and yielding to temptation, leaving me in a recurring state of turbulence.

I counterattack. Keep the house junk-free. Drink twenty-four ounces of water per day. Read food-scare books. Stop eating *before* feeling full, take Pilates classes, work out on machines, take five-mile walks. I hide out at the library, ignoring the gnawing in my stomach until the dinner hour arrives and I can safely return home and face the refrigerator.

I explain all this to Darlie as the waiter serves us two Arnold Palmers. She takes a long sip, then says in a conciliatory tone, "I don't see why you go to all that trouble. You're slender, why should you worry about a few pounds? Besides, size is just a matter of fashion—big is good."

What! I pull off my sunglasses to stare at her. Because I'm thin, she considers there is no problem. Which is exactly why I have never revealed my war with food to her—or anyone. If it doesn't show it doesn't exist. "It's not just weight," I say. "It's about agility and energy and stamina." Why can't she see that it's not only about appearance? Why can't she grasp my desire to maintain the energy that keeps me young and active and alive? "I care about *how I feel*," I say.

"Well, *I* feel just fine! I take my medication and get my rest. I take care of myself. You are in constant stress about eating while I enjoy life. Not much of a contest." Darlene sits up straight, and I can tell she is as much invested in our talk as I am. "I'm okay with how I am," she says. "I hide things to avoid your judicious perusal of my eating habits. You watch me like a hawk. You watch yourself like a hawk. If only you'd let it be."

Darlene appears to be taking the conversation with aplomb. I, on the other hand, am wound up in a coil, ready to strike. She doesn't understand. I am unable to let myself go like that. It's against my principles, against my nature.

"There's a lot you don't know about it," I say, standing up. "I'm going to get ready for dinner."

I stumble down the corridor in a state of agitation, hands shaking. I can't bear it. Everything happy happy. I stand under the warm spray of the shower, and as the water runs soothingly down my back I feel my limbs relax; soon a feeling of shame comes over me—shame of my cowardliness. I've always valued openness between us, yet at the first confrontation I turn and run. I hear the door open and close as Darlie enters. I stay under the warm spray for some time, letting the water curl around me. When finally I emerge from the bathroom wrapped in a towel, I find Darlie crunched in bed.

"You're right," I say sheepishly. "I need to let it be, to drop the charades. To at least be honest about my constant struggle with eating."

But Darlie is not listening. The drooping figure on the bed looks so forlorn, I'm stricken. Her face is drawn, shadows circle her eyes. Coco is pressed against her side, but she doesn't appear to notice. "What! What is it?"

Darlie opens her mouth; it droops but nothing comes out. I get the impression she is hesitant to speak, as if putting her thoughts into words will make them too real.

"While you were in the shower I called Smithy. He is filing for divorce."

"What?" I can't believe it. After thirty-eight years.

"He left the house three months ago. I didn't tell you. I was certain it was just a trial. I knew he'd come back." With this her shoulders sagged, and a rush of tears brimmed and ran down her cheeks. "I called him on my cell phone. I couldn't stand it, not knowing. Just to say hello. Find out when he planned to return."

Smithy gone for three months and not a word! So this is why she has avoided every mention of her husband, about whom she's usually so loquacious. Not a sign, not even to me, her best friend. I didn't guess the truth. How could I be so dense? Maybe I do not understand Darlie at all.

I sit on the bed and slip my arm around her shaking shoulders. Darlie tilts her head toward me, leans against my shoulder. This is not the breezy, cool, impenetrable person I'm used to, the career woman, the social manager, the trip instigator, and haute cuisine connoisseur. I feel all remaining resistance and defense ebbing away and, flooded with affection, pull her closer.

THE PEORIA CONTINUES ITS LAZY MEANDER through the Illinois countryside. The next day we dock at Starved Rock, and a group of us sets out to explore the nearby canyon. The trail leads across hills of white pine, Canada yew, and northern white cedar, spread along outcrops of sandstone cliffs. Gabriel and I often leave the group and wander off to photograph a crashing waterfall or spectacular rock formation. "Do you know," Gabriel says as he hobbles spritely along on his short legs, "In 1680, the once powerful Illiniweks were besieged on this butte by warring Iroquois tribes and sequestered until they finally starved to death. Colonial expansion wiped out most of the remaining population along the river." He is full of facts about the Illiniweks.

"How do you know all that?"

"I read."

We stop to inspect the relics at the Woodland Indian Museum, a sandstone building sided with blocks of glass about which he knows the entire history. He is well informed, this fellow, can explain the burial rituals of the Illiniwek tribes and the geological development of the dramatically carved Starved Rock canyons. An old photo of an Indian couple sitting stiffly side by side on a frayed couch, beat-up refrigerator in the background, catches our attention.

"Native Americans rarely get divorced," he tells me, studying the photo. He stands next to me, his head barely reaching my shoulder, gaze tilted upward. "Not because their marriages are happy, but they understand that there is strife in every union and assume their partner will have faults. My old aunt insisted, when my mother considered leaving my dad, that when divorced people remarry, they merely exchange one set of problems for another, that another partner will have just as many faults, just different ones."

He turns toward me, leaning on his cane. "It's also true of friendships. Consider you and Darlie. She assumes a positive approach to life, takes things as they are, whereas you tend to analyze, intent on getting to the bottom of things. You complement each other. In successful pairs, often one fills out the missing pieces of the other, so they fit together like a puzzle."

"It sounds as if Darlie's trait is an asset and mine's a fault."

"Not at all. Darlie takes things lightly; she has no need for analysis. You like to penetrate and uncover possibilities. Merely traits, without judgment." He looks at me steadily. "You accept each other's foibles. That's what bonds you."

"Maybe," I say, pressing my lips together. "But I can't help worrying about her."

He removes his green hat, stuffs it into his fanny pack, and runs his hand over his bald head. "I am blessed. My undesirable traits are exposed on the surface, my crippled leg, my stunted growth. So the rest of me is clean—my weaknesses are entirely on the surface." He shoots me a mischievous look.

"Oh, so you have no faults?"

"Have you detected any?"

"Not yet."

"Good answer. You might say my disabilities force me to be honest, as I can't conceal them."

As we meander through the museum, I admire the gentle, breezy way Gabriel shapes his thoughts, his head slightly tilted, piercing the workings of things around him, how he understands me with only a few words—I start the first sentence, and he can anticipate the entire paragraph. At the upper level, we pause to study the replicas of fossil mastodon footprints. "I wonder what those awkward creatures did with themselves all day," I muse, peering through the lighted glass.

"They slept, ate, shat, and copulated."

I know he is trying to shock me. "Smart ass." I can use an off-color word as well as anybody.

As I look down at his crippled form, this man twenty years my junior, I wonder why we get along so well. Maybe because we share a commitment to truth and an instinct for sensing deception. Like Gabriel, I like to call it like it is and can usually uncover a phony in a minute. Gabriel, I have noticed, attaches no blame to subterfuges and evasions, attributes them to the person's past traumas or conflict, or possibly an innate inability to overcome deep-seated fears.

It occurs to me that I can learn something from this man.

After watching a video on the earliest inhabitants of Illinois showing the remains of the prehistoric Cahokia Mounds, we set out on a hiking trail through the nearby hills. Now Gabriel launches into his story. A sadness flickers over his face as he describes how he lost part of his leg at age eleven when the car his mother was driving swerved off a bridge, killing her and rendering him a cripple. How he never had a chance to forge an army career, following in the footsteps of his father and two brothers, his childhood dream. How he studied hard for six years to become eligible to work with those suffering from post-traumatic stress disorder. How after a year at a Buddhist monastery in Ladakh, India, he became a Buddhist, shaved his head, and never looked back.

"Life goes on, my friend." He twirls his cane smartly, and now he laughs. "I acquired this cane at an African refugee camp in Niger. It's my power stick; with it I am whole. Maybe it's conceit, but I actually feel it enables me to do anything I care to."

I walk next to Gabriel in a state of contented exhaustion. A pleasant hike, lunch in the lodge, and exploring the museum have lifted my mood to new heights. We spot the familiar outline of our paddleboat moored at the dock, its white-and-red hull dominating the shore. Its decks are lined with colorful figures sunning themselves. Several small boats circle lazily on the river, as if going nowhere. At one end of the dock two little girls in tie hats bending over the water drop crumbs and watch the minnows devour them in snippet bites.

"Would you like me to cook some of those little fellows for your dinner?" Gabriel offers as we reach them.

"You kill them and I'll beat your ears in," cries the one in the red hat, before tossing in another handful. Gabriel and I laugh, and the girls laugh too.

**THREE DAYS LATER DARLIE IS PACING** the cabin looking like she's about to face a firing squad. It's the night of the Latin dance contest, the night everyone has been anticipating. "Why did I ever let myself be talked into this?" Darlie turns to me, hands clasped together, a look of desperation on her face. She has spent the last hour before the mirror, applying makeup, heavy eye shadow, crimson lipstick, clip-on rhinestone earrings, surveying the image of the red-and-black flamenco dress reflected back at her. All day she's been expectant, animated, sure of herself. Now she lowers herself on the bed with a low grunt. "What was I thinking?"

It was Willie from the band who persuaded her, after learning from the tour director that she had once won the Latins at the Robbinsdale dance pageant. Oh, just a local affair, no competition at all, she assured him, but Willie had whipped out his guitar and watched her twirl, slowly gaining speed. He nodded as she picked up the rhythm, melting into the music, her body gradually assuming an unexpected power. "I'll recruit José from guest services to partner you; he's experienced in the Latins," Willie says. "I think you can do it, Darlie. Go for it!" By the end of the afternoon, he had signed Darlene up for the contest.

And now, after days of rigorous practice, she is about to go out there and, she is certain, make a fool of herself.

I place my hand on her arm. "You can do it!" It's the friend in me, not the truth sayer speaking. In truth, I fear she will embarrass the audience as well as herself. Never, during years of teaching in the same high school and socializing with the same crowd, could I picture her as a dancer—she who dislikes excess activity, who circles for half an hour to find a parking space next to the store entrance, who avoids queues and only walks in parks that have benches.

Willie is pounding at the door. Fifteen minutes! With a weak smile, Darlie wipes her palms on a red handkerchief, throws me a pleading look, and follows Willie to the upper deck to join the band for last minute preparations.

I make my way to the recreation hall. The stage is draped with red and black tasseled curtains, and posters of matadors swirling their capes cover the walls. I've been on pins and needles—she refused to let anyone watch her rehearse—and locating a chair in the front row I wait impatiently as people crowd in and fill the seats.

A figure slips in next to me, and I turn to see Gabriel, who is wearing a red scarf tucked into his shirt collar.

"I am anxious to see this," he exclaims. "I had no idea our friend could dance."

"She *used to* dance. Forty years ago. To expose herself in her state is unwise. I'm not sure I can bear to watch."

"You'd be surprised at what people can do when it's something they love."

One by one the contestants line the stage, the women costumed in long flounced skirts and shawls with long gold fringes, the men in red cummerbunds—and bow to the audience. Darlie looks straight ahead with a determined air. As I regard the tight bodice, the mass of her flared skirt, and the roundness of her arms, I am swept by a feeling of horror. Maybe I should have dissuaded her. But Willie had been so sure, so confident, assuring us that her talent would bring the house down.

At their turn to perform, I watch as Darlie's partner, wearing black tights and a waist-length tuxedo jacket, sweeps up her hand. He stands tall and long-limbed, erect, his head rigid, his legs daggers. The music begins with a flare.

My hands are sweating.

I stare in amazement. What I see sends chills through my body. Head held high, Darlie swings around the floor, responding to each pull and tug of her partner, moving with precision and grace. The dynamic flamenco rhythms carry her with ease as she twirls in her flowing red dress, stamps and throws her shoulders back, head arched to the side. The ruffled skirt swirls around her legs, red splashes that follow her every movement as she spins as if carried by a force from another realm. Each pause and stretch displays authority, a light, ethereal connection to the rhythm as she spins and stomps her feet in perfect unison with her partner. I can't believe it, hold my breath for the moment when it will all fall apart and the skeleton of steel that possesses her will give way as she runs out of steam, and my poor friend will melt onto the stage floor like a pound of butter.

I could not have been more wrong. Darlie's natural rhythm and obvious pleasure in blending with the insistent pulse of the Spanish guitar transform her, carry her into a natural expression of restrained movement. The applause explodes; she and José are called back on stage for bow after bow. Holding herself tall, panting, smiling broadly, Darlie throws her arms out to the audience, responding to the warmth coming at her from all sides. She laughs aloud when the long arm of Willie catches her wrist, twirls her to him, and clutches her in an exuberant hug. "You are marvelous!" I hear him declare, "I'm going to take you home to Mama."

They receive second place. The other couple are dance instructors in Chicago—hardly fair competition. I can't get over the way Darlie blossomed into a graceful gazelle on the dance floor, reminiscent, she tells me, of her thin and agile days. I am filled with admiration. I also experience disturbing confusion. Why have I not known about this special part of her life, and what other layers am I ignorant of? First our food issues exposed, now this. What else remains to be uncovered?

"What? Where?" I ask her as we undress later in the cabin, but she falls into bed, and all I manage to learn centers around a summer romance in her twenties in Malaga that included dance lessons and late hours at a local dive by the pier. A smiling mystery that I vow to penetrate when the time is right.

"There's a chef's special dinner tonight, pulled pork with mushrooms and sweet potato soufflé," Darlie says the next evening as we change into fresh blouses and pull on silver and turquoise jewelry. "Are you almost ready?"

"I think I'll just grab a sandwich in the lounge," I say. "Too many tempting sweets at dinner." I have to do something. My eating habits have continued to erode as we cruise slowly down river. I have been gorging, stuffing myself with snacks and desserts. A never-ending battle!

Darlie's next comment catches me off guard. "What happened to the chocolate cream pie the chef let you have yesterday after dinner? The pie left untouched on the dessert table." I swirl around. Darlie stands in front of the mirror, attaching an earring to her pierced ear. "I was hoping for a taste."

"I—it's, um," I stammer.

Darlie regards me curiously. "What's the matter?"

I can't bear to admit it, after my constant ranting about sweets. "There's too much temptation on this boat. I had no intention—it just happened. I ate it."

"The entire thing?"

"The entire thing."

Little does she know how hard it is to sit on the couch with a bag of glazed donuts or apple crisp from the bakery stored in the back reaches of the refrigerator, feeling their existence pressing like gunpowder in your brain, blocking out the book in your lap or the drama on television. A laser call that drives you out of your seat and straight to the fridge for another portion. Before the evening is over the entire batch is consumed, fomenting in your stomach, and there is nothing you can do about it. You know it will happen, the inevitability. You give in, might as well just eat it all at once and be done with it, save the agony of fighting temptation and the shame. A losing battle.

My voice is hardly above a whisper. "When it's in front of me I can't resist."

"I thought you were so disciplined. And you're so thin," Darlie looks shocked.

"It's all these desserts. Since we got on this boat, I've gained six pounds!"

Darlie laughs. "You should be drawn and quartered. Me, I wouldn't know the difference. But Allie, I don't care. God doesn't care. No one cares. You can lose it when we get home."

"It's not that easy, Darlene, you've no idea. It will take weeks. My slacks are tight. I hate the bloated feeling. I feel loaded. I feel imprisoned. I can't bear it. And I can't stop."

"If you feel that strongly, what are you going to do about it?" Her matter-of-fact tone produces a calming effect. Maybe I'm creating a storm out of a few raindrops. Of course, I could reach out for help, but to attend Weight Watchers and announce that I want to lose six pounds—I would be sent to the stocks.

"Allie," Darlie resumes, "only you believe you have a problem."

"That's all it takes."

Darlie sits down next to me.

"It goes way back," I continue. "When I was a child, meals revolved around my eating. I refused to eat things I hated. I barely ate anything. My mother was driven to desperation—she's so skinny, what is the matter with her? I wouldn't give in, and she wouldn't give up. It was a raging battle, with me the center of attention. When the hormones kicked in, I snacked constantly on junk food, those energy builders that pull you out of the doldrums and lift you off the ground. I gained fifteen pounds."

"I'm sure you'll find a way to get back on track, honey. Don't take it so hard."

"You have always encouraged me, Darlie. You told me you would never stop being my friend. In all these years, you have never let me down. You were there when I discovered I couldn't bear children; you stayed with me when Roger drowned in the sailing accident and I couldn't bring myself to get out of bed."

We sit engrossed in memory.

The dinner bell sounds, and the loudspeaker announces a sing-along after dinner in the main lounge. Darlie fetches a doggie bone for Coco from a pouch in the bottom drawer, and we both grin as he drops to the floor and chomps noisily, licking up crumbs with his tongue.

IT'S THE NINTH DAY of our cruise down the Illinois River. The wind is low; there is only a mellow play of breeze caused by the slow movement of the boat and the usual warm spray of sun drenching the land. Today is a free day, with everyone on their own until the next port. I find Darlie on the upper deck at a small table, Coco nestled at her feet. Nearby, a couple is sipping iced tea and peering at an oversized map. Mrs. Heller's young nephew leans at the railing, panning his rubber bullet gun across the water as if looking for targets.

Feeling relaxed and deliciously non-purposeful, I descend the stairs and lean on the railing of the bottom deck, gazing idly at the passing green hills and red and black rock formations lining the shore. I could really get used to this...

I hear footsteps and observe Mrs. Heller stroll up to the railing and stand a few yards away. She clutches the top bar with both hands and observes the river scene with tight lips. "I saw your fat friend on the upper deck," she says after a while, wiping her moist fingers with a tissue. "In case you're wondering."

I am aroused with a jolt, my face turns pink. "What do you mean? You are speaking of my best friend. That word is demeaning."

"I don't see how you can deny—"

"Have you any idea what she puts up with? Ridicule and intolerance surrounding her from all sides. But she has learned to live with it and accepts herself as she is."

"I don't think—"

"And so have I." I take a steadying breath. "You have to understand, food addiction can be a sickness. Don't you think she'd prefer to be slender if she could?"

I am jolted from my anger by the sound of staccato yips from the upper deck, and suddenly a blurred trajectory flies by me, followed by a loud splash. I recognize the white form bobbing below me, churning the water, bubbling little cries of distress. In a panic, I lean out over the railing, focused on the furry little body pumping water furiously a few feet below. Impulsively, I swing my body over the railing, release my hold on the top bar, and plunge feet-first into the sun-soaked water. Seconds later my head emerges, dripping. Twisting around, I spot the white head of fluff drifting away from the boat, a wet tangle of fur, eyes scouring frantically in all directions. As I swim toward it with firm crawl strokes, I hear a splash behind me and twist to see another swimmer heading for the same goal. I get to the animal first, whereupon Coco clings to me in panic, digging her claws into my shoulders. A minute later Gabriel draws up, riding the surface of the water easily with his muscular arms.

"What are you doing, Gabriel?" I cry, tugging a tangle of wet dog hair from my mouth.

"I thought maybe you could use assistance."

"I was on the swim team in college," I spit out.

The *Spirit of Peoria* is easing farther downstream. I hear a siren sounding across the water, can see figures on deck, crowding the rails, men scrambling to detach a lifeboat. Shouts of encouragement reach us: "Hang on! We'll get you!" I can see on the upper deck Mrs. Heller's nephew, Vaughn, a smug look on his face, holding his rubber bullet gun against his stomach. Darlie is leaning over the railing waving her scarf, as if that would help. Impossible to remain still, she must do something, anything.

I watch, kicking to keep us afloat, as Gabriel tugs on one of the life jackets he snatched from the side of the boat. He hands the other one to me. I struggle to pull it on, Coco all the while snorting in my ear, struggling to get up further toward my head while I keep his peddling legs away from me with my elbow. "It's okay Coco, calm down," I say in what I hope is a soothing voice. I'm not good at babying tiny things, but Coco looks forlorn, fur matted against her head, eyes bloodshot and wet, her body shaking against me. Snapping the life jacket closed, I hold her closer.

"You're shaking," Gabriel says, treading water alongside me.

"Seeing our boat move off downstream doesn't exactly build my confidence," I sputter. "What the devil are we doing here in the middle of the Illinois River?" I watch as the *Spirit of Peoria* drifts further into the distance, the figures lining the rails getting smaller and smaller.

"There's land on both sides; it's not as if we're in the middle of the ocean," Gabriel says. "Don't worry, they won't leave us to float down the river on our backs." With his head and shoulders above water, he pulls Coco's claws from my back and strokes her head gently. "Look, the boat is attempting to turn around; a lifeboat is heading this way."

There is nothing left to do but wait. I feel a tinge of misgiving as the stretch of water separating us from the boat grows wider and wider.

"Gabriel!"

"The lifeboat will be here. Relax."

"No one back home's going to believe this," I say.

"I do believe we are a bit crazy," Gabriel says, chortling. "The captain may do some mental tests on us."

"Let's make a bet. Will the consensus be that we are heroes for rescuing Coco or idiotic fools for leaping in after her when the boat officers could have handled it?"

"It only matters that *we* know the truth," Gabriel exclaims. "Whatever that is."

With that we both burst into hysterical laughter, caught up in a fit of giggles that take on a life of their own. I struggle to catch my breath, stomach shaking, unable to stop the laughter. Each time I pause, a series of snorts from Gabriel starts me off again, until I am breathless. Coco, resting against Gabriel's life jacket, looks around as if glad to hear a comforting sound.

The lifeboat is approaching in the distance. The danger is over. I flip over on my back and stare at the sky, feeling my body buoyed by the warm water. Silver streaks lap over the smooth round of my belly, the bulge I'd been fighting to reduce. No longer!

"No more diets," I announce, rubbing my hand over my stomach.

"What! You on a diet? You're joking."

"My aim has always been to eat wholesome food, to avoid the dangers of processed sugar and the weight gain brought by advancing age. A new book has come out showing that by eating only healthy foods, over time your system self-regulates and eliminates the craving for harmful junk. How perfect is that."

"It doesn't hurt to have a plan," Gabriel says lazily.

"No, and no matter what happens, I'll be okay with it."

Coco, who has been gazing at me steadily, moves up and rests against my chest, quieter now. I smile at Gabriel floating alongside me. The water laps warm against my cheeks. I kick easily, feel myself carried along by the current, the water shimmering on all sides with green, vermillion, ochre reflections, charged by the brilliant light of the sky. Gabriel is whistling a tune of childhood. I find the words and join in. "Cruising down the river, on a Sunday afternoon…"

The river pillows under me, meandering toward its destiny, and I relax into it. The rising hills spread out on both sides of us in bronze, green, and brown splendor. I can see the boat receding toylike downstream, can see ant-people circling around the decks. Gabriel carries an expression I have not seen before, a look of contentment and non-questioning acceptance, of blissful containment with nothing missing. Coco is drooped across my chest, feet dragging listlessly in the warm water, gazing with a reassured expression at the figure of Gabriel floating a few feet away. When I look down at him, he shifts his head and gives my shoulder a lick; I don't know if he is reassuring me or giving me a token of gratitude. I listen for invisible river life carrying on unseen in the depths below as we float relaxed and free, gazing up at the cloudless sky.

Suddenly I do not want to go back. The water feels so warm, accommodating; Gabriel at my side looks so happy. *We are loose, half-drowned water sprites going nowhere fast, if only it would last!*

But soon the lifeboat draws up. I hand Coco up to outstretched hands, and Gabriel and I are pulled into the lifeboat amid much consternation.

Surprised to see us looking cheerful, the three crew members settle us in the bow without asking questions, intent on their life-saving mission. Gabriel and I smile at each other.

People on deck cheer as the lifeboat pulls up, and we're hoisted aboard, wet and smiling, surrounded by admiration and loud admonishment—Fools, you could have drowned! Coco is shrouded in blankets, with Darlie cooing, squeezing, crying dry tears.

In the background, a series of snorting laughs. Darlie peers through the crowd to see Vaughn leaning against the wall, rubber gun at his side, looking smug. Abruptly, she thrusts Coco into my arms, moves off, and I see her pin Vaughn against the wall with her weight, pressing the hand with the gun against his chest.

"I saw you throw him in," she cries, her face bright red. Vaughn's smug look fades, and he grimaces: No, he will never apologize, that stupid dog has no business being on the boat, a damned nuisance, he's sick of the thing.

Darlie releases him, grabs the rubber bullet gun, and, with a forceful thrust, flings it over the side of the boat. We hear a sharp splash as it hits the water.

"You have not heard the end of this!" Darlie cries. I am stunned at Darlie's transformation, at the unexpected energy belying her easy-going, lackadaisical manner, her avoidance of exertion at any cost. Maybe I don't know my friend as well as I thought.

**LATER THAT DAY,** after a hot shower and a hot toddy, compliments of the boat captain, I am relaxing on the upper deck when Darlie appears. "I've brought some Fujis and a bottle of sparkling lime water," she says, lowering herself in the chaise next to me and tilting her straw hat against the full afternoon sun.

"Hi, Coco." The dog leans against the edge of my chaise, and leaning over I feel a soft wet tongue against my cheek. Since her rescue from the river in my arms, followed by a great deal of petting and scratching on my part, I have become Coco's new best friend. I pat her silky head and stare out at the calm river curving out of sight in the distance, carrying ghosts of the past in its warm waters. I breathe deeply and feel my body melt into the soft cushion.

"Thanks for the healthy treat," I say to Darlie, referring to the plate of sliced apples on the table between us.

"I'm watching it. Not changing my lifestyle, mind you—dieting is not for me. But it hit me when I saw Vaughn toss poor Coco into the river and I couldn't move faster than a snail. I could have prevented it—" Her voice rings deliberate and clear over the deck—"if I weren't so fat."

At last! A liberating sense of release flows through me. I stare at my friend, composed and free next to me. No matter what anyone says, Darlie is still beautiful.

"Darlie," I say, "you and I are more alike than I realized. We're both pushovers for anything sweet and can't control ourselves. The only difference is that you, for the sake of appearance, conceal your eating habits but carry on as you please, having made peace with your state. Whereas I, for the sake of appearance, conceal my binges and struggle constantly under rigid standards and bouts of nervous self-flagellation."

"But things will be different." Darlie was looking at me with uncommon tenderness.

"They must be." I smiled back at her.

It looks like both of us will be alert to what we put in our bodies from now on. Like forever.

Forever—the lifetime of a friendship.

A flow of air from the riverbank skims across the deck of sun bathers. I draw in the pungent odor of damp weeds and lichen from the river blow. Straightening my sun hat, I regard the black and white *PROMENADE* sign on the wall, the brilliant yellow umbrellas dotting the deck, the scarlet beach bag draped on a nearby chair, my crinkled toes browning in the sun at the end of my chaise.

Life is good. From now on, wherever the river goes, that's where I'm going.

# The Night Owl Sings

**THE WINDOW ACROSS THE ROOM** is a dark aperture; I can't see beyond the ink-black pane, and any eyes out there would certainly have an open picture of me snuggled here in bed. But there is no creature around that is the least bit interested; no one ventures up here to this small cabin concealed in the woods. The property abuts ninety acres of protected Environmental Conservatory land to the north, with neighboring cabins concealed on the southern edge of the lake beyond a thick spread of white pine and tall oak. Any spy out there would be a nocturnal animal, merely curious, observing me through the glass.

I'm not scared up here. The darkness around me feels comforting and solid. I prefer the nighttime, safely peering out at the world from the protective darkness.

Placing the Ondaatje novel on the nightstand, I unpin and shake out my hair and click out the lights. As I lie, cheek warm against the pillow, the rustle of nocturnal life outside grows more intense. A crackle that could be footsteps sounds beneath the window, a low cooing issues from overhead. A wintery wind has picked up across the lake; I can smell the scent of night air from the open window. The air is cool, puncturing the softness of Indian summer, filling me with expectation. Tomorrow the men will arrive, and a new chapter begins.

The cabin sits on four acres in a clearing that slopes gently down to the edge of Starling Lake. It is surrounded by humming woods harboring hidden animal life that rarely ventures into the open, except for brazen raccoons that break through screen doors to steal leftover food. Believe me, I've had many rows with these thieves, even though they try to win me over with their cuteness. Here in this cabin the children, Carson, and I spent summer after summer, a happy, active family. Back then. It's for them I'm undertaking the renovation, not for me. I'm old, retired, husbandless; I have no more truths to find or roads to travel. I dawdle around my apartment in the city, wondering what to do with the rest of my life. Well, I can do this. For them.

The cell phone on the nightstand rings. Who in the world?

"Hello."

"Mom?" It's my daughter, Emma. Her voice comes through sharp, distant. "Hope it's not too late to phone. Sorry I haven't returned your call. You can't imagine how busy—"

"You don't have to explain. No problem." I am careful not to apply pressure on Emma and Todd. They have flown off to their own lives, with their own families and jobs, and I no longer have a family on site. They are buried in soccer games, piano lessons, medical appointments, sleepovers, and the continual shopping, driving, and maneuvering that make up their lives and keep them in a constant state of acceleration.

"I don't think we can join you up there, Mom. It depends on the kids' schedules." Her voice is heavy with doubt.

"I understand." She'd long given up trying to counter their busy schedules, careful not to be too pushy.

"Just called to let you know. Enjoy yourself. I know how much you love the cabin."

"But you must see the new renovations," I urged. "You'll love all the changes."

"Oops, Phil just walked in. Got to run. Maybe in the fall before it gets cold. Goodbye, Mother."

The cell goes dark.

My throat tightens. I sink down on the pillow, envisioning those summer weekends at the cabin when it was bursting with activity, the children loose in the freedom of the surrounding woods, building forts, collecting agates along the shore, rummaging for raspberries among the coneflowers, running in and out of the water with inflatable rafts and surfboards. Gathering for dinner on the porch, after which Carson abandons his model automobile collection and joins us to roast s'mores at the campfire, followed by a cut-throat game of Monopoly or Malarky. The family around me, close, warm.

Back then.

Since Carson died in a freak ski accident twenty-six years ago, I frankly admit, yes, I have neglected the cabin. The gutters are cracked, the back steps crusted with moss, the tile floors chipped and outdated, weeds and bushes cover the driveway. The forest is a living force that strives continually to reclaim ownership the minute I turn my back. But I love the old-fashioned water fixtures, the worn oriental rug, the dated stone fireplace, holding hours of irreplaceable memories.

Then last spring, after thirty-four years of employment, I retired and turned my attention to the cabin with new eyes. It was not a pretty sight.

Nothing to do except get off my derriere and take action. Last spring, as I sat by this very window with a cup of tea, pondering, the idea of a new project fired through me. Just the thing to lift the doldrums! I determined to undertake a major renovation. A new beginning. A fine, sparkling cabin that would bring Emma and Todd back to the fold. Like the old days.

The men have spent the last two weeks measuring, ordering, carting in supplies and lumber, checking requirements. I have design plans in place. I'm a bit nervous to have to tell a bunch of working men what to do, but the renovations must be perfect. God knows what decision I will be called on to make next.

My thoughts as I lie in bed are interrupted by something slapping the windowpane. Immediately, I'm full awake. Something's out there—maybe, just maybe, it's the fox, a sleek creature that has been slinking around all summer, weaving between trees to spy on me. I've seen him on walks slipping through the branches, his reddish fur running thick along his back and his long sweeping tail ablaze with a deep red hue. He might be outside right now, having tracked me down. The thought makes me laugh, throws me into a tailspin of curiosity. Tiptoeing to the window, I peer out but can determine nothing in the moonless dark. Must be a twig. I return to bed, draw the comforter lazily around my chin, and wait for my body to create a cocoon of warmth under the covers.

From outside, *hoo hooo hoooooo hoo hoo,* a velvet wail in the night, cuts through the air like a companion voice in the darkness. I've never seen the owl, but its call is familiar. I recognize the soulful sound, and it shoots through me, reminding me of all those summers when everything was young.

A vagrant breeze slips through the open window and brushes over my face, and just as I am about to smile, I fall asleep.

**THE NEXT MORNING,** I am up early, brewing a cup of Tazo. Outside, the lake reflects sparks of the lifting sun, and the canoe bumps softly against the dock. I catch a whiff of wet leaves and fishy lake life. The day promises sunshine and action. The men will be here soon. Lulled by the fresh air, I have slept soundly, am ready to hop on the next gust of motion and dig in.

It wasn't easy to get the renovation project off the ground. At first, I flew around in a tizzy, seeking advice, combing the internet. I researched building designs and consulted architects. And then I found Thor.

As I dip a donut hole into my cup of tea, I hear a noise in the yard. Thor and his two assistants are here! Thor, with his thin torso, sharp Adam's apple, and swig of short sandy hair lying flat on his forehead, is a puzzle. When I first met him in the Silverton Lumberyard office, I found him dry, so uncommunicative that I figured him somewhat dense, but the manager assured me that Thor was the best contractor in the area. I discovered right off that this guy was not into formalities. No formal contract, simply, "We'll be there," as he handed me a one-page invoice. What's this? No itemized list of projects, materials, labor? Did he operate on the buddy system? How could I deal with this?

Within minutes the cabin is abuzz with energy. They will be expanding the kitchen area, adding a room-sized porch, enhancing the main door with a wooden archway, and building a new redwood deck with railing and lattice sidebars. The old white metal cabinets in the kitchen will be replaced with new hickory models, and the floors and ceilings resurfaced with new oak paneling. I can hardly wait!

After consultations, trials, and adjustments, the work is under way. I trot upstairs to the loft, drape my jacket around the back of the desk chair, open the laptop, and pull up my latest poem. Below I can see the men unloading stacks of two-by-fours and measuring for the new foundation. Thor, dressed in heavy work overalls and a worn leather belt cinched tightly around his waist, has a serious, don't-bother-me look. Thor's son Lenny, who is learning the trade, keeps his attention safely on his work and says little. The third worker, Fred, is a burly fellow of around thirty-five, with an edging of blonde hair bulging from his tan bucket cap and a scraggly yellow mustache that droops over his upper lip. He looks like he could lift a tractor. I distrust his air of floppy nonchalance.

Later I learn from the lumberyard that Fred spent time in prison eleven years ago. His crime: While working on a cargo ship on Lake Superior, he beat up a fellow dockhand, breaking his arm and throwing him into a pile of metal panels, which cracked the fellow's skull behind his ear. The memory has faded, but Fred has kept a low profile since his return.

What have I gotten myself into?

**THOR ISN'T EASY TO DEAL WITH.** I hate to complain—hard-working Thor seems to know what he's doing. But he's an action-not-words guy; direct, to the point, that's Thor. *Yep* and *Nope* are his favorite words, never an explanation. But I need explanations! I must contend with terms he tosses out liberally—joists, two-by-fours, flashing, hip roof, dado, fascia, backhoe. Even when I press—Could you put that in different words?—he merely repeats the same thing. When he says in a clipped monotone, "The end siding will run up to the soffits," and "The wall truss will replace the two-by-fours right under the eight/ten pitch, so it'll fit real good," I struggle to repress my frustration.

I consult the dictionary a lot.

"What are soffits, Thor?" I ask. His face puckers, his mouth squeezes into a knot. He looks like he'd rather be fending off a drove of alligators. He thinks awhile, spits out a few words. When I request a sketch, a job list, or a breakdown of materials, Thor gives me a sour look, clearly not used to such persnicketiness.

Eventually we establish a halting work pattern whereby I go off and decipher his ramblings on my own, and he goes ahead and does what he figures will work. I try to keep on top of what he's doing, to grasp all the loops and curves. I want to be involved, to be part of the team, to ensure the end result will live up to expectations.

I experience constant irritation. Often they ignore my desire for detailed information, respond with unintelligible construction terms, change their work routine abruptly without letting me know. Their plans alter with the breeze. Damn it, how can anyone be expected to operate under these conditions? What a bunch of loons. A non-communicative leader, a skinny kid, and an overgrown delinquent—how is this ever going to work?

Still, as I watch the three men work steadily, lifting, sawing, hammering, confronting challenges of supply and size, I envy their easy camaraderie and the way they understand each other with a mere word or nod, connected in a mutual goal of accomplishment. I have no choice but to trust that their haphazard comings and goings, which are beyond me, will add up to a slick, rejuvenated cabin.

To smother my doubts, I pull on a boonie hat and set off into the woods. "I'm going for a walk," I yell to Thor, who is on the porch foundation hammering two-by-fours.

"If you get to Culbertson's, find out if he got that fox," he calls back.

I stop short. "What do you mean?"

"Old Ed Culbertson's been out with his shotgun looking for the fox that's been nosing around his place at night. He aims to kill it before it gets to his turkeys."

I wonder if it is the same red fox I've seen lurking in the woods ever since I arrived. Strange maybe, but I've had the distinct impression the fox is watching me. Once, without the slightest sign of fear, he approached within ten feet, stood squarely, and returned my gaze. His ocher eyes brimmed with a mysterious intelligence, his pointed ears twitched, as if catching a thousand nuances of life filtering through the air. He looked at me with an air of purpose. I gazed back at him, afraid to move, as if to break contact would cut off my source of oxygen. Finally, he blinked and was gone.

Quickening my steps, I follow the narrow deer path through the woods along Starling Lake. My aim is to find the fox and somehow warn him. It makes no sense, but that's my plan. He mustn't be killed. There is something about that fox—an otherworldly mien, a penetrating gaze that fascinates me.

I follow the path around the lake through a thick range of oak, aspen, maple, ash, and pine trees that glitter with gold, auburn, and velvet brown. At last, the forest breaks into a wide grassy meadow of wheatgrass, milkweed, and yellow buttercups spread out in opulent cover. Whiffs of sweet blossom fill my nostrils. Once a cultivated field, the old farm buildings have long disappeared, the land reclaimed by nature. I brush past a thicket of asparagus billowing like feathers in the breeze. Black-and-orange butterflies, flying ladybugs, and speckled moths flutter among the wild elderberry bushes. Overhead, two hawks circle, dipping and crossing each other in sharp runs. As I approach, a trio of thrushes flutter on a low branch, squawking and shoving. I seem to be the only human life in existence, caught in an outpouring of nature. I am invaded by an overwhelming sense of well-being.

I want to linger, but my anxiety about the fox returns, and I get on with my charge. I detect the cool odor of the spring-fed lake before it comes into view. Emerging from the woods, I look out over the water gleaming still and smooth under the crisp autumn air.

Sidestepping down the slope to the water's edge, I squat and dip my hand into the cool water. Suddenly, from the corner of my eye I spy a movement along the shoreline, possibly a falling branch or an errant breeze. Then a reddish shape flashes from behind a clump of pine trees and patters lightly to the edge of the lake. I freeze and hold my breath. It is too far away to be certain, but it is, yes, clearly an animal, maybe a dog, but no, the fur is too scruffy, the tail too bushy. The brilliant red color is unmistakable. The fox! I can't believe my luck. Slowly, I lower myself to the ground. Don't see me! Don't run off!

As I stare, the creature laps steadily from the lake in long, deep gulps, then, muzzle dripping, raises his head and looks around. His eyes fix on my kneeling form. I don't move. He holds me long and hard with his gaze. I wait, my blood racing. The shelter of the woods hovers mere feet away, and I'm afraid the vision will disappear into its depths. But no, probably struck with curiosity or bravery, the fox starts padding toward me, ignoring the squirrel that scampers up a tree, tail whipping. The red apparition stops a few yards away. I remain transfixed. The remains of a deep wound is streaked along his side. But his tail is erect, and the soft eyes continue to survey me, his reddish bronze fur glistening in the sunshine.

Then, to my amazement, the fox glides to the lake, scoops up another jaw full of water, trots up the bank, and sits in the grassy area near me. As I slowly lower myself to the ground and draw my arms around my legs, he licks his paw, runs his tongue over his muzzle, and looks out over the water as if he considers a moment of contemplation a good idea.

I must warn this beautiful creature! How to communicate the danger? At last, with a helpless gesture, "Stay away from the Culbertson place," I say aloud. "He's out with his gun to get the next fox he sees." I feel better saying the words and see him turn his head in response.

As the fox regards me, I have the unmistakable feeling he understands. He shakes his head indifferently as if to say, *If I get killed it is no matter*. He looks as if he knows exactly what he is doing and there is nothing for me to add.

Since my voice has not freaked him, I try again. "If you go there, you'll get shot."

He looks at me with an air of amused serenity. Under his soft gaze, I feel an understanding, not for my warning, for which he seems to have no use at all, but for me and my desire to connect. Now he sinks to the ground, curls his luxurious tail around his legs, and gazes serenely out over the water, as if he has nowhere else to go right now.

"Foxes don't relax in the open like this," I say aloud. I am unconcerned at my outrageous behavior, here in the wilds where reality is not obvious. "They're either out chasing meals or rounding up offspring or sleeping. They don't just sit doing nothing."

At this the fox chortles, an unexpected cello sound. I take this as a contradiction. *But don't you see, I am not doing nothing*, he seems to say, as a sly smile creases the edge of his jaw. *I am enjoying the sunshine. Being inactive can actually be doing quite a lot*. His words form quickly in my mind; I am finding this fox amazingly easy to read.

"If we weren't talking, we'd be doing nothing," I begin to counter, but before I can finish the thought, I realize that he has a point. Sucking in my breath, I feel energy flowing through me, lifting my chest. I am aware of how refreshing the air is, how deep the colors of the forest, and how much I am drawn to the fanciful creature next to me. It hits me that there is much I could learn from this fox, that he holds a cache of wisdom that I yearn to probe. If only he could tell me what to do with the rest of my life.

We look together out over the water gently nudging the shoreline. The earthy tang of dry leaves and rotted wood drifts across the lake, and occasionally a sudden sharp cry sounds from the nearby woods.

Slowly I move toward him. "Red," I say aloud, giving him a name. He doesn't move. His ocher eyes twinkle, and I feel he approves. Then he breaks his gaze, gets easily to his feet, and with a sweep of his tail trots off into the brush.

Never has an interchange caused such anticipation. I feel certain that Red and I share a destiny, but I can't grasp the implications. Or figure how in the world I am to reconnect with this promising muse.

Back at the cabin the yard is empty; the men have left for the day. Climbing to the loft, I sit at the desk, determined to get some writing done. I stare at the laptop—if I wait long enough maybe an answer will shoot up on the screen. I sink into the quiet. I think of Red. I feel the air on my face. I am aware of the woods teeming with hidden life, a world of activity taking place around me, camouflaged, stealthy, alive within the stillness. My fingers begin to move.

**SEVERAL DAYS LATER,** the yard is abuzz with activity. I watch as Thor pounds boards into place and Lenny, his nineteen-year-old son, measures planks on the sawhorse while Fred lugs packets of shingles from the truck. The midday sun, unimpeded by clouds, lights up the outline of the porch, its rectangular form already adding a handsome new architectural shape to the cabin. It's lunchtime; the men are about to break.

"Looks good. It's really starting to take shape," I say, filled with anticipation.

"Yep."

Thor lays down his tool, walks up to the outside spigot, and briskly rinses his hands, followed by Fred and Lenny. The men dry off on a ragged towel hanging on a nail by the back door, then shamble into the house and gather with their lunch boxes around the old mission table Carson and I found years ago at a local antique store.

It took some persuasion to get them to come in and eat in the comfort of a bug-free, fanny-friendly room. At first they ate their lunches outside, sprawled on scratchy logs under a dusty oak tree. But I coaxed them inside, my curiosity increasing as the personalities of these men became more and more evident.

Now, they settle around the table, pulling out sandwiches and a six-pack of Mountain Dew. Thor, at six feet, looks like a Nordic scarecrow, with his mosquito-sharp nose, his long legs splayed out, his coveralls splattered with putty and paint. Next to him, Lenny munches a baloney sandwich, his thin arms leaning on the table, eating quietly, a soft smile on his face. With his crew cut, thin features, and shy expression, he looks green compared to the two older men, but he works non-stop without complaint.

I lean at the counter in the open kitchen and munch a peanut butter and tomato sandwich, keeping my distance, hesitant to move into their intimate little group—small talk ceases when I'm around. I recall my grandmother's admonition: Don't get too friendly with the hired help or they'll slack off.

No, it won't do! These guys work long hours in the hot sun, do not complain, and demand nothing. I'm beginning to appreciate their modesty, straight talk, and strong work ethic. Here we are, me at the kitchen counter and the men across the room, two islands side by side. I curtail an urge to take my sandwich, draw up a chair, and join them at the table.

After they've finished, the table is strewn with jumbo bags of chips, M&M wrappers, empty cans of Mountain Dew, and crumpled napkins. Thor and Lenny stuff leftovers and trash into their lunch bags. Fred tosses his crumbled chip bag across the room, and it arcs into the trash can.

As they start out the door, Thor turns. "The shipment for the Danbury house will arrive any day. We'll be going to work on it," he tells me.

What? My plan is to remain at the cabin for the weeks it takes to complete the work. "When will you be able to work on my cabin?"

"Oh," Thor says, "we'll fit you in."

My expectations sink. Fit me in! Juggling two jobs. Well, that's just fine! Who knows when they will return? At last, the renovation is starting to show results and the crew abandons me, the work dead in the sawdust. I don't know from one day to the next when they will be off to another project. Damn! This casual, it-will-all-work-out attitude is sloppy, no other word for it. I have no faith that my renovation will be completed as planned. These clowns clearly don't make it a priority.

"I need the work here finished by the end of August."

'No problem," Thor assures me easily. I can only hope his words coincide with reality.

I stare at a yard strewn helter-skelter with materials and tools, half-empty crates, and discarded refuse. The cabin is piled with dusty lumber and gallon cans stacked against the walls. The two golden maples that every fall burst out in brilliant display have been hauled away, along with the children's favorite rope swing. The old rock wall the entire family built by hand is nowhere to be seen.

What have I got myself into? Maybe this wasn't such a good idea. Still, faced with no ready alternative, I determine to bury my anger and maintain a friendly air.

**THE NEXT DAY IS STRANGELY QUIET** without the men stomping around. Time for a walk. As I forage for raspberries, a strange lowing sound draws my attention. I leave the path and trudge cautiously through a thicket of tall trees into the woods. I stop beside a pile of decaying logs and listen. Nothing.

Then the low tuba cry sounds again through the treetops. I continue, high stepping over logs, twigs snapping under my tennis shoes. There it is again—a sharp gurgle this time. Something about the plaintive cry cuts through me. I find myself in a meadow spread with sedge grass and foxglove.

Walking along the edge of the woods, I spy a gray-brown form pressed against the trunk of an oak tree, half-hidden behind the leaves. Two large citrine eyes beam on me. I stop. Silence. Then another *hooo hoo hoooooo hoo hoo* shoots out, full of desperation, and now I see the cause. Behind a web of low branches, a great horned owl is pinned against the tree like a living dartboard, a pencil-thin arrow protruding from its mass of feathers. A red river of blood has trickled down one side and covered the overlay of feathers.

I feel panic. What to do? Pull the arrow out and risk tearing the owl apart? Run to fetch help? I must do something; I can't let this magnificent creature perish.

While I ponder my next move, a tall, angular figure strides unexpectedly out of the woods, swinging his arms, a quiver slung over one shoulder. He's followed by a younger man wearing fatigue pants. Something about the tall man's swagger, the red-checkered kerchief tied carelessly around his neck, and shiny leather pants project an ominous look.

Seeing me the stranger stops, leans against a tree, and plunges one hand deep into his pants pocket, a carefree smile on his face. He looks deliberately from me to the owl caught above in the branches. The hint of insolence around his mouth is unmistakable. "This your bird?" he asks sarcastically.

What is this guy up to? He can't be more than twenty-two, yet there is an air of arrogance about him, as if he is master of the forest.

"Owls aren't owned," I counter, moving closer to the tree where the owl hangs in a wad of feathers. "He's wounded."

The stranger remains propped against the tree. "Yeah, my arrow got him good. If he's not too ripped up, he'll look dandy over the mantelpiece, don't you think?" He pulls out a leather bota, tips it to his mouth, swallows. "At least I won't go back to the house empty-handed." Then he guffaws. I can't imagine what he thinks is funny.

"Are you aware this is private land?" I say loudly. Actually, the land is under the protection of the Land and Water Conservation Association, but I'm not about to quibble.

"We have the permission of Sam Leighton, the county commissioner, to hunt here. A friend of mine," the man declares. He approaches the tree, followed by his companion. The owl hasn't moved. The man hoists himself onto a low branch, snaps off some of intervening twigs, and grabs hold of the arrow. My nails bite like glass into my palms, but before I can utter a word, he jerks the arrow toward him, and the owl, with a wild screech, balances for a second in mid-air and tumbles to a lower branch, where it manages to find a tottery foothold. Then it drops to the ground, a sorrowful heap of limp feathers.

The man kicks the owl onto its back, reaches into his backpack, and pulls out a large bowie knife. Every tendon in my body tightens.

"You can't kill this owl," I cry out. "The state of Minnesota prohibits non-game birds from being hunted or trapped. Don't touch him!"

Quickly I move to the mangled body of the owl, cradled in the leaves, eyes still moving, and plant myself in front of it.

"You better watch out," his companion says. "My friend Drake here has a temper."

"The owl's not dead," I cry angrily. "There's no need to butcher him. I'll report you to the DNR!"

"These aren't your woods," Drake spits out.

"Let it go, Drake," the other one says. "We've got other fish to fry."

With a struggle, the man called Drake recovers his composure. "I won't be bullied by a woman," he says. "I'm claiming that bird, and there's nothing you can do about it. I'll be back with a gunny sack." He disappears into the woods with his friend.

I fall on my knees, emotions racing between rage and fear. I suspect the owl is dead or soon will be. Then, to my astonishment, one of the feathers moves, and slowly a mottled gray wing inches out from the leaves. Transfixed, I watch as the bird with a heaving effort rolls onto one shoulder, tucks his feet, laboriously pulls himself up, and stands weakly. One wing droops, the feathers smeared with blood. The extent of the injury is hidden behind a mass of feathers, but the body appears intact.

My heart is pumping. I must figure this out fast before leather pants returns. Cradling the creature in the fold of my jacket, I enter the woods and leave him in the hollow of a dead log, his yellow eyes gazing up at me.

No sooner do I arrive back at the clearing than leather pants clumps in, followed by his glum-looking friend. He is carrying a rifle. He stops dead in his tracks on seeing his prize missing.

"Where the hell is my horned owl?"

I look up nonchalantly, assuming the sober air befitting my decades of advancement over this young whippersnapper. "Would you believe it? The creature was only stunned. He's flown away."

The two men stare at me.

Drake darts a deadly look into the woods, then swings his gaze back to me. "Wait a minute. That's impossible!"

"The arrow only pierced the edge of his body." I keep my tone matter-of-fact. "He struggled to get aloft, but his wings carried him. He's gone."

"You old biddy!" The man slams his gun between two branches, where it stands upright like a steel gauntlet. At this, my anger begins to dissipate. I have said my piece; time to pull out. I feel my knees trembling and decide that the only way to stop this butcher is to stand tall and show no sign of weakness.

"Must have been a flesh wound," says his buddy, tugging on his beak cap. "We aren't after owls anyway. No big loss. Let's skedaddle before it gets dark."

117

Reluctantly, Drake swings the empty sack over his shoulder, grabs his gun, and jerks around, tossing me a long, shriveling look. The impish smile is gone.

"I didn't throw him in the lake," I call after him.

The Raptor Center in Willerton, when I arrive with the owl, assures me that it has no vital organs damaged and can eventually be released back to the wild. I am thrilled at the prospect of tramping the woods and hearing a hearty *hoo hoo hoo hoo* reverberate over the treetops—There's my fellow!—serenading me with his melancholy call.

**THE NEXT MORNING,** I grab an apple from the fridge and head into the woods. My purpose: to find Red, possibly locate his den so I can somehow figure out how to connect with this mysterious creature.

As I reach the shore, a loon glides motionless over the glassy lake surface, then suddenly plunges into the water and disappears. Scanning for its reappearance, I spy a dark spot the size of a locust in the distant sky, and gradually a silver and yellow object breaks through the flimsy clouds, buzzing aggressively as it whirs closer. Wobbling and tipping dangerously to one side, the sea plane lowers until the metal belly skims the water, sending up white foam in all directions. Then it chokes and putters to a stop.

What happens next throws me into a tailspin. Who would expect, up here in the peaceful isolation of the north woods, that a seaplane would land in front of my nose, the door open, and out would step—Chip!

I watch stunned as the figure—attractive even from a distance—steps off the bow and onto a sandy stretch a few yards down the shore.

"Hello!" I yell, waving my scarf.

"Tru! Is it really you?" He trots up, snappy in a blue bomber jacket. He looks older, his face tighter, hair now gray, but I notice he's kept his figure and athletic stride.

"What brings you to Lake Starling, Chip? And by air."

"I'm doing research on the northern Minnesota lakes, and this one is part of the test pattern." He stands, hands on hips, smiling at me with the familiar insouciant air. I feel my emotions stir for a brief moment.

"You're looking great," he says. Then he steps up and throws his arms around me in a tight bear hug. At the feel of his warm body, I sense my muscles loosening. Spools of the past unwind in my mind, images of skiing down white mountain slopes, scarves whipping like sails behind us, of meaningful smiles, of being held until my blood raced. But there is no going back. I hastily reason the long-buried memories back to lifelessness, become myself again.

"You up here on your own?" he asks.

"Yes, there's work to be done on the cabin."

He appears extremely glad to see me, a bit overdone given his abrupt exit all those years back. But his friendly manner overcomes my hesitation; after all, haven't the years brought us both to a wiser, more lighthearted maturity? And haven't many former couples reunited as friends after time has healed the past?

Chip leans against a rock and tilts his head. "I quit my grocery distributor job. Now I do geological research for the State Meteorological Commission. Latest assignment is in the Pine County area." He sweeps his arm in a circle.

He looks older than what must be his—let's see—seventy-two years. Has it really been over twenty years since those intoxicating days when, newly single, we danced into a new life?

"The pay's not great. I haven't completed the advanced certification. But being on my own suits me," he says. "I like traveling with no supervision and no pressure. The work is boring, but it gives me freedom." He strokes his chin, regarding me.

"You're not that old, Chip. You still have many years to learn."

"Not that many. I've done my stint. Life is to be enjoyed, and there are plenty of people out there to enjoy it with."

Behind the thinning hair, the slightly paunched figure, I can still glimpse the unfailing energy and twinkling expression, the old boyfriend.

"Chip, I have to go. There's a delivery scheduled this afternoon." I turn to leave.

Chip flashes me a grin, flicks a twig from his sleeve, adjusts his cap, and heads down the beach toward the plane. Here we are in our senior years, and he acts so carefree and flippant. Will he ever change?

"Imagine you being here; what luck!" he calls back. "I'll be in touch!"

The next morning, Chip whizzes up the driveway in his grandmother's old Pinto and skids to a halt. I watch as he stomps up to the porch and swings open the porch door.

"Hey, Tulu." Chip walks up in his blue bomber jacket, gray hair loose around his ears. I recognize his pet name from the old days. He seats himself next to me on the wicker couch, fans open his jacket, and grins at me with the lopsided smile I know so well. He does look good, smiling and tan in his satiny blue jacket. I detect the scent of fresh cotton and crushed leaves. An alertness beats through me.

"I'm off to work, thought I would stop by and see the old cabin again. Should be done in a few hours. I'll be staying at my aunt's house for a couple of days."

"What aunt? What house?"

"My Aunt Tilda lives in an old farmhouse down Highway 73, not far from here. She moved up here permanently after my uncle died." He straightens up, moves closer. "I'll be here for a few days to explore the area. Why don't you come over tonight? We can settle in and drink Cabernet Sauvignon by a crackling fire. I'm all by myself. What else have you got to do?"

"I don't think we have anything in common, Chip. In fact, we never did. Even back when we skied and partied and made love."

"We have enough. Come on. I'm so close. And you here alone and all."

"I have work to do."

"You used to be fun, Tru. You've become too serious," he says. "You should take things as they come. Life is short. I've fulfilled my responsibilities, and in six months I'll be retiring. I intend to enjoy my freedom."

"That's fine for you, Chip. I'm not that frisky."

"Okay, how about a serene walk in the woods? Just two friends. I can show you a meadow of lush marsh marigolds beyond the creek that will blow you away."

I feel a tug of frustration at Chip's devil-may-care attitude. With no ambition, no work ethic, he's like a kid, floating along enjoying whatever comes his way. After we'd been together for a year, he broke it off. One day he buttoned his Levi's in front of the full-length mirror, lifted his bare chest, liked what he saw, and informed me that he thought he could do better. No hard feelings.

"And you must be lonely…"

"I'm not!" I say irritably. He seems to be the one who avoids being alone. Besides, seeing Chip would have no depth. He would fly off post-assignment, and we would resume our separate lives.

Still, I consider. I know he's only looking for a good time, up here on his own and all, that to take him seriously would be folly. But with the men off again working on their miserable McMansion and my writing wound down to zero, I'm at loose ends. How could it hurt? It occurs to me that I have never spent a dull moment in his company. *Don't be such a stuffy goose.*

"All right. I'll stop by your aunt's for a bit after dinner."

**DO I FEEL DARING,** frightened, defiant, uncertain, regretful? I feel none of those as I trudge home late that night, the feel of the sheets still warm on my skin. Stirred by the perfumed breeze, the hum of the crickets, the touch of the open air, and the revival of the old chemistry, as if time had flipped back twenty years.

"It is what it is," Chip had said contentedly as we lay next to each other. "You're still attractive, you know. And we still click. You feel that too."

I left his house feeling amazingly free. It had been stimulating to relive the past, lost up there in the woods where nothing seemed to matter except the moment. The charm was still there, the warm, carefree sensuality that had never failed to draw me in. But the old attachment was gone, the dependent waiting, hoping, expectations. I saw through his bravado, outlined in the bright light of advanced years.

As we parted, Chip slipped his arms around me. "Look here, since we're neighbors, I want you to have this key to my aunt's place." I saw a gold flash between his fingers, and he slipped the key into my hand. It was hot from his palm.

"No kidding, Tulu, come over any time. I plan to be here a while."

Now I walk slowly, having refused to let him accompany me home. The evening air is hushed. I feel alive, too awake to even think of sleep. I skip a few steps, kick a branch off the path, listen for signs of creatures communicating in the darkness. I don't know where I'm going, but it doesn't matter. Chip will be gone soon, and our brief rejuvenation absorbed into the breath of the surrounding woods.

**ALL MORNING I HEAR** the reassuring sound of pounding, screeching drills, the slap of boards. The second shipment of wood for the big house in Danbury has not arrived, so the men have resumed working at my place. They work silently, moving non-stop until I hear someone mention lunchtime. Traipsing downstairs, I grab my egg-salad sandwich from the fridge and, for the first time, join them at the mission table. Maybe it would be good to get acquainted; after all, we operate as a team. No point in sneaking upstairs to eat by myself.

"Mind if I join you?" They scoot over to make room for me.

"Fishin's pretty good here in Starling Lake," Thor comments after I'm seated. "But my wife and I do our fishin' at Green Lake up north."

I smile at the idea of people who already live up north going up north to vacation. "I'm from the Twin Cities. I thought *this* was up north."

"Too crowded here," Fred says. The tufts of sandy hair protruding from his cap give him a playful look. "Doesn't cost nothin'. Tent, beer, bait, and a fishing boat, that's all we need."

The talk rambles, the men eating quickly. I am afraid my presence will stiffen the air, but the conversation runs smoothly. We discuss the work in progress; I inquire idly about their past jobs; they mention the Fourth of July parade in Hemming. When the sandwiches are finished, Lenny offers me miniature bars of Twix, and I pop one in my mouth. Swallowing his last bite, Fred pulls out a pack of Marlboros and looks up with a crooked smile. "I'll smoke outside," he says, glancing in my direction.

They clear remains from the table, then return their lunch pails to the truck. I bring out napkins and salt and pepper shakers for the next day's lunch, humming under my breath.

A routine sets in. Gradually, the men seem to adjust to taking requests from a construction-ignorant female. I observe their pragmatic approach, the way these guys cleverly handle the screwups and revisions that plague the best-laid plans.

I sit on the back stoop watching a red-streaked sunset sink across Starling Lake. Somehow, surrounded by woods and the broad isolation of the lake, none of the barriers that society builds to define personal territories seem to matter. The men are growing on me, and they seem to accept having me around.

It looks like we just might get along.

**TWO DAYS LATER,** I hear voices shout below my window, the rev of a car motor. I hurry downstairs to see Lenny being supported under each shoulder and lifted into the truck.

"He was out gathering firewood and got himself hurt. We're taking him to the medical center," Thor calls from the driver's side. They maneuver Lenny, who is clutching his leg, into the back seat. Fred hops into the front.

"Let me know how he is," I call as they drive away. The yard becomes suddenly still.

An hour later Fred drives up in the truck. "Lenny's foot is being stitched up just fine. The blades of the bear trap missed his major arteries. I need to get out there and remove the thing." Grabbing a canvas bag and pliers from the back of the truck, he sprints across the yard toward the wooded path.

"I'm coming with you," I yell.

"No, it could be dangerous!"

Ignoring him, I tuck a pocketknife into my pocket—just in case—and follow him into the woods.

After some five minutes we come to a fork, and following Lenny's description, Fred leads the way to a copse of tall oaks at the bottom of an incline.

"It should be among those trees." Fred begins scouting through the brush. "Near the path—I've got it!"

I move over to where Fred is kneeling at an iron contraption sticking out of the debris. "This must be the one. See, these steel jaws can cut off a limb. Luckily, Lenny was wearing heavy shoes and didn't lose his foot."

"Look." I point to a pile of feathers beyond the oak tree: the bodies of at least twenty birds—phoebes, bluebirds, and red-winged blackbirds—freshly killed.

"What do you think you're doing?" Two forms appear carrying rifles and canvas knapsacks. "That's my property."

The defiant snarl, the slick leather boots—I recognize the owl hunter, Drake.

Fred marches up to them. "There's been an accident. These traps are dangerous."

"That's the idea, punk," he says, ignoring Fred's friendly grin.

"This bear trap should be removed," Fred says. "My buddy almost lost his foot this morning."

"That's not my problem." The hunter doesn't appear to notice me.

"Look, the use of steel-jawed traps is banned," Fred told him. "How many have you set?"

"None of your fucking business."

"Those dead birds yours?" Fred inquires. "It's illegal to shoot them."

"They sure are. And so is this fox here. A real beauty." He pats the knapsack hung over one shoulder. "And I'm out to get a bear that's been seen stalking around here. You amateurs can bug off."

Fox! My heart freezes. "I've seen this bloke before. He kills everything in the forest that crawls, walks, or flies. I saw a barred owl he killed," I cry, spittle coming out of my mouth. "I told him it's illegal. Talking to him is a waste of time."

"You two get out," shouts leather pants, brandishing his rifle. "I have rights. I have power, and I'll jolly well use it."

Fred's face takes on a look of stubborn rage. The shorter man begins to back away. Fred springs over and with a swift gesture pulls the rifle from leather pants' arm and flips it into the brush, then swirls and crashes his fist directly into his stomach, quickly followed by a swing that lands with a thud on his jaw. He looks down, breathing heavily at the figure that lies squirming at his feet.

"I'll take this trap. And I'm going to report you," he splutters.

"His name is Drake, from Willerton," I put in.

"Your hunting days in these woods are over, Drake. Now get."

Before the hunter can rise to his feet, Fred grabs the trap, and we start off down the path. Behind us low voices converse excitedly, but we don't turn. I glance at Fred, green bandana twisted at his neck, yellow mustache drooping scruffily around his mouth. He grins at me, looking satisfied. I want to hug him. This guy is a handy fellow to have around.

THE NEXT DAY AS I CROSS THE YARD I hear footsteps and turn to see Fred rounding the house, coming straight toward me. His blonde hair is ruffled, and the scissored scar on his neck stands out in the bright sun. He wears the expression of a kid who has been discovered with his hand in the cookie jar.

"About yesterday, I want to explain. That is, I guess I shouldn't have punched that guy out. It just—"

"No, no. Are you kidding? That poacher deserved what you gave him and more."

"I exploded, that's it. I have this temper, always have…"

"You did the right thing."

"I shouldn't have gone berserk like that. I—I should tell you, well, I was a mixed-up kid. After my alcoholic father took off and I was sent to a foster home, I gave everyone a hell of a time. I fought like a banshee. Beat up a man so bad he lost an eye. Got put away for that. But he jumped me, ripped off the $4,000 I won gambling. My kid foster brother needed big-time teeth work, and I couldn't see any other way. I know it was a stupid thing to do."

I feel myself melt. "You needn't look so abashed. Okay, you have a temper. How long has it been? Years?" He lifts his shoulders and throws me a hesitant smile.

Here's this thirty-five-year-old clumsy guy with hair that looks like a dry mop, and I am finding him more and more endearing. I repress an urge to tell him he's a decent guy, not the rogue some think he is.

The next day Lenny returns, to everyone's immense relief. He is clearly pleased to be back and sits at the workbench, crutches at his side. "I can do my work, not to worry," he assures me confidently. As I gaze at his earnest face, I want to slip an arm around him, but instead I make sure he is well supplied with cold cans of his favorite, Dr. Pepper.

**THE EVENINGS ARE BECOMING SHORTER.** The sun is lowering on the horizon as I tramp along the dirt road to Chip's aunt's house, flashlight tucked in my jacket pocket for the walk home. The September air is brisk against my face. This morning Chip stopped by on his way back from inspecting a northern chain of lakes.

"I'll be home this evening. Come on over and we'll watch a film."

Sure. A night out would be fun, and I do enjoy Chip's company.

I find the yellow mailbox easily and follow a curving dirt drive up to a rough-hewn farmhouse, where I see two cars parked side by side, one a scruffy orange, the other a metallic blue. Maybe the aunt is home after all, although Chip mentioned she had gone to town for a few days to keep company with her friend Bertha after her friend's surgery. Mounting the steps of the front porch, I search for a doorbell and immediately feel foolish—these old cabins don't provide such amenities.

Moving to the front window, I make out two figures inside, their features softened in the low light. Chip leans on the counter with a tall frosty glass in his hand, and a woman in a pink chenille top and tight jeans stands with her back to the window, running a hand languidly through her long blonde hair. Somehow, she doesn't have the look of an aunt.

Full of curiosity, I knock on the front door. Chip opens, flashing his winning smile, although I detect a grain of hesitancy. His hair is tousled in a sexy way. The aroma of wine and cheese spouts from a fondue pot on the counter.

"Hi. Eh, come on in. Good to see you." As I step in, I feel the warmth from the large stone fireplace and glance around at the roomful of old, heavy furniture, built in the days when things were meant to last for generations. "This is my friend Celia."

The other occupant of the room is seated on the couch, legs tucked under her, smiling up at me. "Hi there."

"She is a new member of the Schussing Singles ski club. And this is Tallulah, a former member of the club."

"Tru," I correct. He's never called me Tallulah. Evidently, he has a need to stick to formality.

"Celia's only been downhill skiing for a year, but she's improving fast. Has natural ability."

I observe the blonde tresses streaming down her back, pulled from her forehead by a purple velvet headband, and the slightly crooked teeth protruding through her smile. Despite a heavy brow and uneven features, her golden hair and slim, graceful limbs lend her an appealing air. This woman is young!

"Chip, I didn't know you were having company."

Chip coughs, shakes his head, looks down at his yellow sweater. "Celia stopped in unexpectedly."

Hesitantly I sit down and accept the glass of red wine he pours from a decanter on the table.

"My plans changed," Celia explains. "My sister's husband will be back from Toronto, and she doesn't need me to drive her to Raysville after all, leaving me free as a bird. How about that?" She fondles a silver pendant around her neck. "So, I came on up to see lover boy."

The wine, the murmuring fireplace, and this blonde obviously at home as she sprawls territorially on the couch—clearly a liaison. He must always have a woman, I remind myself. Distance is required here.

"Celia's never been here before."

"My GPS couldn't even find the place." Celia laughs up at him. "Chip had to direct me the last five miles by cell phone." She claps her hands as if the joke is too much, gives her legs a long stretch, and takes a deep swallow from her wine glass.

"Tru joined the ski club around the same time I did. She owns a cabin down on the lake. I was there a couple of times…years ago. Long time…" Chip's voice trails off, stretching into eons.

After me, Chip was involved with several women in the club. Some were convinced they were the end of the line, while a few undemanding ones were experimenting with midlife adventure. Chip bounced around the pool of available women like an overripe ball, forging monogamous relationships one after the other.

"You and Chip once dated?" Celia asks with a toothy smile, jingling an armful of silver bracelets.

"Yes," I say uneasily. I have no desire to discuss the cozy days when it was just Chip and me with his girl. "It was a long—"

"Chip and I have no secrets along that line." Celia hurls a booming laugh into the room. "We totally agree: No commitment for us."

"What about family?" I ask, aware of how conventional I sound.

"Oh, family—we've both raised ours. Now we're free to do what we want, date whomever we want, even while we're together."

A shock wave shoots through me. Of course. This is Chip, a nice guy, charming company, warm lover. Too good, evidently, to restrict to one companion.

"Does this...work?" I ask in what I hope is a tolerant voice.

"An open relationship?" Chip waves a hand in the air enthusiastically. "It's ideal. Who says you can't love more than one person at a time? As long as you're honest with each other."

Celia straightens and curls her long legs around each other, serpent-style. "I have a boyfriend in Chicago. He's a pharmaceutical salesman and travels a lot, and we get together whenever we can. That leaves plenty of time to see Chip."

But of course, for Chip it's natural. No strings, no restrictions, couched in openness and honesty. The complications of expectation and sacrifice removed. Yet the arrangement seems disjointed. Inevitably, someone will be hurt—relationships are never exactly equal. A partnership based purely on enjoyment, with no commitment to weather the bad times, is bound to be doomed.

"It's the only way to go, Tru." Celia extracts a cashew nut from the dish and presses it between her teeth. "After three failed marriages, I've had it with monogamy."

*Why don't you two grow up?* I want to say. "I'm not sure I'm secure enough for such an arrangement," I say instead, determined not to be swayed by sophistic reasoning.

"You just have to want your partner to be happy," Celia says.

*What about* my *happiness?* I long to shout. How can I be a good partner if I'm miserable? But logic is out of place here. I shift to an adoptive mode. Live and let live, no judgment.

Chip smiles and lowers himself on the couch next to his friend. "Celia's got the idea," he says. She presses next to Chip while he sinks luxuriously into the cushions, his metallic blue bomber jacket hanging carelessly open, one arm resting along the back of the couch, looking substantial and warm.

"Well," I say, standing up. "I really can't stay. I have to secure the boat before it gets dark." Big lie, but then Chip hadn't mentioned a girlfriend. One that comes on like a fire engine.

"We're going hiking at William O'Brien tomorrow," Celia says cheerily from the couch. "I hope you'll join us."

I marvel at her confidence. Her wide smile irritates me. She is too sure of herself—and too fallacious. I study Chip, who is smiling. He has become an older version of himself, but lacking the easy nonchalance I always found irresistible. Maybe I could learn to be that easy, that free…

But no! One pays a high price for such so-called freedom, not knowing how long you can keep your place or what to expect as you balance on the moving track, uncertain where it is leading or where to get off—not for me.

On the front porch I lean against the railing. Then the door creaks, and Chip steps up behind me. "I didn't know Celia was coming," he whispers in the shadows. "She's not my girlfriend. She followed me up here. I don't know where her head is. A little too sure of herself if you ask me. We don't have a thing."

A thing?

I experience a sudden urge to know who this guy is, what makes him tick, how he can live permanently with the unpredictable. "Tell me," I ask in a low voice. "Do you think you'll ever settle down?"

"Me? Never. Since my wife divorced me, I am done with duty and following someone else's rules. Where did it get me? Never again."

"Of course, you don't want to repeat your mistakes," I persist. "But do you really think you can get by—live—without responsibility? Accountability? Availability when it matters?"

"I'm no good at that," he says, shaking his head. Maybe he is constitutionally unequipped. Maybe he's indolent. Or a confirmed hedonist who has tossed conventional standards into the failure bin and coasted on what remains, utilizing his male charm to navigate a sea of single women.

I walk down the path into the cool night, my cheeks hot. Despite a strong foreboding, I have the feeling I'll be seeing him again.

EACH MORNING I WAIT EAGERLY for the sound of the men's truck. Over lunch, the men tease me about my writing. "How about an ode to the screwdriver?" they ask. Outside the screech of a starling—identified by Lenny—so shrill that we raise our heads. Then we hear something clawing at the windowpane and watch fascinated as a clump of fur scales up the house, nose cutting the air, tail waving wildly. Another mad screech as a second squirrel scurries after it, and we hear a medley of squawks and shrieks on the roof above us.

"A lot going on out there!" I exclaim.

"Sounds like my mother-in-law," Thor quips.

Lenny squeezes a chunk of watermelon between his teeth. "Joe Ramsey's uncle is training me on his quarter horse for the Midwest Horse Show in Stanley," he tells me. "I'll have four good feet to walk on." Lenny cracked a joke!

Upstairs at my desk I read my new poem, crisp black letters staring at me from the screen with a defiant do-not-touch air. I hatchet the last three lines and become absorbed in the text, searching for just the right word. The scraping, hammering, and muffled voices of the men in the yard hum like a distant melody as they scurry back and forth. I've been amazed at Thor's efficiency as he inspects shipments carefully, makes sure every joist is secure and every brick line exactly laid. Fred fells trees with precision, each landing exactly where planned. Even Lenny works steadily, not giving up until the last board is in place. There seems to be nothing these guys can't solve; I marvel at how relentless they are in getting things done and done right, no matter how difficult.

Things are advancing, sending waves of warmth and vitality through the house. It's good to feel the presence of the men constructively employed outside while I toil away inside, to exist in an atmosphere of sanity and purpose.

**ARRIVING AT MY FAVORITE SPOT,** an overlook on the south end of the lake, I lean against a smooth rock and look out over the water glittering below. The sky is overcast. As I pan my binoculars, a shape catches my eye, a reddish shadow moving at the edge of the woods near the shore. I adjust the focus, and the form sharpens into a head, a soft muzzle, a long scrappy tail—it's Red, my red-coated guru. I clutch with relief. He has not succumbed to the deadly tactics of leather pants! He prances along the ground sniffing, halts, cocks his ears.

I am caught by a strange euphoria that illuminates the landscape, but it's only the sun bursting through the clouds. At that moment, the fox turns his head and starts to move in my direction.

Soon he appears at my side. "I was wondering when you'd come here again," he says quietly.

"I've been hoping I'd find you!" I say. "I have so many questions. I want to know more about you. Why do you appear to me like this? Why are you singling me out? What is your aim?"

"It's up to you to come up with the answers," he says as he seats himself next to a moss-covered rock, his legs planted straight in front of him.

Laughing, I move down to a patch of soft ground beside him. "Okay, first I need to know the question."

"Here's one: What is it you want?"

"I want simplicity. Life is flat. I want something more."

"There's a contradiction there." The fox regards me intensely. I can tell he wants me to continue.

I hesitate, my mind careens. "I want…" I wait as the words come to me. "Okay, I surrender. I am giving up wants and regrets. Regret is a want, you know."

"You're catching on." The sun has swallowed a passing streak of grey clouds, leaving a clear cover of blue sky.

"It's a waste, all that worry and guilt. I want peace. I want real connections with others."

"Yes." My companion waits patiently.

"No," I say, "I don't want those things. I have those things."

"That's the ticket." With what looks like a smile, Red runs to the water's edge and plunges into the lake, whips around playfully. "Come on!"

I fling off my shoes and wade in up to my knees. "I can't. It's freezing!" I jump around, laughing in short gulps. The cold squeezes my legs and awakens every inch of my body. I throw my arms wide, take a deep breath, and plunge all the way in.

Red laughs.

"I did it!" I shout, lifting out of the water.

"Naturally," Red replies. He swims out into the lake, head aloft, ears perked, then takes a deep swallow of air, as if relishing the cold.

He watches me breaststroking after him, alive with energy. No sooner do I catch up than he declares, "If you need me, I'll be at the pipal fig tree." Churning through the water to shore, he runs up the bank and disappears into the woods.

There are no fig trees around here; he's teasing me. The fellow is getting out of hand. My feet are light, my mouth tastes sweet. I'm aware of the vibrant hues of cream, russet, and amber rocks along the shore, the rich black of the tree trunks, the clear azure sky gleaming above me. Everything vibrates with vivid colors, as if lit from within. The separation between levels of existence—between ground, insect, plant, animal, mineral, cosmos—diminish in front of me, linked in a seamless flow.

I awake with a start. As I lie in bed under the covers, the vividness of the dream swirls in my head, more alive than anything in the room, more substantial than the gray shadows of dawn outside the window. I'm reminded of the fairy tales my mother used to read when she tucked me into bed that gave me a sense of safety and comfort.

Reality has been transformed…or maybe it's me who has metamorphosed during the night. While I am musing on this, a light closes in the center of my mind, and I drift into emptiness.

IT'S FINISHED! The crew has been hauling tools into the truck while Lenny sweeps rubble from the deck platform. Thor approaches. "Guess we're pretty much done," he says in his drawl, wiping his hands on a worn towel. The cabin has taken on a new, majestic look. With Fred and Lenny, Thor and I walk around to view the transformation from all angles. "Think we're done," he repeats with a satisfied grin. We admire the new porch that faces the lake, the new cedar deck with baluster railings, the half-log sidings gleaming with fresh redwood stain. The cross-hipped roof over the addition shines with golden speckles from the sun, producing an architectural element of balance and surprise.

I feel the men's eyes on me as I inspect their handiwork. "Wow!" I cry. "It's perfect! Oh, it's stunning." The men look pleased. We beam at each other. "What an accomplishment!" I exclaim.

"Think so myself," Thor grins, uncovering a gold tooth at the side of his mouth. "Yup. Turned out real good." We look like we've won the World Series. Fred and I shake hands spontaneously, grinning like idiots.

We saunter down the drive, me chattering excitedly. "I'll be up here a lot. I'll get tickets to the horse show next summer."

"I'll be back tomorrow to clean up that pile of junk," Fred tells me. "And stack up that there wood." He unbuttons his jacket and starts to whistle a tune from *The Music Man*.

As I watch the two vehicles pull off down the long drive, elbows jutting out the side windows, I sing out with gusto, vocalizing a garbled rendition of seventy-six trombones and a hundred and ten cornets leading the big parade.

I laugh for no reason and clap my hands. Corny for an old gal, but I don't care!

**THE SUMMER IS ENDING.** There's a crackling, a charge of life circulating in the woods, a harbinger of change. Chip stops by occasionally, suggesting walks to the beach or a drive to the quarry ruins outside of town. This morning he left, finally convinced that I can't abandon my writing to see him, that I have much cosmetic work left to do on the cabin.

I've made up my mind. I know exactly what to do. Grabbing the brass key from a table drawer, I march down to the dock and gaze at the smooth lake surface glimmering in the sun. The key sparkles in my hand, a beautiful rainbow reflecting every color in the sky, gathered into this one little object.

Inhaling deeply, I fill my lungs with oxygen, lift my arm, and with all my might throw the key far into the water. The metallic shape spins, drops, and skids below the surface. I watch as it sinks and vanishes into the lake bed.

With a feeling of satisfaction, I stir up a lazy log fire and settle on the couch, book open on my lap. The closeness of the oak-paneled room bathed in firelight cloaks me in a cozy glow. I haven't seen the men for over a week.

"I'm seventy-three," I told them during our last lunch.

"You do great."

"You're in better shape than my mother."

"You're in better shape than my wife."

I miss those guys! The sound of their truck each morning as I scamper down to check their plans for the day, the stories and jokes over lunch, the hours of purposeful bustle, the flow of life in the making.

Suddenly, I don't want our association to be over.

There are endless projects to be done. Thor and I located the perfect spot for a gazebo overlooking the lake, and Fred wants to install a new dock on wheels. And then a sauna for Emma and Phil, a log playhouse for the children, and on and on.

The thought shoots through me like a fireball—I will spend entire summers here. Yes, that's it! No more driving back and forth to the city. Friends will visit. I know Rita, my best friend who collaborated with me at the *Star,* will drive down from Duluth. And there's a two-week creative writing retreat on Madeline Island I have decided to take. I could even arrange marathon writing sessions here at the cabin. How exciting is that?

Best of all, there is now an irresistible place for my family to congregate. I know where to obtain a second-hand sailboat—I'm not too proud to lure them with watery entertainments. There will be sounds of children cavorting, group dinners from the grill, board games on the porch as red, yellow, and orange sun flares spread on the horizon. With Carson hovering in the rafters, joining in with his deep laugh and amused sarcasm, just like the old days.

Back when. A dream.

As I open my book to continue reading, the phone rings.

"Look Mom, I'm afraid we won't be able to make it up there. Probably not this year. You don't understand how much is going on in our household."

"I do get—"

"Maybe next year we can squeeze in a weekend. The lake is wonderful. But with the kids getting older. You know."

"I'll be here. I've decided to stay awhile."

"What?" Emma sounds annoyed. "Are you going to spend October up there in the wilds? You shouldn't be up there alone. We can't be responsible."

"But I'm alone where I live now!" My voice is firm. "I'm staying, dear. The cabin is winterized. In fact, I will be moving up here for half the year in the future. Don't worry, I know what I'm doing. This is my life now. I'd love for you all to join me. Come on up anytime. You're always welcome."

I hang up before she does. A first.

TOMORROW I WILL TUCK THE CABIN in for the winter and leave for the cities to plan for the following summer. I have tons of ideas. Desiring to watch the sunset from the crowning spot on the lake one last time, I set off following the narrow deer trail along a creek that runs crashing in the spring, but now meanders lazily into the wide arm of the lake. The crisp October sunshine covers the banks and warms the forty-degree air. I listen to a plaintive *hoo hoohoo hoo hoo hoooo hoooo* from the treetops—my barred owl. I hear him often as I traipse through the woods. At least I like to think he's the fellow I rescued and that he is following me.

I stop, alert, breathing in the earthy lake scent. Around me sounds the buzz of insects circling the branches. I hear the crunch of invisible feet shuffling in the underbrush. A pair of creature eyes glitters from a pile of fallen branches. I exhale a long, loud poof of air—my contribution to the pulse of existence. How could the world be so glorious, the scattering of clouds so luminous, the lapping of the water so hypnotizing, everything so alive, including me?

The path leads up a hill to a rocky cliff high above the shore. I settle on a rock and immediately spot the orange coloring and perked ears of my fox sitting some yards away, wearing an air of tranquil composure.

A pair of hawks circle overhead in ever tightening loops, then shoot off in different directions across the seamless blue sky. A deep stillness closes around us, like the soft hum of the universe. I feel complete in this creature's presence.

Red stands up, and I can tell by the beam in his eyes and the erect tilt of his ears that he has something in mind. He regards me for some minutes, and I read the message encrypted in his gaze. *You don't need me.*

With that, he approaches the edge of the cliff and gazes down at the bed of black and ruby rocks running along the edge of the lake. In a sudden flash of apprehension, I move closer. I don't like his air of determined finality, the way he stares calmly into space. While I stand uncertain, he leaps out, hits the water with a deep splash, and sinks beneath the surface out of sight. A few moments later he reemerges, vigorously shakes off wet drops from his head, and without a backward glance swims off into the center of the lake, head pointed straight ahead. While I watch transfixed, the bronze head gets smaller and smaller, then disappears, and the water closes the space and resumes its still surface as if the fox never existed.

# Armed Flight

**AN EIGHTY-EIGHT-YEAR-OLD WOMAN** does not burrow into dusty old boxes that have nothing to do with anything without taking something of a risk. It's the photo that draws me, thumbing through old packets to find pictures for my granddaughter's graduation display. I pull out a folder holding ticket stubs, reminder notes, a train schedule, a frayed journal, and then the photograph. I had all but forgotten, but there he is, the sweetest face imaginable. So long ago.

I draw out a wrinkled sheet. Written in longhand it says:

*Jeremy*
- *initiates no activities*
- *little insight, doesn't get things, doesn't understand half of what I'm talking about*
- *a fuss-budget, hates hassle, the slightest obstacle sends him into a tizzy*
- *hates spontaneity, likes things ordered and predictable*
- *conversation rote, repetitive, boring*
- *is negatively focused, runs down politics, his home situation, industry, etc.*
- *is quiet in company*
- *loathes conflict*
- *acts helpless when we travel, the maneuvering is beyond him*
- *youngest child, used to being taken care of*

Jeremy. My partner, my love, my nemesis. There had been plenty to dislike, and it needed to be recorded for some reason. What went wrong all those years ago? How had he managed to ruin things? Vague shadows rise from the page, images of the past coming into focus, details sharpening under the bright closet light. Twenty-seven years is an eternity. I certainly can't recall with clarity or reliability those days, back when I was divorced and single and the dating scene swarmed with confident, wounded men and desperate, searching women.

It began as I was perusing ads in the *Twin Cities Reader*. Jeremy advertised for adventure and companionship. I wanted closeness and understanding. I should have known right off that we faced an insurmountable wall.

**DURING OUR INTRODUCTORY CALL,** he doesn't have much to say; I almost hang up.

"We don't have to meet unless you want to," he says, noting my hesitation. That does it. The hint of aloofness I came to abhor appears at first to be based on some superiority as of now invisible in the shadows of the phone line.

"Might as well," I say, matching his nonchalance. What could you tell by a twenty-minute phone conversation? After all we're both looking, and we're the same age, sixty-two. Maybe if we meet we will uncover some areas of commonality.

The restaurant is crowded. When I walk in, he gives me the sweetest look imaginable, as if he has been waiting for me all his life. "Audrey?" he asks, jumping up and pulling out a chair. He is wearing a soft green sweater and khakis, and I find his still-youthful, slender figure immediately attractive. His smile—gentle, warm, with a twist of reserve—subdues my lingering reservation. I want to know more.

At the end of our second date, we kiss. I am drawn to his gentle ways, his sensual mouth, the supple way he moves in jeans and a black t-shirt. I want to hug him and draw him close. We share brief histories of scarred upbringings, failed relationships. During one weekend at a lodge on Caribou Lake, I convince him to consult experts on arterial disease at the University of Minnesota Medical Center. It only takes a little coaxing on my part; he agrees it is worth a try. I go with him, hold his hand. To our delight, the alprostadil injections into the genital area before lovemaking do the trick, and Jeremy is able to perform at a level that is fully satisfying. He is ecstatic. At first sex bonds us tightly, becomes, you might say, the bedrock of our relationship.

During our first months together, I am full of confidence. He's a degreed elementary school teacher. Perfect, I think, I'm a secondary history teacher. Since retirement he's undertaken handyman work part time and sets about fixing things around my house, most of which didn't quite work. He likes to have me arrange our various activities, planning weekends, scouting out classes on Native American history and the latest spacecraft missions. We fall into a routine whereby he stays over at my place twice a week, often the entire weekend. There are jaunts to a north woods cabin, just the two of us; Saturday night parlor games with my friends Steve, Annabel, Johnny, and Beth; Sunday mornings at the Unitarian Fellowship I attend, with Jeremy agreeably following my lead. I adore him. He relishes our life together, so much conviviality and light.

Then, a year or so along, something changes. The novelty and rapture with my new love and the whirlwind of good times in the couple's world begin to fade. I become dissatisfied. I want more.

Jeremy keeps me at bay. He says he likes things just as they are; what more do I need? I mention affection, intimacy—emotional connection. "You're too offhand," I tell him. "You take everything with such nonchalance."

Like the time he called at the last minute. "Sorry, I can't make it tonight. My brother's in town." No phone call, no response to my several emails. I hadn't heard from him in over a week. What was going on? "When can we get together?" I could feel the distance between us lengthen as I waited for his answer. He wasn't sure how long his brother would be around. "Maybe next week. I'll have to see. Gotta go."

We talk. He doesn't understand. He fends off my attempts to squeeze love and caring from him. I care, I care, he insists. My rational explanations about childhood deprivation and lack of affection fall on deaf ears. He becomes bored, fatigued. He even breaks up with me, but is miserable, changes his mind.

He appears to view my love as a threat. The more I explain, the further he retreats.

Oh, I can't say Jeremy doesn't try. But he gets sick of it. I keep pushing. It is clear there on the pages of my journal: I want him to be different. Not merely a pal, a companion, a date out for a good time. I press him, but I do not believe professions of love that are pried from a jar.

We decide to take a trip, to spend a block of time together in playful abandon, which I secretly hope will bring us closer.

Me: "Are you enjoying it here in Palm Springs?"

Him: "It's okay."

Me wailing protest.

Him: "Why can't I say what I think, be who I am?"

**HE OFTEN PROCLAIMS HIS LOVE** of being alone, doing his own thing. Fine, maybe we can do our own thing while we're together, just be ourselves without the social dictates. But when I start reading while he is at my house, he objects, even though he has no subject of conversation to suggest. He sometimes says things in response to me that are so off the mark I wonder if he has the foggiest idea what I've been talking about. Never, heaven forbid, does he venture deeply into anything personal or revealing. Like talk about the suicide of his second wife or question me about my grueling divorce or my string of failed relationships, which believe me, I am not about to dig up.

I don't give up trying. "The least you can do is consider my needs. I would happily do the same for you should you ever reveal any, which isn't likely."

"Well, what would you like me to do?"

"Oh, how about sending me a loving card?" But he says the wording wouldn't express how he feels, and he won't sign anything he doesn't mean. I can't tell whether he is being obtuse or asserting his independence.

**I STAND, SHAKE OUT MY STIFF KNEES,** and move with the packet to a comfortable chair in the den. The evening light is retreating from the windows, and I switch on a high-powered reading lamp that sends a glare over my lap and continue reading, spurred by curiosity and a desire to figure out why after two years the relationship failed though we each wanted to make it work.

There are many clues. Here are some examples.

One: We fly to California to attend my cousin Conrad's wedding. I spot Jeremy the minute he enters Conrad's rented beach house carrying the wine he'd volunteered to fetch for the hostess. I haven't seen him all day, having come over early to help with the food, and feel my blood quicken at the sight of him. The party is in full swing. I want to introduce him to my newly arrived family members, but he disappears. Finally, I spot him on the other side of the room, looking handsome and sporty in the new green pinstripe shirt I talked him into wearing. For a minute, I find it hard to believe that this knockout guy is with me! He is conversing with a man in a golf jacket, but he doesn't look my way. I go to the bar and help myself to a sloe gin fizz. Why doesn't he try to find me? His aloofness pierces me to the core. Well, I can match it! I avoid him for the rest of the evening. He wants to be alone, well he's got it. Later in the car he swears ignorance. Questions why I left him on his own in a sea of strangers. One of us just doesn't get it. I prefer to think it is not me.

Two: The night he slips out of bed in the wee hours and goes home without a word. I haven't a clue. Whatever we have argued about escapes me. When he finally calls two days later, he is contrite. His explanation meanders without landing on anything specific, replete with words like *mood* and *anxious* and *tired*. I hang up, filled with foreboding. He is slipping away. But why? A few months ago we had our sleeping bags zipped together and enjoyed a heavenly six-day camping trip in the Quetico. I begin to calculate. If I accept things as they are and give up all complaints, maybe everything will go back to normal. If only I can accept normal. I cannot figure out why, but this I seem unable to do.

Three: I don't hear from Jeremy for ten days. He is with his son, who is visiting from Oregon, and they are wrapped up in gatherings and excursions together with Jeremy's brother and wife. I don't like being dropped; I would have found a way to include him had the situation been reversed. I have met his brother and wife. Why am I excluded? I take this as another distancing move, which sends me into a swirl of uncertainty.

It's clear I want to see him more than he wants to see me. I know he cares for me in his own way—why isn't it enough? Maybe if I could be satisfied, he would stop backing off.

Four: We sit on a boulder alongside the St. Croix River, lazily munching sandwiches under a stretch of shade. When I bring up the subject of our relationship, Jeremy states that it will last as long as it is good. I jerk up and the egg salad catches in my throat. So this is a good-time deal! I protest, railing and arguing. This time I've had it, and I tell him so. Eventually, we make up. With just a little more missing.

I confide in my girlfriend. The air is slowly seeping from our relationship; it is getting flatter by the day. The friend advises me. So he likes to eat at Perkins alone. He asserts his independence. Let him be. You take his every move as personal, relating to you. If you want to keep the relationship, accept him as he is. Encourage him, and maybe he will flower. Yeah, sure, by then I'll be a wilted vine.

"I have many old hurts," I tell him.

"Are they ever going to go away?" he asks. He's tired of being criticized. "I can never do anything right." Or, "I'm just not the right person for you."

I tell myself we can work it out.

But the words *not the right person* reverberate in my brain, stirring a sharp pain. Maybe I'm not the right person, whatever that is. Can my indignation at his desire to eat alone at Perkins be explained in any rational way? Is this doomed to be another relationship failure?

I reflect on my dates with the newly widowed Ralph, who was seriously wife shopping. He needed someone and now. I scurried fast out of his reach. And there was Andy, whose wife had broken up their home and family for no good reason, and I could tell by the way he distanced himself, backing off the minute I nosed in, that he had sworn off commitment for good. The most depressing was Joe, the sexy truck driver from Sioux Falls who avoided lengthy conversation and didn't seem to understand my hints for signs of affection. A brief "love you" was all I got at the end of lovemaking, right on cue. I made him pay for that.

It's possible that my girlfriend's words of warning hold a wisdom unknown to me. Maybe my demands are one-sided. But no way can I tell Jeremy how strongly I feel, no way could I lay it flat out in the open. His respect would wither; his feelings for me would crash into nothing. Why aren't the days of canoeing and evenings of charades with Jack and Evelyn sufficient? Is it so necessary to obtain more?

**SEEING A THERAPIST WAS MY IDEA,** and Jeremy went along. He'd do anything. He liked the way I instigated things, kept life interesting. He also wanted us to work out but did not have a clue.

"Well, Audrey"—the therapist regarded us from his dark leather chair—"Jeremy has expressed a wish to deepen your sexual relationship. Would you be agreeable?"

"No, I don't think so. I'm okay with making love less often as we've been doing lately."

"Jeremy, how do you feel about this?"

"I don't understand why she feels this way."

"What's behind your reluctance, Audrey?"

"We're not in a committed relationship. We're buddies. We date, that's all. I don't want to be more invested than that under these conditions. I don't want to be that close to him, to care that much. I would lose some of the distance I've managed to create."

Jeremy shook his head. "I think we have more than a dating relationship."

"I don't think so."

"I thought you wanted us to get closer."

"*We* wouldn't get closer. *I* would get closer."

The therapist looked at us over his glasses. "Why don't you want to make a commitment, Jeremy?"

"He wants the fun," I put in, "doesn't want to do the work."

"What do you think, Jeremy?"

"We have an exclusive relationship. But I'm afraid to care for her too much. Maybe we will never work out."

"What do you want for yourself?"

"I want it to be the way it was in the beginning. I'd like her to be happy like that. We were really good then. I'll do whatever she wants."

"Is there anything that would make the relationship more fulfilling for you, Audrey?" the therapist asked.

"I want more openness from him."

"Address Jeremy."

"I want more intimacy with you. You balk at that. And when things get uncomfortable, you bolt. You always need to have one foot out the door. This makes me anxious, and I lose all sense of equilibrium."

"I get overwhelmed by your continual demands. You're like a bottomless pit, nothing is ever enough. I tell you I love you. But you're constantly battling."

"Do you believe Jeremy loves you?" the therapist addressed me.

"I don't think he does. Not his fault, it's not there."

"And Audrey, are you okay with this?"

I stared helplessly at the therapist. "It's not my first choice, but it's what I've got."

**THE GOOD TIMES WITH JEREMY** become fewer. I confront him with his own line of resistance. I deny my affection so that he'll want more and seek it out. I become less available, less responsive. If I become distant, he will experience what it's like, and he'll finally understand and capitulate. Down to the bottom. Tit for tat.

**FOUR MONTHS LATER,** Jeremy walks out my front door for good. Several friends are due to arrive for a dinner party. I am in the kitchen, preoccupied with not burning the caramelized onions, sponging the can of pickled mushrooms off the floor, digging deep into the top shelves for cut-crystal serving dishes.

"Can I help?" Jeremy shuffles in.

"Well, I'm out of garlic salt." I probably could do without it, but I can see he's at a loss for something to do. He seems to be floating through the house in a vague cloud. I have no time to reach out to him; besides, I am still in retaliation mode and refuse to give him attention he doesn't deserve. Off he goes to Safeway. Flustered, trying to get everything ready at once, I fly back and forth setting the table for eight, making sure the butter dish is clean, that salt and pepper holders are at each end of the table. Then I dash to the bookshelves to select a poem for the assigned after-dinner readings. I don't see the flash of his back going out the door. When I reenter the kitchen fifteen minutes later, a can of garlic salt stands alone in the center of the kitchen table. I dash into the bedroom. His overnight bag is gone. His brown jacket is gone. And so is he.

I cry for two days. I paint the living room a pale cream, stomach lurching as I move the roller back and forth, cursing his cowardly way of breaking off without a word. I feel as if my insides have shriveled and left a hole big as Bryce Canyon, where we'd spent his birthday.

I want him back. Call that crazy! Why, when we bicker and argue, when I lie beside him in bed crying silently, do I feel so lost? But it overwhelms me, the missing—his adorable way of sidling down beside me when we're with friends, the way he laughs at my attempts at humor, the lemon fragrance of his freshly-washed shirt, the feeling of his arms around me.

But only part of me yearns, the part that hovered over him waiting to be affirmed. Not the part that takes charge of life and forges ahead full steam. It's the former that suffers, that wakes empty in the night and stares at a blank ceiling, that endures silently the suffocating ache in the stomach. It's the latter that gradually, as time dissolves the relationship's gloss and reality takes on a new shape, is able to grasp the utter futility of it all.

I paint the entire downstairs, order a new set of wicker porch furniture, and sign up to teach a community class in French poetry. I purchase a miniature poodle and name him Prosper. I mail Jeremy's suede slippers to him without a note—another door closed. I scratch his brother and friend Rolf from my address book. Occasionally I imagine I glimpse his good-looking figure speeding by in a car or his easy lope in a shopping mall mixed in with the crowd on the level below. Probably not him.

**THREE MONTHS LATER** I call Jeremy's number, but when he answers I hang up. My cell phone rings a minute later, but Prosper is whimpering from the next room. He, at least, needs me.

**IT'S GROWING LATE.** The sun's light is retreating from the room where I sit over a dusty box. So much to digest, the past spread before me in glaring reflection. As I close my journal, I discover a piece of notepaper squeezed between the last two pages as if inserted at a later date; it's hard to tell. It's in my handwriting and it contains these words:

*Audrey*
- *Needy*
- *Needy*
- *Needy*
- *Needy*
- *Needy*
- *Needy*
- *Controlling*
- *Needy*

I pull out and reexamine the fastidious list of Jeremy's failings as a human being, evidently drawn in an effort to render my partner, my love, my nemesis as undesirable as possible and, therefore, my loss perfectly understandable and exactly what I wanted. It was not me, it was him.

As I continue to turn the crinkly journal pages, I am stunned at what they reveal about my compulsive attempts to mold what I had into what I wanted, to turn Jeremy into the right kind of loving partner. Jeremy was not the shallow coward I imagined, nor I the justified victim. It's no fun, I can tell you, to look back at yourself and see either a mental case or a pathetic fool.

That evening, as the sun sets in the backyard, I watch as the edges of the journal pages catch fire and the remains of old memories begin to be slowly consumed, done away with. Best to move on. I stare at the fire pit, just as a nine-year-old I sat on the dock and saw the Mickey Mouse watch my grandparents gave me for my birthday sink and disappear to the bottom of the lake, swallowed, as I wanted to be myself, to be anywhere but on the dock. Oh dear, they will say, you took it off in the water. It's always the same. When will you learn? In a thousand years you will never learn!

With a sudden gesture I reach in, grab the pages that expose my former life, and smack them against the ground until the flames are extinguished. Then, clutching the journal against my chest, I make a vow: This time I won't forget!

I feel my own hand warm against my face, and I don't cry at all.

# No Greater Love

"**WHAT FUN WE HAD** on those family vacations in the old days, Angela! I miss that."

They perched on the edge of Angela's bed bent over a red velvet album of old photos: children digging canals in a sandy beach, waving hats from a sailboat, parents holding children in their laps in front of a sparkling Christmas tree. They sat knee to knee, turning the pages one by one.

"So, do I, Pinky. But we've moved on to our own lives. You at the university and me, here, I am married." She reached over and pulled an envelope from the nightstand. "Here are the latest photos of me and Brian in our new house."

"That's what I want to talk to you about. Seriously, my favorite and only cousin, I'd like to know what's happening with you two."

"What do you mean?"

"Your marriage, dopey. I know I'm only eighteen, but I can judge things. You and Brian aren't doing well, anyone can see that. Neither of you seem to be happy. Bogged down, I'd call it. Are you sure Brian is the one for you?"

Angela was shocked at the directness, although she shouldn't have been. She had been subtly warned by others. She and Brian had little in common—different backgrounds, beliefs on opposite ends of the political spectrum, he a staunch Irish Catholic and she an oblivious atheist. Angela had waved off the objections. "No two people are identical. It's our differences we *like* in each other. This is the man I want to spend every minute with. I feel charged in his presence, I am eager for the sight of him every time we're apart." Never had she been so certain. "We'll work things out."

She felt in every tissue of her being that this man was right for her. The prospect of a married future thrilled her. It's what a woman did, what her family and all who mattered expected; it affirmed her. Brian, a Loyola University graduate, with his brilliant mind and gentle, compliant manner; and Angela, driven by a sparkling energy and ambition. Each supplied traits the other lacked. A match made in heaven.

They would live in happiness forever.

She'd known since her apartment mate Terry had won two $350 tickets to the Emerald Ball, and they had gussied up in lush formals and long gloves and met Terry's boyfriend Tyrone and his friend Brian at the Regency. Known when Brian had led her to the dance floor and slipped an arm around her back in a touch that ran down to her toes, as he drew her into the music in easy turns, in perfect sync with the rhythm, their feet skimming effortlessly over the floor. She couldn't stop looking at him, couldn't believe this handsome guy had chosen her.

It seemed so long ago! Seven years they'd been married. They had moved to Angela's hometown of Minneapolis for Brian to assume a computer programming job with Bain and Underwood. One photo showed him dressed in his new navy suit and tie, standing in front of the Chesapeake building on his first day of work. Another, snapped by Pinky at Charlie's restaurant, showed them with her parents grinning around a backlit table with a white tablecloth.

Angela barely recalled the dinner, but the row they'd had in the bedroom while getting ready came back to her vividly. As she was fastening her earrings, Brian entered the room.

"Those scruffy shoes won't do."

"We're going to dinner with your parents, not a wedding. I don't see why I have to be so formal," he said gruffly, going into the closet to retrieve his shiny new shoes.

"Why, what's the problem?"

When pressed, he admitted that sometimes he would rather be back in San Francisco—at the corner bar with his cronies, Joe and Lester, shooting the breeze, getting high—rather than all this formality, watching every move. What was the point?

"Didn't you dress up for social events as a kid?"

"There weren't any social events. In high school I went to mass and catechism. I spent two hours a day practicing the piano. In college the parties were casual. I can teach you the Irish jig."

Brian tried to explain. He was not sure he fit in. What did he know of Mediterranean cruises or Hilton Head retreats or Alaskan helicopter fishing? He'd been brought up in an outlying district of San Francisco, with its run-down streets and tight blocks of identical stucco apartment buildings. He had not been allowed to mingle with the perilous gangs that gathered on the corners, but remained safely in the apartment. The landlord maintained everything; he had never changed a light bulb, couldn't distinguish a drill from a handsaw. Here he was, transported to Angela's turf, to a lake house in a suburban Wayzata neighborhood where he knew no one.

He could never live up to her demands and expectations, and as far as he could tell the best way for the marriage to succeed would be for her to be happy. He would offer it up.

She would try to understand. He needed to make an effort.

"Sure, he's likeable and good looking. That's not enough." Pinky said insistently, holding up one of the photos.

"Really!" Immediately Angela swung to her husband's defense. She slammed the album shut irritably and turned to face her cousin. "You're wrong, Pinky. I love him." Pinky, so outspoken, so young. Too inexperienced to see beneath the surface, to understand the truth that can develop between two people. She relented. "You're such a screwball, Pinky. What do you know about marriage?" Fond of her cousin as she was, sometimes it took patience waiting for her to grow up.

"Seriously, what does he contribute to your life?" Pinky leaned forward earnestly. "Brian says nothing, doesn't want to go anywhere, takes no initiative—he follows you around like a trained seal. He has no interests. You can't ride through life in the bedroom." Pinky shook her head defiantly, her circular drop earrings swaying.

"You don't understand," Angela retorted. "Brian is agreeable. He's devoted. He supports us. He conforms to our suburban way of living even though he prefers city life." Angela regarded her cousin defensively. It was disconcerting to hear her own doubts expressed by this young free spirit. "I do miss emotional support," she said after a time. "But Brian's not a bad guy."

Pinky grabbed Angela's wrist. "I had to tell you what I think. You don't hate me, do you? You two don't look happy, that's all."

"I appreciate your concern, honey, but marriage isn't all about happy." *But an important part*, she reflected, caught in a haze of uncertainty.

She had to face reality. She was unhappy, and Brian seemed to be stuck in a mire of stoic resignation.

Pinky pulled the photo album into her lap. "Let's see some more." But after the shots of their honeymoon with the two of them in front of the Acropolis and sipping tall drinks under an olive tree, there were no more. The remainder of the pages were empty.

**DR. SVOBODA LEANED BACK** in his chair, hands splayed over his knees. His black turtleneck, the tumble of blond hair falling down his neck, and the splotched beard covering his chin gave him a casual look. Several floor pillows lay scattered along the walls, covered by the spray of light streaming through the windows. The three of them faced each other across a bare carpet.

"Who's going to start?

Angela recrossed her legs, took a deep breath. It was time. She'd have to say it. "I'm not sure I want to continue this marriage."

Finally, it was out. She feared the words would release an explosion that would blast their lives into little pieces. The dark lines around Brian's mouth, sitting next to her, drew tighter. "Brian and I have little in common. We never go anywhere or do anything. We have nothing to talk about."

"Can you be specific?" Dr. Svoboda asked. "What is it you want from Brian?"

Angela pressed her lips together. She needed *more*—whatever that was. Her mind churned as the other two waited. "I—well, I need an active partner. Not a shadow reflecting everything I do. Brian has a brilliant mind, but the practicalities of life evade him. He says little, just hibernates in front of the TV. He gives me my own way, but I give up too much to get it."

Brian regarded her with a guarded expression, as if facing the unknown.

"Do you think Brian has always been unresponsive?" Dr. Svoboda asked.

Angela paused. Here was a new twist. She squeezed her hands tightly in her lap. "I—no, he didn't use to be. Back in California Brian was a popular storyteller; all it took was a few drinks." Maybe marriage with her had not served him well. Her doubts grew. "He grew up in a tough inner-city neighborhood in San Francisco," she continued. "Now he lives in the Midwest suburbs, cut off from his roots, his friends, his mentors, his religious network. Brian is used to a landlord taking care of things. He doesn't know how to live in a house on a lake."

"Why don't we let Brian speak for himself?"

The other two looked at Brian expectantly.

"What is it that you want from me?" Brian asked finally, turning to look at Angela.

"I'd like you to let me know what you think and what you want— who you are! To assert your interests. Stop agreeing to everything I say.

Sometimes I need resistance. I'd like thoughts that challenge me, prod me to reflect, offer a new light."

Brian sat immobile, staring at the carpet. Then he slowly ran one hand across his forehead and down the side of his face and looked up. "Angela runs the show. This is her territory. I want her to be happy. When she's happy, I'm happy. I want us to be as we were in our early years. She was content then. I'll do whatever she wants." His green eyes looked directly at Dr. Svoboda. "I'm in this for the long run, with God's blessing."

They waited for him to continue.

"She has so much energy and independence," he continued in a hushed voice. "She holes up with her Gloria Steinem and Betty Friedan books and everything has to change. She wants me to be her lover, her provider, her advisor, her companion, her soulmate, to furnish everything that life has to offer. She's a bottomless well. I take life as it comes. I'm not sure anything I could do would satisfy her."

Angela felt a jolt. Could she be that needy? The implications stared her in the face.

She lowered her head. "No, I don't really need all that. I just want you to love me."

"Of course I love you."

It was the *of course* that hit her. Facile words without weight. He showed no interest in her life, her doings, her feelings, had no understanding of who she was or what made her tick. He was content with the predictability of home life.

"You give no affection. You're the most undemonstrative man I've ever known," she cried.

"I show feelings in my own way. I'm loyal, I'm devoted. I'll never leave you."

"I need a partner. She looked at Dr. Svoboda, then Brian. "With you I feel alone."

"I try to do what you want."

"What do *you* want, Brian?" the therapist asked.

"I don't need anything. I have a successful job and a good home, far exceeding what I could have imagined. I count myself lucky on that front."

"Be honest," cried Angela. "You go around looking grouchy all the time. I'd like to know what's going on with you."

Brian's smoky green eyes glimmered. "Maybe I'd like things to be different. But I want a harmonious life, a contented wife, not this constant upheaval. I'd just like you to take things as they are and not always be rocking the boat. Nothing is perfect. I can accept things—why can't you?"

She swiveled to face him. "Brian, don't you see that your stoic endurance has buried you beyond reach?"

"How do you feel about what your wife just said?"

Brian thought a minute. "We were poor. Everything went into my education. Since I excelled in school, they pushed me to study hard. My teachers claimed it would be a sacrilege not to develop my God-given ability. I was the first in my family to attend college. The first to marry out of his faith. I broke the mold and am trying to live up to the sacrifices my parents made. I am a lucky guy, in many ways. It's not my place to be demanding."

Angela looked down at her hands. To her surprise, the palm she'd been scratching with her nails had drawn a line of blood. She could see, in the clarity of the room, that he had nothing except her; whereas she, who had her whole life around her, was the one who was ripping their marriage apart. Her throat squeezed into a tight knot, and she could not get a word out.

"I don't know why you can't take me as I am," Brian said at last.

Angela stared at the floor and shook her head vigorously, as if to shake up the swirling molecules in her brain so they would settle and readjust in some reasonable order. Things were happening. She had the feeling an opening had been forged, although how this might play out, she had no idea.

Dr. Svoboda uncrossed his legs and stood up. "Time's up. Good work. We'll continue this next week. Meanwhile, Brian, think about how you can assert your own needs more. And Angela, I want you to examine the effect of all your expectations."

**ONE EVENING AS THE FINAL STRAINS** of *The Brady Bunch* theme faded, Brian clicked off the television. "The sessions with the therapist have got me thinking. I've never given much weight to my own needs. I'm a simple guy. But if we're to keep the marriage going, I have to speak up and not leave it to you or the heavenly father to make it work."

Angela lowered the newspaper she was reading. Such unprompted introspection was not like him. What was he driving at?

"We're not getting any younger. Angie, you're twenty-eight. Don't you think it's time…?"

Angela felt her body tense. Brian had brought it up once, but she insisted the time was not right, and he had let it go. Now his voice had a ring of insistence. "Brian, I don't know. As we hit the seventies, the country is sinking into chaos. Divorce and open marriage are all over the map. Recently, over one hundred thousand people have marched in Washington for ratification of the Equal Rights Amendment; anti-racist and gay-liberation riots are everywhere. Not a time to bring another being into the world."

"There's always something."

"Besides," she said, "I'm not sure I'm good maternal material."

"Nonsense," he said warmly.

"I've become very involved with my job at the Eberly shelter. I like working with battered women. I'd really like to build a career. I'm not sure children would fit in. To tell the truth"—she took a deep breath, but she had to say it—"I don't want children."

He stared at her in disbelief.

"Brian, I'm no good with kids. I'm impatient with child games and the slow pace of doing mindless things. Many couples choose not to have children these days. Some women don't fit the mother role, and I'm one of them. I have a limited capacity for nurturing. I'd make a lousy mother, believe me. And I would be the main caregiver. I'd be doing it all."

To her surprise, Brian leapt from his chair with unexpected vigor, his face flaming. Going to the sidebar, he opened the cupboard door, pulled out a highball glass, and poured into it the remainder of the silver shaker sitting on the marble countertop. Raising the glass to his mouth, he took a long swig.

"You won't even consider it?" he asked, his mouth tight.

Her throat too tight to speak, she stared at him, shaking her head.

After draining his glass, he returned to the recliner and sat on the edge, leaning on his elbows. "I want to be a father. As an only child, I vowed to have a large brood. I adore children. I'm Catholic. Bringing souls into the world is God's will."

"I know. I should have said something," she faltered, "but I didn't know myself." She moved to the miniature fridge behind the bar and pulled out a Pepsi, feeling the urge for a kick of caffeine. She took a long swallow and felt a sharp tingle in her chest. The sight of Brian's drained, sunken face filled her with guilt. But she couldn't deny her feelings.

Brian got up abruptly and, finding the silver shaker empty, reached down and pulled out a fresh bottle of Madeira. He twisted the corkscrew, and a loud pop filled the room like a gunshot.

"Couples get married and have children," Brian resumed.

"I just can't do it."

"Where there's a will there's a way."

The self-righteous look on his face infuriated her. His rigidity, the way he pulled life choices from a box of biblical scriptures, blocking alternatives.

"You assume that all women want to be mothers. Wrong." But it was hopeless; she felt defeated by his inability to understand.

"The Lord will make it work." His expression was set in deadlock.

Growing hot, she wiped a sleeve across her forehead. Then she lurched across the room and flew out the back door and across the lawn, running, running, stumbling onto the dock, until she came to a breathless halt at the end. In front of her the steel gray lake lay flat in the lowering dusk. *Stop, calm down.*

She sank on the dock cross-legged and let her thoughts roam at will. The dock installation had been a gift from her parents. You must have a dock, they insisted, or what's the point of living on a lake? Brian would not set up the dock, claimed it wasn't *essential*. That was the word. They could sit in the lounge chairs at the water's edge and enjoy the lake just *fine*—another key word—dock or no dock. As for a boat, well, Brian was waiting for a closeout special, sometime later, always later. Non-essential category.

Reminders from the past burst into her mind. The event that had nearly changed the direction of her life. Those years following the adoption, free to resume her life unencumbered, she was certain she and her parents had made the right decision. The baby had a good home, and she could continue to build her life and justify everyone's faith in her academic promise. She had been saved from a faltering relationship and avoided an embarrassing scandal.

She liked the idea of family, of growing and working together, the interaction and fun. But the strain of disciplining, handling the continual chaos—she would never be able to cope.

A decision had to be final. With abortion or adoption out of the question, there could be no compromise about giving birth. One bore a child, a live human being, or one didn't. One couldn't give birth to half a child or change your mind and become suddenly childless. There was no way to allow each of them half of their wish. Not like splitting a house: the upstairs for you, the downstairs for me.

It was a dead end.

**"THIS IS FUN. I HAVEN'T BEEN TO THIS CLUB FOR AGES!"** Angela, hands resting on the white linen tablecloth, smiled at the man sitting across from her. Her oldest friend in the world. Porter grinned back at her fondly. Their fathers had worked side by side for years at her father's microchip company. As youngsters, they had often sailed the reaches of Lake Minnetonka, followed by family dinners at the Fairlawn Country Club. Both had attended the University of California, Berkeley, two years apart.

"It's been too long. Angela, you're beautiful. That full red hair amassed in clouds around your face—every time I see you, you're more lovely."

Flattery will get you everywhere," she laughed. "You look good yourself. You were so skinny when we were kids. Remember the time after Easter dinner when your father shot the wounded eagle in his backyard, and I threw such a hissy fit and ruined the party? You stood up for me."

Porter grinned. "Everything gets to you, Angela. It's what I love about you."

He knew her so well. What a comfort, how she could tell him anything. Nothing she did bothered him, no matter now unorthodox or goofy. She pulled back her hand to pick up her drink. She had hardly seen him since her marriage eight years ago. The intimacy she felt with him was like savoring a favorite food or snuggling against a warm pillow.

Beyond the dining room window, Silver Lake stretched in all directions, and Angela glimpsed on the far shore a line of stately houses hidden behind a cloud of oak and maple trees.

Porter was watching her. "You and Brian live close by. Why don't you get an associate membership here? Wouldn't hurt you guys to take up golf."

"I'm not sure I could get Brian out on the green. He's the indoor type. He plays chess on Friday after work in Mike Sweeny's basement. It keeps him busy."

"Has he time on his hands?" Porter asked. "If only I had such a problem. My job keeps me on the go."

"How I envy you, flying off to far continents to solve corporate problems. And enjoying the sights, by the look of the postcards you send. Exactly how much of your gallivanting is job-related, Porter?"

"You've got me." Porter gave Angela a wide smile and gazed at her mischievously. With the clean-cut line of his dark hair, marble brown eyes, and seersucker sports jacket, he looked as if he had stepped out of an *Esquire* ad. "Is there any reason I can't incorporate both work and pleasure?" he asked. "I oversee company branches in hubs like Copenhagen, Shanghai, Hong Kong, and Seoul. When I'm stuck here at the home office for too long, I go crazy. So off I go, squeezing in trips of my own between assignments."

"Are you sure you don't squeeze in assignments between trips of your own? Didn't you recently spend three weeks in India?"

"Yes, indeed," Porter exclaimed. "Fascinating country. Look, here's a photo of the Taj Mahal." He pulled a packet from his jacket inner pocket. "I took a four-day escorted trek across the desert. It was like being transported to another world." Porter leaned back, adjusted his Armani tie, and smiled widely, displaying even white teeth. "We traveled on camelback over the golden dunes. You can't imagine the beauty and mystery of the desert. What it's like to walk in fresh sand, visit a remote gypsy village, exchange stories with the Indian guides around the campfire, and sleep nights under a star-blazing sky."

Angela thumbed through the photos. The sight of foreign lands, of exotic cultures, hinting of the unknown, heated her blood. Then, "Who's the woman in the yellow scarf? The one with her arm around you?"

"That's Clarisse. We met in New Delhi three days before the trip. Afterward we palled around India together. A lovely, divorced lady, at loose ends, looking for adventure before deciding what to do with her life. Quite a free spirit."

He tilted his head at the white-shirted waiter who glided up to his elbow. "Cherry chicken salad for the lady, and I'll have the T-bone, rare, with asparagus and extra béarnaise sauce on the side."

Porter continued to relate his escapades on a multitude of safaris, cruises, and mountain tours.

Angela listened dreamily. "It sounds wonderful…" Taking a sip of wine, she looked beyond the window at the distant sky, a wide stretch of blue softened by a blaring sun. "Porter, why don't we get together more often?" She plucked a roll from the basket and set it on her bread plate.

"Darling girl, you name the place and I'll be there." He replaced the packet of photos in his pocket. "I'm quite an unstable brute, unsuited to settled, committed life." He let out a mock sigh. "Whereas you have the security of a family, the assurance of a steady partner, and a life built on consistency. Does that satisfy you?" He looked at her as if he already knew the answer.

Angela flushed and bit her lips. "The thing is, I don't want children. I'm much too tied up right now completing the credits required for a professional-level position in social work. But with just the two of us we're not really a family."

"I regard two people as a family."

"Brian wants many kids," she said, "and for me to fit in my work around motherhood while I mind the hearth and keep the pots cooking."

"You didn't resolve this before you got married?"

"I know! But everything happened so fast after we met." She looked down at her lap.

"And Brian took having children as a matter of course," Porter suggested.

"Yes. I kept putting it off, promising to deal with it later. Later is here."

"Tell me, do you have a good life together?"

"No!" It burst out with more vehemence than she realized.

"Angela, before that stiff waiter returns with plates of tempting food, I must confide something. I'll speak frankly. You and Brian are different people."

"Our differences used to bind us together, like two parts forming a whole. But it doesn't work anymore."

The waiter appeared and slipped two dinner plates on the table. "Can I bring you anything else?"

"No, no." Porter waved him away impatiently. "Brian is a very likeable fellow. But I don't think he's for you. You deserve more. I say it as a friend."

"Maybe I don't want more."

Was this true? She stared at the walnut salad on her plate. She had reasoned that if she could understand her husband and do her part, the balance could be restored, the marriage saved. But maybe Porter was right. Maybe marriage wasn't all it was cracked up to be. Pinky and her boyfriend had decided to live together freely. Several of her girlfriends were already divorced, bewailing the doom of the isolated housewife, how much they missed a far-reaching life of substance.

"Oh, Porter, I'm crazy to travel. The summer after college when I spent a year touring Europe on a shoestring was one of the most exciting times of my life. There are so many places I want to experience. How I envy you!"

"I don't wonder you envy me. I'd envy myself if I didn't already have everything I want." He snuck a side look at her. "Next week I leave for the Australian Gold Coast. You and Brian should get out of your rut and try it."

"Brian despises the hassle, the orchestration of travel," she said, "And he hates to fly, prefers his feet safe and sound on solid earth."

"So, you'll never fulfill your dreams. Very sad. No, waiter, we don't need anything, and please don't interrupt. Just fill the water glasses when needed."

"It's not Brian's fault. His mother devoted her life to his every need. He's not used to taking charge."

"Angela, there's a whole world out there. Look at me—I travel widely. Last year I spent a month at Esalen at Big Sur in California. There are group sex parties shooting up everywhere. These days you can do anything you want."

It had a ring of freedom, of possibility. But something in her cringed. "Porter, I'm not sure what I want."

After dessert, they strolled quietly along a path behind the golf course, breathing in the fresh air. Porter pulled her arm through his. "All right, Angela. Stick to your man," he resumed, "but I suggest a little flirtation never hurt anyone. Look at me. I have liaisons with women I meet everywhere. I'm not the most handsome fellow in the room, but I handle myself well and claim my share of charm. There are many women out there looking for adventure. Friendships don't have to be platonic."

The freewheeling lifestyle he described did not surprise her. It surrounded her everywhere—women speaking out, protests filling the streets, in the papers, on broadcasts, in the very air. Women breaking free. Challenging the roles, the limitations, the barriers to high-level employment. How much this affected her, Angela wasn't sure. "Brian and I are doing all right. Maybe we're not so close—"

Porter tugged on her arm. "Angela, pet, marriage is not for everyone. Marriage squeezes everything into a common denominator and eliminates the unexpected, the novelty, the intensity, the very things that make our short stay on this earth uplifting. If you want to live, stick with me."

"Porter, you're incorrigible." She shook her head. But a light radiated through his nonsense. A faraway oasis of dreams.

So far she could almost touch it.

"Angie, Babe, I have something for you." With a sprightly tilt of his head, Porter dug his hand in his jacket pocket and pulled out a long envelope. "Look here, I'm being sent to Nepal to research economic openings for my company. I have in my hot hand two plane tickets. One of these tickets is up for grabs. And you, my lovely, have the opportunity to grab it. All above board. Strictly platonic. First class, expenses paid." He waited. "I suppose you'd rather go to Bora Bora."

"I find all vacations appealing, since I never go anywhere."

"Nepal is exotic, ancient, spectacular. Come. We always have good times together. You know Brian will let you do anything."

"Why me? What about your girlfriend?"

"No girlfriend at the moment."

"What about one of your friends with benefits that you have scattered everywhere? Why not ask one of them?"

"I'm washed out on relationships, even the so-called easy ones, which they never are. I choose you," Porter exclaimed.

"I won't deceive Brian."

"Don't be ridiculous. That's not in question. We're friends before the trip, we'll be friends after the trip. All right, no hanky-panky." With an imperious smile he reached out and took her hand. "And if you should change your mind, after a night on the town and flagons of wine, and want to crawl in with me, I will be glad to oblige." His voice lowered. "What Brian doesn't know won't hurt him. You're too appealing to limit yourself to one man. We've known each other so long, like siblings, no danger of infatuation. A perfect setup."

"Porter..." Appalled, she drew her hand away.

"Oh, I'm only kidding. Just come."

Porter had always had a cocky side, along with a daring that often went over the line. Once they had whisked away an old blind man's cane as he sunned himself on a park bench and choked with laughter as the man searched frantically, crawling on the ground, waving his hands. The amused look on Porter's face when he replaced the cane and the man's hand gripped it eagerly. She winced, thinking of it. Now she wondered if Porter had always had a dark side. He was displaying a raw callousness in his mature bachelor years, and she wasn't sure she liked what she saw.

"Angela, you're young. You should live a little."

How could Porter assume she would fly off with him and leave her husband? And the promise of an open door, leaving her the freedom to walk through—or not. It was presumptuous. It was out of the question.

*Of course, if she really wanted to…*

She cursed her ambivalence, her lack of spine. She wouldn't consider it. She wouldn't.

**ANGELA THREW OPEN THE HEAVY DOOR** of St. Theresa's and flew inside. She needed something; she needed to talk to someone; she needed to talk to him. Scurrying down the corridor, through another door, up the aisle, she scanned the rows of pews until she spied a figure on the far side of the chapel, face hidden in shadow. All she could make out was a pair of legs crossed at the ankles, then his face, his broad shoulders, the outline of his green sports shirt.

Whatever could have brought Brian to St. Theresa's on a Saturday? "I thought I'd find you here. What are you doing sitting in the dark?" she asked.

He sat motionless. "I come here sometimes to think. I feel at peace here."

"I have very bad news." Drawing a deep breath, she searched for what to say, dreading to say it aloud. "It's my parents. The car they were in, the one they bought last month in Tuscany, was crushed by a local bus. They were, they were—Brian, they were killed."

"Oh, Angela!"

Until that moment, Angela had felt numb, operating mainly on automatic. On hearing her husband's voice, she felt a surge of grief rise to the surface, strangling her. She experienced a pressing need to be close to him. Wiping her hands on her slacks, she lowered herself into the pew beside him, aware of how small she felt sitting next to his tall figure.

They sat for some time in silence. Angela began to sob quietly. She sensed Brian waiting patiently beside her. All she had to do was reach out.

"Tell me what I can do." His low voice from the shadows was calming, she felt an influx of relief.

Angela found her voice. "Brian, what am I going to do? They were home to me. I think home is in your blood, it can't be replaced."

"You have a home now with me."

*Home—why was it always in the past, why did one calculate everything on the formative years, as if one's adult life were determined by the results? Home consisted of wherever you belonged and were safe.*

"I feel like a child right now."

"We are children in some ways all our lives." He stood up, stuffed his hands in his pockets and looked down at her tenderly. "That's why we need God."

For once she didn't disagree. "We all need a mother from time to time," she said. "That's the way I'd put it. Men grow up and marry and continue to be mothered by a wife. A woman grows up and marries a breadwinner and must be a mother to herself, as well as others."

"An honorable job, motherhood," he said.

"What if a woman isn't suited? What if she doesn't have an inkling?"

"Of course she does. Women carry it in their genes. If they need nudging, they can learn." She sucked in a choking breath and almost believed him. "Men can be caring, too," he said. To her surprise, he took her hand and pulled her to her feet, a gentle touch that bathed her in warmth. "Let's go home."

Outside it was raining. Driving through the streets in Brian's Chevy they were hit by a barrage of jumbo raindrops that smeared against the side windows and across the front windshield. There were details to clear up, arrangements to be made. Recovering the bodies from Europe. The funeral, the service. Brian insisted on taking off work. As she watched the windshield wipers sweep back and forth, back and forth, exposing intermittent panels of clear glass, she scooted over and with a deep sigh relaxed against his shoulder.

ANGELA STOOD ON THE DOCK and gazed out over the lake's smooth surface, which reflected a flotilla of low dark clouds. There was no sign of activity; the light rain had driven people indoors. She seemed to be the only living creature on the lake. Since the interval with Brian at the church, the world seemed to tilt in a different direction. The sense of parents always there at her back existed no longer, she was alone with the challenge of her marriage. Alone with Brian.

Her thoughts were interrupted by Brian's call from the house. "A letter for you." The blue envelope looked intriguingly personal, probably some tricky sales pitch in disguise. Pulling a Pepsi from the fridge, she picked up the envelope, ripped it open, and pulled out several sheets of blue paper. She didn't recognize the signature: Lynn Dorsey.

She read slowly, absorbing the contents. At one point she started over, wondering if she had misunderstood. But there it was, the impossible, the one thing she had not anticipated. She sank back against the counter and lowered the letter. After all these years she had forgotten, the event buried in the archives of her mind, aroused only in rare moments when she saw a baby girl laughing on the beach or being hugged by a doting mother. Moments when she felt something open within her.

She staggered out to the back deck and leaned trembling against the railing. The moist breeze from the lake hit her hot cheeks. How had she been located after all these years? They had cut all ties. Her parents had insisted on an iron-clad contract with the adoption agency that ensured her identity would never be revealed, the separation final and untraceable.

And looming: How was she to tell Brian she had given birth to a child? Faced with the implacability of his strict moral code, she'd been afraid to confess the past, to create a rift that could poison their life together.

She entered the living room clutched with anxiety. Brian was seated in front of the TV.

"Brian," she said in a tight voice. "Something has happened."

Immediately he stood up and flicked off the television.

"Maybe you'd better sit down. You look sick." He stood back so that she could pass him to the sectional, but instead she clutched the letter to her breast and moved to stare out the window.

*How could she face him? She had deceived him by her silence. Where could she find the words?* "I don't know where to begin." She slowly turned. "Brian, when I was seventeen, I made a mistake. A serious one. I'd had the same boyfriend since eighth grade. We were best friends. You can't imagine how close we were; we did everything together. The other kids teased, called us the royal couple. I adored him. He, well, he gave me attention I'd never known before. He found a shy, sensitive girl and gave me a life."

There was a hushed silence. She forced herself to continue, to get it out in the open. "I gave birth to a daughter. Raising a child was out of the question; I still had four years of college. Oh, there was no pressure, it was a unanimous decision. My parents handled everything, fabricated a sinus condition that took me for some months to Arizona."

Brian's expression remained deathly serious.

"The baby was born here at a local hospital to avoid out-of-state legalities with the adoption. The adoptive parents were screened by the agency. I would never be part of the baby's life, never see the family again. The files would be locked. We wanted the episode over, an accident that should have been avoided but that produced joy for a deserving couple. My boyfriend agreed, and we went on as if it never happened."

Brian sank back down, elbows on his knees, head bent forward.

"I was young and ignorant, Brian," she continued. She told him that attending different colleges ended her relationship with the boy. They experimented with dating others and discovered that they existed in a high-school rut that traveled round and round the same track, that the circumstances had changed and so had they. "And now this letter."

"Can I read it?" His mouth clamped in a stiff line.

"It's from the girl's mother." She held out the letter.

*Dear Mrs. Dineen,*

*You will be surprised to hear from me after all these years, but I really need your help. Your daughter, Madison (that's what we named her), has been a real blessing, and I thank you a thousand times for allowing me to have her. I'm sure it was out of love that you gave her to a family who could care for her as she deserves. I suppose you felt you were unable to, although maybe you could have managed somehow, as people do, and had the experience of being a mother to the most delightful, obliging child in the world.*

*My husband abandoned us several years ago, leaving us penniless. I was forced to take on housecleaning to keep us going. I didn't mind. I'd do anything for Madison. At thirteen she is a star gymnast at her school and one of the prettiest girls in her class. She is on her own a lot, with me out scrapping to keep food in our mouths and trying to keep my boyfriend happy too. She is so very independent. You would be proud of her.*

*Last week Madison went into a coma after falling from the high bars. Worse, she has caught some horrible disease in the hospital they can't figure out. This is why I come to you, her mother, who gave birth to her. The hospital needs your medical records to help find out what could be wrong with her. You could help save your daughter's life.*

*The adoption agency wouldn't give out information, but I wheedled your whereabouts out of the snarky woman in the back office. Could I come to your home and pick up the records?*

*Yours truly,*

*Lynn Dorsey*

She searched Brian's face for a reaction, but his expression remained closed. He sat motionless, staring into the empty gulf that filled the room.

"How could you?" came as almost a whisper.

"I couldn't care for—"

"How could you not tell me?"

"The event had been erased from my life, Brian. And from my mind. It had nothing to do with you, with us."

"It's about trust." He stared straight at her now. "I can't believe that you would give up your own flesh and blood, a precious gift of the divine."

"I was seventeen."

"It could have been managed, with sacrifice on your part."

"You mean the Lord would provide. I don't think like that, Brian."

He didn't look at her, and she felt an ocean widen between them. Despite a conviction that she had every reason to bury the past, a crimson flush crept up her neck.

Brian had a faraway look on his face. "I've always wanted a large family. I believe that every new life is a gift from God."

*In that case, why didn't you make certain the woman you married wanted the same thing?* she was about to ask but stopped, struck with uncertainty. He was right: She had not been straightforward. She had been cowardly.

Before she could say more, Brian stood abruptly and left the room, leaving an ominous silence. For a stark moment Angela felt their life crumbling into hopelessness.

She stepped out to the garage where the old Chevy Brian loved and her spanking blue Volkswagen rested side by side under the dim light of an overhead bulb. Sitting on a stool next to the cluttered workbench, she tried to pull herself together. Arguments to persuade him swarmed through her mind, arguments that any rational person could comprehend. *The episode was a stupid youthful mistake, buried to save the lives of the living. I did not want the child. It has nothing to do with us. What's the point of making it an issue now? What difference does it make?*

But the words rang hollow now that he was gone, stewing about all the reasons she should not have deceived him. She longed to talk to someone, but who? There was Pinky—too adolescent. As for Porter, Mr. Free-for-All, his way out of adversity was escape.

Maybe this crisis would be a catalyst to something different—anything would be better than the emptiness that in the last years had penetrated the lake house. Maybe Brian would yield, would see her side, would forgive, maybe she would furnish this woman with the medical records and that would be the end of it. Maybe…

She closed her eyes, tears spilling down her cheeks as all sense of control drained from her. After a few minutes, she heard a whine, felt a wet nose pressed against her leg. She looked down in surprise to see a sleek black and brown form looking up at her—Biff from next door. She slid to the cool floor, mindless of the dirt, and throwing her arms around the Doberman's neck pressed him against her, squeezing her eyes shut as she felt his moist tongue on her cheek.

They sat entwined for some time, Biff's rump swaying gently. Beyond the open door the lake radiated blackness. She was on her own.

**ANGELA WATCHED THE FIGURE APPROACH** with a twinge of expectation—yes, it was Dora Moser, looking beautiful and summery in a cool blue sundress. Her blonde hair waved gracefully back from her face, showing off finely turned features and a pair of keen blue eyes. Fifteen years her senior, Dora had a refined, European look that stood her apart from the casual American housewife.

At the sight of her, just when she had been longing for someone to talk to, the tight pressure in Angela's chest lessened. They had been neighbors since Dora and her husband moved next door two years ago from the east coast. When Dora became a widow ten months later, Angela showed up at her door, launching what had become a close friendship. Angela felt an instant rapport, drawn to her composed manner, her sympathetic expression, the way she gave one her full attention. Angela felt she could tell this woman anything. Angela found her troubles pouring out as if a valve had been loosened: her youthful pregnancy, the sudden appearance of the adoptive mother, Brian's pressure to have children.

Now, as they started their walk through the park, Angela launched into her story.

"Yesterday, Lynn Dorsey actually showed up at our front door. I'd already sent her the medical records, hoping that would be that, she would leave, and we would be done.

"That was good of you. You've done her a great service."

"But that's not what happened. She listed a string of misfortunes. A couple of years ago their house burned to the ground due to a faulty wire, and a week later her husband took the dog to the vet and never returned. Gone like the uninsured house. Later the husband wrote that he would send them money when he could—if he didn't commit suicide—that he was sorry, but he had lost massively at gambling and they were better off without him. The money never arrived. That was the last they heard from him.

"Now Madison's medical bills had left her destitute, and she needed money."

"That's quite a story," said Dora.

"But there's more. The woman insisted that Madison had a right to know who gave birth to her. She brought out a portrait of Madison, a pretty, serious girl with sad eyes. She loved the child dearly, but she'd done all she could, was no longer able to cope."

"Dear girl! She dropped quite a load on you."

"This is not the family the agency described to us."

"You told me the files had been sealed after the adoption. The agency must answer for revealing information about you."

"The agency claims an investigation determined that no one gave out privileged information and questions Lynn Dorsey's story," Angela said. Dora reached out and pressed her friend's arm. "I've hardly slept since her visit."

Dora slowed her pace as a motor scooter whizzed by. "Dear friend, I have something to tell *you*. Last afternoon, a woman showed up at my house in a maroon Buick and asked for directions to the Dineens. She had on a red dress and carried a large tote bag with bamboo handles. I thought nothing of it at the time."

"Lynn Dorsey!"

"I watched her hop into the Buick and head toward your house. In the driver's seat was a dark-haired man in his forties. The back window rolled down and a youngster peered out. I'd say she was thirteen or so."

Angela's head began spinning as the implications of this hit her. She stopped walking. "Dora, it fits! I haven't told you all. After she left yesterday, I phoned the Banes Memorial Hospital where the girl is supposed to be deathly ill. Madison Dorsey had been discharged a week ago, completely cured."

"Angela, this is serious." Dora reached into her purse and pulled out a folded strip of newsprint. "After they left, I noticed something on the curb that had evidently slipped out of her bag. It was a newspaper clipping with the headline *LOCAL CEO AND WIFE KILLED IN ACCIDENT ABROAD*. The article related your parent's death in Tuscany and described your father as wealthy."

In a burst of energy, Angela grabbed her friend by the shoulders. "So! The woman had expectations far beyond the non-existent medical bills. The entire miserable story is a sham."

"The woman is counting on your desire to help and possibly meet your daughter. What will you do?"

Angela smiled. Her cheeks held a pink glow, her eyes sparked with zeal. Nothing had been solved, but things were happening. "I don't know. But I'm going to find out."

**ANGELA ENTERED THE ROOM** and snapped off the television. Brian looked up inquiringly. "You look peaked. Don't you feel well?"

"Oh, it's nothing. I've been without energy lately, a bit nauseous. It will pass," Angela replied. "Brian, we have to talk."

An impasse had set in. Angela was in a state of perpetual annoyance. Brian remained in a state of resigned neutrality and moved through the house silently, sitting in mute stoicism at the dinner table. The rise of a biological child from the ashes of the past hung in the air like black smoke. They were not able to press charges against Lynn Dorsey; asking for money was not a crime, and no threat or pressure had been applied. Nothing could be done.

Angela sat on the edge of the couch. "This regards Lynn Dorsey. She showed up again this afternoon asking to be reimbursed for hospital expenses due to a recent back injury that prevents her from working. She hinted that if we didn't help her she might be forced, much as she hated the idea, to give the child up. The boldness of the woman is infuriating. She also brought these."

Brian shuffled through the pile of childhood photos of Madison, plus a teacher's note praising Madison's school work. Angela gazed at the image of a girl around eleven, hair glimmering bronze in the sunlight, hands clasped in front of her, looking directly at the camera. There was a lightness, a steady gleam to the girl that belied her abject circumstances. Something inside Angela stirred…

Brian's expression softened. "I don't see how we can refuse."

"She wants to bring Madison to visit. And she wants money. Oh, Brian, we've learned how deceptive she is. Once we give in, I'm afraid we'll never hear the end of it."

"It wouldn't hurt to meet her. For the child's sake."

Of course, Brian would become attached—she could see he already regarded the girl with sympathy and some ownership.

"Just meet Madison and see how you feel," he suggested.

"Brian, I didn't want a child when I was sixteen, and I don't want one now."

"The mother seems desperate. Maybe we should help her."

"We don't know she'll use the money for the child."

Clearly, the mother and child were poor. Brian claimed the welfare of the child was the main issue, and their only move should be to assist her, either though helping her with bills or, if it came to that, taking the child under their wing in whatever way possible.

It's not the girl's fault," he said gently. "The woman doesn't love her, or she wouldn't be talking about giving her up." He leaned forward. "All the more reason she should get away from an unhealthy environment. We can help her find the right path or straighten her around if that's necessary. If she's as needy as she seems to be, maybe she'd be better off with us. Think what we could do for her." He looked at Angela with urgency. "I'm willing to do whatever you want."

It rested on her shoulders. There was no thunderbolt from the sky, no hand reaching down from authoritarian realms to tell her what to do or to realign the pieces of their marriage in harmonious order.

Angela uncrossed her legs and leaned back against the sofa cushion. The Westminster clock on the wall ticked loudly; time was crowding in. To bring a child into their home—such a huge step. Brian moved over and sat on the cream sectional next to her. "Angie, if she's what she appears to be, you would learn to love her."

"It takes more than love! It takes skill."

"You don't think you'd be a good mother, I get that. But I disagree. You try hard to do the right thing. You're a good person, that will come through. Do you think other women don't have the same fears? The perfect mother doesn't exist. You will learn."

He inched closer and put an arm around her. "I will be here, you're not in this alone. We could at least give it a try."

Madison belonged in their home, with them. He was determined to do the right thing.

So was she.

"Brian, you may be right. But I'm sorry. I can't do that."

She didn't trust anything about Lynn Dorsey. The situation smacked of lies and manipulation. To give in would be opening a Pandora's box of trouble and heartache. She swallowed the remorse she felt at letting Brian down as she walked to the mailbox and slipped in a letter to Lynn Dorsey forbidding the woman from contacting her again.

THE NEXT DAY was too hot for a walk, and they elected to meet instead at the Rosa Tea House. A sprightly waiter seated them at a glass table overlooking a garden patio and poured water into two jar glasses. He balanced a tray in front of them, rocking back and forth on his feet. "So, beautiful ladies, what can I get to brighten your day?" He waved two glossy menus in the air.

"Just tea," Dora said. "I'd like Tazo green."

"Same for me," said Angela. "With milk." Tea would soothe the lower pain in her abdomen. And lift the droopiness that had been slowing her steps lately.

Dora adjusted the drape of her skirt and folded her hands in her lap with an air of composure. "You look sad, Angie. What's going on?"

"The death of my parents left me a hefty inheritance. There's so much to take care of. It's overwhelming."

Dora smiled slightly. "So, you have inherited a good amount of money. Should I feel sorry for you?"

Angela shook her head. "It's a responsibility. How am I to manage? I need help with health and life insurance, medical directives, real estate matters, taxes, career decisions, that kind of thing. I've never felt so alone."

"Your husband?"

"Brian knows little about those things."

"Have you tried him? It's possible he can handle more than you give him credit for."

"Well, not exactly. I assume…"

"Angie, I think you underestimate Brian. From what you tell me, he's more capable than you think. So are you." She laid a hand on Angela's wrist. "I've heard a great deal about Brian—and I've learned during my bumpy life that the stars lie within ourselves."

Angela stopped twisting her bracelet. Dora was attempting to tell her something. The stars—she saw them shining within Brian. Was it possible to fill the holes and cravings of her life with her own light?

"Brian says he's willing to do whatever I want. If I want to go places, we'll go. If I want him to be more attentive, more outgoing—he doesn't know what I want exactly, but he's behind me 100 percent."

"It would be hard for him to change who he basically is."

"But his willingness counts for something. Maybe a guiding hand would ease things along." Angela held her hand out in front of her face, fingers splayed. It looked very small.

The waiter slipped the tea and saucers in front of them. Slowly, Angela circled a spoon in her teacup. "Did you find marriage this difficult, Dora?"

"Of course. Nothing worthwhile is easy. But I loved being married, and since Hans died I miss it terribly. He and I went through a period of disillusionment, where our respective faults flared up and crushed our dreams. But we found that if we supported each other when one fell short, if we faced reality with understanding, our shortcomings would lose power. If that failed, there was only one thing left…" She stopped.

"There was only one thing left…" Angela repeated encouragingly, her heart quickening.

"To give up expectations. To let go of what you can't change." She touched Angela's sleeve. "You can't change him. You must learn to accept Brian as he is. Everything that follows is built on that. If you need more from him, gentle guidance works better than getting upset because he's not who you want him to be or someone he can't be."

"Sweets for the beautiful ladies? Butterscotch scones? Petit fours?" They shook their heads.

Angela felt the sun's rays from the window press against her skin, infusing her with strength.

"The sunshine makes me feel good," she said smiling.

"I think you have a great deal of sunshine in you. You're young. You'll do fine if you believe in yourself. Just remember, Brian has feelings, although he may act otherwise. I'm sure it's not always black and white for him. And from what you've told me, he doesn't have anyone to confide in."

"Brian is more alone than I am. This city where I grew up is my home. His home is with me."

As they left the teahouse, Angela was invaded with a new lightness and squeezed her friend with both arms.

"I wish I were as wise as you are," she said warmly.

"Life instructs. You're learning, my dear friend."

**IT WAS A BRIGHT JULY SATURDAY,** and the entire neighborhood was out sweeping pathways, mowing lawns, weeding flower beds. Brian and Angela stood in the garage gazing at the moldy boxes, dusty tools, and leftover garden supplies, the walls pocked with putty repairs and stains. Painting the garage had been Angela's inspiration, a project they could do together, and to Angela's gratification, although he had never painted so much as a flower box, Brian had agreed. They would tackle the garage first. If this succeeded, the entire house needed painting, if only she could convince her husband that fresh air and activity surpassed indoor entertainment and repose.

Angela watched him drag the folding ladder across the floor and struggle to set it up against the garage wall as if he didn't know which end was which. But she said nothing, not even a playful tease about his helplessness they could both chuckle over. Besides, she was having a good time just hanging out in the garage with him, creating a sparkling new space.

Angela made a move to assist him with the ladder, but no, let him manage on his own. "Not much light in here," he remarked, looking over his shoulder.

Again, restraint was in order. She would not run and take care of it. "What would help?" she asked instead, lining up paint brushes on a folded newspaper.

After a few seconds he suggested, "Why don't you screw in a flood light?"

"Excellent idea," she exclaimed, prying the paint can open with a screwdriver. "The bulbs are in the basement storage room." She poured the smooth cream-colored paint carefully into a roller pan, heard the click of the door as he entered the house, moved the roller back and forth in the pan, heard the door click again, then scraping sounds along the ceiling. Shortly thereafter the overhead light went out, and a fresh beam appeared, flooding the garage.

"There you go," Brian said, flicking the light on and off from the wall switch.

"It works perfectly," Angela said. "Good idea."

She spied the flicker of a smile on Brian's face as he climbed the ladder and began gingerly moving the roller back and forth under the ceiling, spreading rows of paint in even laps. The sight of her husband perched on the ladder in a pair of her father's old jeans and faded olive t-shirt with a rip under one arm made her smile, so different from his usual clean-cut, proper, uptight self.

Laying a drop cloth along the floor, she knelt and began applying paint, covering the blotted wall with a white glow. She started to hum an old ditty from her young camp days. The chitter of birds arguing sounded beyond the open garage door, through which the odor of sweet alyssum drifted, mixing with the smell of fresh paint.

"How do you like doing handyman work?" she asked Brian as he swiped the roller back and forth.

"Fine."

"I find this kind of work soothing. It clears my mind." No response. "What chores did you have when you were growing up?"

"None. My duties were to study, practice the piano, and attend catechism." He scraped the roller on the edge of the pan and resumed painting.

She stood up and began running her brush along the wall corner. "Let's have a conversation. It'll pass the time."

His arm, back and forth, back and forth. "Sure."

"What do you want to talk about?"

"It's up to you." Was it possible he wasn't just being accommodating, that he actually *liked* having nothing to say and nothing to do? The thought staggered her.

She drew a breath. "I'll tell you about the new support group we're offering as an adjunct at the Center for women suffering in abusive relationships. They're a whipped, damaged lot who live in fear. My co-leader and I decided to begin the meeting with a three-minute meditation. After one minute a woman leapt to her feet, the others followed suit, and they all claimed they would quit the group if they were forced to sit in silence one more second."

"I suppose it would be hard, if you're not used to it," Brian offered from the ladder.

"Yes, they couldn't bear it. Silence forces them to turn inward, to view their lives straight in the face. To feel all they'd been going through."

"I need a rag."

"On the workbench." He clambered down, stuffed a cloth in the back pocket of his jeans.

"Brian, are you interested in what I'm telling you?"

"Yes, of course."

"Do you want to hear more?"

"Yes."

"Do you realize that not commenting or questioning makes me think I'm boring you?"

"No, no."

"Brian, it would help if you asked questions," she said gently. "Like 'How did the rest of the group go?' or 'What do you hope to accomplish?' Anything. To keep the conversation rolling."

"I don't want to sound inquisitive. You tell me what you want to."

"But there's too much to tell. I could go on about the Center for hours. I need encouragement, a sign of interest."

"Well. Tell me more."

"Can you ask me a specific question?"

"It makes me out as a know-nothing."

"Actually, it makes you sound interested and involved."

He dipped his roller in the pan and raised it dripping to the wall. "Well, so, what is your role in this new group?"

She laughed. "Good question. I'll have to think about that one." The putter of an outboard motor roared by on the lake and receded into the distance.

"I get what you're saying," he said. "How about you ask me questions?"

"All right, Mr. Smarts," she went on. "I've plenty. First of all, why are you still wearing your wristwatch and getting paint all over it?"

He glanced at his wrist, looking abashed. "Huh. Nobody's perfect."

"Never mind, I've done much the same thing. I once dropped a diamond pendant my father gave me in the lake. I told him it had just disappeared. I lied. What a coward I was!"

Brian dismounted, removed his watch, and wiped it with a clean cloth. "Right as rain."

"Great. Here's another question for you. How many miles in a light year?"

"Roughly six trillion. The distance light travels in one Earth-year. I studied that in high school."

His memory awed her. "Too easy, huh? Here's another one: They're looking for soccer coaches. Why don't you give it a try? You'd be great working with kids."

"I've only played unsupervised soccer on the playground. What do I know?"

"You merely have to learn the rules. You're a sports fan. It couldn't be hard."

"I'll think about it." His voice was hesitant, but she thought she detected a flicker of interest.

By the time they finished, the sun had dropped low in the sky. Brian went into the house to take off his dirty clothes and shower. Angela regarded the line of paint cans and stained papers strewn along the floor.

"Brian!" He poked his head from the door. "Would you please help me clean up?"

A month ago, she would have taken care of the cleanup herself. Easier to just do it—wrestle later with the resentment. She watched in satisfaction as he stored the ladder in the corner and began boxing up the paint supplies.

They stood together and gazed at their handiwork. With sparking new walls, the garage had been revitalized. After a thorough cleaning and the installation of new shelves, it would have a brand-new look.

"Doesn't it look fantastic? You've done a wonderful job, Brian."

Brian's expression was lively. "We'll have to build a new garage for the dirty cars."

They laughed, giddy with fatigue.

"Maybe I'll try it." His green eyes glistened.

"To be a professional painter?"

"No, pinwheel, the soccer coach job. Wouldn't hurt." She was too surprised to speak. "Maybe you could call tomorrow."

"Just phone the Minnetonka Community Center," she responded evenly. "They'll set you up."

He reentered the house. A minute later the door creaked back open. "I'll do it. And the next question's mine: What's for dinner?"

Angela laughed. From the yard, a cardinal let out a screeching cry. Impulsively Angela echoed it, squeezing her mouth into an O and giving a high piercing whistle. Let's see how he likes that! After a minute of what she imagined to be a surprised silence, the bird gave another cry. Now that's how to carry on a conversation, she said to herself, marching happily into the house.

Later that evening as Angela was in the kitchen preparing a tuna casserole, she heard a commotion from the garage. When she raised her head, there was Brian standing in the open doorway, a tall, swaying figure, his wet face alive with exertion. Droplets dribbled onto the floor from his clothing, and he was breathing heavily.

Something about his expression had changed.

"What happened?"

"I went for a swim." He slapped his arms loudly with both hands. "Very invigorating." A proud, audacious look came over his face.

"You what?"

"A swim."

"You don't swim. You never go in the water. What's going on?"

"The water looked inviting, and I needed to cool down. Besides, I wanted to get away to figure things out, and there was nowhere else to go. So I went into the lake, clothes and all. I wanted the shock. I waded out to my chest and quick-walked all the way to Richardson's dock and back. It was good to be out there on my own, with the frigid water to buck me up. I may not swim, but I can manage the cold lake any time."

"But—" It was so unlike him.

"Oh, and there's a skunk hiding in the chokeberry bushes by the boathouse. If it's not gone tomorrow, I'll call a fellow at work—"

He removed his water-soaked shoes and took the towel she held out. "I've been thinking," he said, oblivious of the wet clothes against his skin. "My birthday's coming up next week. I think we should throw a party."

The day of Brian's birthday, the hors d'oeuvres were set out on the back terrace, the umbrellas raised and tilted into the sun. Brian had insisted: no mention of his birthday. He didn't want all the fuss and hoopla, just a get-together with friends. He looked handsome and summery in his white pants and beige sports shirt, face tan from pushing the rotary lawnmower over the yard—something he did now every other Saturday, winding steadily back and forth, looking pleased with himself. After bringing out orders of martinis, gin fizzes, and scotch sours on a tray, he seated himself and crossed his legs as people exchanged stories of their various backgrounds. Dora, with her slight accent, charmed everyone with lengthy tales of growing up in the Swiss mountains, moving to Zurich after her parents died to live with an aunt and uncle when she was twelve, where she helped out and eventually ran their original art shop.

Brian, after draining his second martini, launched into his story: "My grandfather grew up on a farm," he said warmly. "He raised pigs. He had a guard dog, Bobby, who was the apple of his eye. One day he found one of the pigs in the back pen, dead. Bobby had ripped its throat apart. The dog had never done anything like that before, and this pig was known to be cantankerous and mean. But my grandfather couldn't put up with a pig-killing dog, and he gave Bobby to a fellow in another town 260 miles away. Two weeks later Bobby showed up at the back door, shaggy and hungry. He had trudged 260 miles to get home. My grandfather decided that from then on mean-spirited pigs had just better look out."

Angela couldn't believe it—it had been ages since she'd seen him enjoy himself as he had that evening, speaking with natural effusiveness, a humorous twist to his mouth. Like the old days in San Francisco during their dating years when everything had been new and exciting, and they roamed the city and partied with close college friends. What had gotten into him?

Pinky described the sugar plantation in Antigua where her boyfriend had grown up with two siblings and a loquacious parrot. "Homer's the smartest person on the planet," she exclaimed, blowing a bubble with her gum and laughing. "He's completing his PhD in animal husbandry. We're going to live on a farm."

"These advanced degrees are a waste," Porter commented, crossing his legs. "It's social connections with those in high places that get you somewhere. Me, I lack ten credits for a BA, and nevertheless, look what I've achieved: CEO at a major corporation."

"Homer works hard for his degree, it affirms him," Pinky cried.

"Not everyone can do that, Porter," Angela put in.

"Homer's going to do big things. He and I, we'll be together for always, you know." Pinky drew one leg under her and looked at Homer affectionately.

"So, that makes you his what—girlfriend?" Dora inquired. "I don't know the terms they use these days: partner, lover, significant other, best mate?"

"Terms are restrictive," Homer said. "We're together because we want to be, not because of some idiotic pledge on paper. I love Pinky. We understand each other and we have a good life together."

Pinky laughed, a high squeal. "I guess we're a couple of hippies. Like the author Germaine Greer, we reject marriage. We'll never ever have to break up because we have all the freedom we want and there would be nothing to gain by being apart."

"Atta boy," Porter exclaimed. "We now live in an open society where you can do your own thing. I'm single because I can't bear to eliminate all the women I'd have to give up if I tied myself down. What's wrong with that? Why deprive myself? Why deprive the female race? And for what? Obliged to be home every night at a certain time, spend weekends on chores and yard work? Not for me."

"And Brian and I choose to live out here in the staid suburbs." Angela said with some irritation.

"Your choice, my lady." Porter brushed a fleck from one of his white shoes. "So, Brian. When are you going to get a speedboat? You do live on a lake, after all."

"When we can afford it," Brian replied.

Angela shook her head. "It's a major project: installing a boat lift, hauling, fueling and maintaining, storing a large boat."

"The truth is," Brian said, "I don't know how to handle a speedboat. I'd never been on a boat before the cruise with Angela and her parents in the Bahamas. Buying a boat is down the road."

"Oh," Pinky cried, bouncing in her seat, "you must get a boat! I want a speedboat for waterskiing! Homer and I will be out all the time, won't we Homer?" She reached over, planted a kiss on Homer's cheek, then swung out of her chair and announced she was going to inspect that enormous maple across the yard.

It wasn't long before the conversation, which had resumed with a crackling of ice dropping into glasses and the bowed figure of Brian circling the chairs, was interrupted by a terrified cry spiraling through the yard. Brian dropped the decanter on the table and rushed toward the sound of crackling twigs and the swish of leaves scuttling over each other. A strained, gargled voice climaxed with a grunt as he arrived, and a form came crashing through the branches of the maple and landed in a heap on top of him. He pushed Pinky's limp arms from his chest, shook his head to get his bearings, and, ascertaining that no bones were broken, carried her inside and laid her on the bed. After fetching bandages and cream from the bathroom, he and Angela worked side by side, cleaning the wounds, applying disinfectant, binding up the sprain in her wrist, and taping the cuts. It was amazing how exhilarated Angela felt, the way they worked together like that as a team, predicting each other's requirements, moving back and forth like two dancers circling rhythmically, like two seabirds drifting on the same wave of air.

Afterwards, Brian received several pats on the back for his rescue. "I make a real good pillow," he said smiling.

Pinky recovered sufficiently to allow everyone to enjoy a dinner of baked pork tenderloin in the dining room. The drinks flowed, and conversation was lively; the close call had filled everyone with giddy relief.

Afterward, standing on the front steps, Angela and Brian watched the guests file out to their cars parked in a string along the circular drive.

It had been an eventful day. Fall was turning the leaves a crisp golden, and a bold wintery orange moon peered down on the rooftops. Change was in the air.

As the last car drove off, a figure appeared, and they recognized Porter striding around the side of the house, his purple Vikings sweater slung over one shoulder.

"Did you miss me? Had to fetch my sunglasses," he said cheerfully. "Dineen, you really should make better use of the lake. You might as well be living in town. As for you, my dear Angela, you really need to get out more, cooped up here is not your style at all." They regarded him, Angela with irritation, Brian wearing an expression of benign tolerance.

"You may be right. Glad you found your sunglasses." Brian nodded. "Goodnight, Porter." He turned and entered the house.

Porter turned to Angela with a grin. "I don't think that fellow has an adventurous bone in his body." He moved closer. "Angela, why don't you come with me to Jamaica? I've rented a house for two weeks on a white sandy beach, complete with pool, cook, and chauffeur. It would be a waste to stay there alone."

"It might do you good to be alone for a while," Angela said.

Ignoring the sarcasm, he grabbed her around the waist and pulled her close. "Say yes," he whispered. She could detect the alcohol in his breath, feel the pressure of his chest against hers. Then he kissed her, his mouth open, soft. "Come on, we're friends," he said, looking into her eyes. "It's up to you to say what kind. Brian won't mind if you get away for a while."

Angela backed away, every nerve alert, and stared at him. When he saw the look on her face, his expression fell. "Aw, Angie, you know you—"

Angela struck him across his chest, then her two hands gripped his shirt as she pulled his face close to hers with a swift gesture. Porter raised an arm protectively.

"Porter, I won't have it," she cried, shaking with anger. "Not only are you out of line, you have been rude and boorish all evening."

"Whoa! My dear girl, you must watch that redheaded temper of yours." A frown creased his forehead. "An expense-paid vacation in the Caribbean—it's a good offer and I don't make one like it every day."

"I'm done, Porter." She dropped her arms. "Get into your Lexus and go home. I don't want to see you anymore."

Porter gazed at her, and finally, with the sullen expression of a scolded dog, he headed to the car, sweater swaying across his back.

Angela strode through the house to the back deck, past empty glasses and stained coffee cups, and leaned against the railing. Many evenings she'd watched as purple and gold streaks on the horizon stretched and dipped slowly behind the Earth and the golden moon spread its glow over the night sky. Something about the steady, reliable presence of the overhead sky, splashing every night with its everlasting reconfiguration, calmed her.

She thought she heard footsteps. No doubt it was Brian heading for his chair in the living room, but no, the steps grew louder and there he was, leaning against the railing next to her. His hands grasped the top rail as he gazed into the distance.

She didn't speak, reluctant to break the tranquility of the night sky. After a while she said, "I won't be seeing Porter again."

"Oh? But you're so fond of him."

"He invited me to go to Jamaica with him."

"It would be a nice getaway for you."

"Fine," she cried with a surge of anger. "I'll go with him and have myself a fling. I'll notify him tomorrow."

"That's not what I meant. So, you refused?"

"Yes. His behavior is offensive."

"If you feel that way, I don't think he'll mention such a thing again."

She whirled to face him. "He got fresh. Brian, he kissed me. I no longer know him."

Brian flushed and rose. "Is he still here?" He took a few steps across the deck to get a look at the driveway. When he saw it empty, he returned to Angela's side and took a breath. "Angie, that's going too far. Old family friend or not, that's it, I don't want him coming around anymore."

"It's not just Porter's flirting," she said in a softer tone. "I can't tolerate the way he insults people, the way he insults you. Why do you put up with it?"

"Because he's important to you," Brian said, gazing out at the lake. "I chose to overlook his barbs. I tolerated him for your sake."

A smile softened her mouth, and she inched closer and laid her chin against his shoulder. "Is that so? To tell the truth, it's not such a hardship to part from him. I have you."

He darted her a quizzical look.

"I was proud of you this evening."

"I guess I'm a hero. Comes naturally, you know," he said, turning his face to hers.

She breathed in the lemony scent of him and felt her body relax. "Brian."

"Humm?"

"I'd love it if we were together more. I mean, if we did things, ventured into the big wide world to take a look. Would you be agreeable?"

"What are you driving at?"

"Why don't we go somewhere this summer? We could visit your cousin Conor on Long Island. You used to play with him as a kid. We could explore Manhattan, slip out to an ocean beach. It would be fun."

"I have three weeks of vacation coming. When should we go?" He drew back, looking at her with a humorous gleam.

"What?" she cried in surprise. It was too good to be true, too easy… Taking his hand, she began to play with his fingers. "Do you know how handsome you look tonight? You were the best-looking person at the party."

He laughed. "No need to butter me up. I've already said I wanted to go."

"It's good for you to hear the truth, although I shouldn't say such things, or your head will blow up like a blimp."

"No danger of that. I've never been king of the parade. You must be prejudiced."

"Do you remember that party when Sandra Draper couldn't keep her eyes off you? I burned with jealousy."

At this he laughed aloud. "I have news for you. I spent time with Sandra Draper before you and I met. After my first date with you, it was over."

"I see. Well, Mr. Heartbreaker, I have some unexpected news for you as well. I've been waiting for the right moment."

"And what is that?"

At last. The time had come. She felt a fluttering in her stomach. "I have something to tell you." Without looking at him, she turned and leaned her elbows against the railing. The night sky looked down at them through its golden eye, a moon so calm, so sure of itself, flooding them with magic. "You know I've had bouts of nausea these last weeks?"

"Yes."

"I happen to be pregnant."

His head turned slowly in her direction, his eyes riveted on her face. At last, he stuttered, "But—that is—you don't want children…"

"I may not be a great mother. But many muddle through—I will more than most. There are books, classes. As long as I can continue to work, and if you agree to help out—we can do this together."

"I can hardly believe what I'm hearing. Are you sure? No, don't answer. You're sure enough. Anyway, I want it enough for us both."

"I want only one child, though."

"Agreed."

They stared for some time at the lighted houses blinking on the far shore, too struck to speak. Angela slipped her hand into his. "Of course, I expect you to do me favors," she said mischievously.

"What would that be?"

"First, I'd like you to lift your arm. Then, without straining yourself, to put your arm around my shoulder." He gazed at her. "Then I'd like you to pull me close, and after a while, when the mood takes you, embrace me passionately, right here on the deck for all the world to see—of course it's dark, but it's the principle—and kiss me with your entire body."

"What if you're not in the mood for all this aggression?"

"You'll be able to tell. Somewhere between the hug and the kiss, you'll feel it. You'd better hope you can keep up."

"Okay, if you're going to play the fox, I'll be glad to take the role of wolf."

No more talk, only the close night sky and the echo of earlier voices left over from barbecues and boating parties drifting over the lake, noises that spoke of community, of celebrating, of secrets, all unknown, as nothing is ever safe and assured, Angela knew, but standing on the balcony in the moonlight she determined to give it her best shot.

"HAPPY FAMILIES ARE ALL ALIKE. That's from Tolstoy."

"Where did you learn that, Sage?" her mother asked.

"My English teacher. She likes me because I read so many books. She thinks I'm bright."

"You may be too smart for your own good," said her mother, setting two fresh cups of coffee on the breakfast table. "Be careful or people will think you're a showoff."

"But *you* don't mind, Mom. You like that I'm intelligent. I think we're happy, and yet we're not like everyone else."

She skipped up to Brian, leaned against his chair and plucked at his shirt. "You're not like everyone else, Dad. You're weird."

Brian pulled her onto his lap. "It takes one to know one, smarty," he said, rubbing her back. His red-topped girl, his little sprite.

"You sit in your chair hour after hour without getting up. You don't even go to the bathroom. I would go bonkers."

"You, my little gazelle, can't sit still for more than two minutes."

"I'm only twelve years old. Not a fair comparison."

He laughed. "You could convince a beggar he doesn't need money. No wonder you're the head of the junior debate team."

"I like to argue," she cried, jumping up to grab a handful of strawberries from the table. "It's fun."

The July morning was warming rapidly. The air brimmed with scents of honeysuckle and phlox, and the lake below glistened fresh and serene under the lifting sun. The table was spread with plum jelly, sausages, a large plate of pancakes, a pitcher of fresh milk, and cups of steaming coffee. The spaniel, Duke, lay by the door with a resigned expression, eyeing every move at the table.

Climbing onto her seat, Sage scraped a buttermilk pancake onto her plate and smothered it with maple syrup, then harpooned a juicy sausage patty as they passed dishes back and forth. A man and boy in a boat puttered slowly by on the water below, fish lines aloft.

"Good breakfast," Brian remarked as he took a sip of coffee and leaned back in his chair.

"You eat a lot, Dad," Sage said, stuffing a large bite into her mouth.

"That's because I'm tall. A man needs a lot to keep on his toes," Brian said.

"I'd like to see you on your toes, Dad. You'd fall on your head."

"I'll have you know that I marched in the school band and never missed a step."

"Your father has great rhythm. The best dancer in our Arthur Murray class. When is our next lesson, Brian?"

"Friday. The day before Sage leaves for Wisconsin."

Sage beamed at him. "I leave on Saturday. Oh, I can hardly wait!" Sage tossed her head back and grinned. "Two whole weeks! Aunt Pinky and Uncle Homer said I can ride the horses and even help groom them. You'll drive me, won't you Daddy?"

"You bet, kitten."

They heard Angela running the faucet in the kitchen. Sage scooted over to Brian and leaned against his arm.

"Why do you do so many cool things for me?" she asked.

"Because we love you."

"Mom doesn't love me as much as you do, Daddy. She's always got her finger in some pie somewhere else, doing things more important than me."

"That's just the way she is. Everyone loves in their own way. She'd sacrifice anything for you. She's just not used to reaching out. But her heart is as big as the ocean."

Brian buried her in a hug before she scampered down the stairs into the backyard. He watched as she streaked across the lawn, with Duke bounding ahead, tail swinging. A feisty little thing, his daughter, always bursting out with a humorous remark, full of spirit—where did she get that? Certainly not from him. It was no secret; he adored the ground she walked on. Smart, energetic like her mother, never a dull moment. Pure delight.

She threw a Frisbee across the lawn, and he laughed as Duke leapt into the air like a bullet, legs askew. How blessed he was: a beautiful, bold daughter and a sympathetic wife who understood him, who was happy in her job at the Eberly Housing Center. And him—heck, he had recently received a substantial raise, not bad for an ordinary guy.

It had been a challenge moving out here to Minnesota, packed with Scandinavians and Protestants, where no one had heard of the Clancy Brothers. Pouring his efforts into satisfying his wife's idea of a full-fledged, active, entertaining, house-savvy husband. Ideas which she seemed to have abandoned, he noticed, as the days slipped by.

After dinner, they assembled in the living room to do a practice run for Sage's upcoming school debate. She was defending the topic "Disabled Students Should Be Integrated into the Mainstream Classroom," with Brian providing the challenging arguments.

"Excellent, especially for a first try," Angela declared after the first round. "Well-supported points, both of you. Sage, your arguments were sound, but if you tell your opponent they're crazy, you'll turn the audience against you. And moderate your voice; save your hog-calling for the farm. Brian, show more force, more conviction. Enthusiasm will give your arguments power." She set her bottle of sparkling water on the table. "But I'm impressed. Now try it again."

Beaming, Brian laid out his prep papers, confident he'd give Sage a run for her money.

"You don't stand a chance, Dad," Sage cried, stuffing her hands in her jean pockets. "I have points I haven't even used."

"We'll see about that!"

"I'VE GOT IT," ANGELA SAID, scooting to the front door. When she opened it, there stood a young lady in her twenties, wearing a navy sundress and clutching a white straw handbag, bright auburn hair flashing in the sunlight. She was smiling uneasily and clutching a letter in her left hand.

"Yes?" Angela smiled. Something about this girl's friendly smile and fresh scrubbed face inspired confidence.

"Is this—are you Mrs. Dineen?" the girl asked, a look of hesitation on her face. "I was thrilled to hear from you," she began. "To be invited to your home… I have something to tell you."

Angela stepped back in confusion. "Well—aah—come in." She had no idea who this stranger was. As the girl walked past her, something in her walk drew her attention, something that smacked of trouble. *To be invited…?*

"Wait here." She left to round up Brian and Sage, who appeared shortly. "Let's all sit down." Sage seated herself in the wing chair, looking pleased and a bit smug.

"So, tell us what's going on," Angela said apprehensively.

The girl sat erect, hands clasped in her lap. "You much be Sage," she said, looking over at her.

Sage swirled to her parents. "Don't be mad! I asked her to come. I knew you wouldn't be mad long. I had to meet her! When I found those old letters from Lynn Dorsey stuffed in a back drawer, I thought they were just some old love letters, but then I learned about Madison, and I wrote to the return address, and it was forwarded and Madison called and here she is: the sister I've always wanted! And you said in a letter—I saw it, Mom!—that you regretted not being able to see her. And she's so pretty, and I can tell how nice she is. Oh, please don't mind! I promise to do my chores without being told for the next fifty years."

Angela was hardly able to breathe. Words stuck in her throat; all she could utter was "What?" She looked from Sage to the stranger, who had a worried look on her face. "You're—?"

"Mrs. Dineen, I thought Sage was speaking for the family. I'm so sorry. I wouldn't have…"

"You're Madison."

"Yes."

The set-back eyes, the reddish hair, the tall stature—it made sense. This girl could certainly be her daughter. A pretty thing, well spoken. Lacking the abrasive insistence of the adoptive mother. As the shock wore off, she felt herself mellowing.

"Lynn—that's what I call her—doesn't know I'm here. I don't live with her. I'd like to say that right off."

At the mention of Lynn Dorsey, Angela felt unease, then anger as she thought of the woman's deception. This could be a continuation of the shakedown, the girl but a decoy in sheep's clothing. Despite her air of simplicity, the appealing smatter of freckles dusting her face, and the charm of her quick modest smile, Angela's alarm grew. The wholesome, makeup-free look didn't fit with what must have been a turbulent and impoverished upbringing. But now that the girl was here…

"I guess I shouldn't have—" Sage began.

Angela broke in. "Sage, we'll deal with your scheming later. Now, let's hear what Madison has to say."

"Madison, we were not aware that Sage contacted you," Brian said. "But you're welcome. Why don't you tell us about yourself."

They listened spellbound as Madison described how her adoptive father had left when she was seven, her mother abandoned her years ago, and from age eleven she lived with her elderly grandparents, who although poor were good to her, saw to her every need.

"They're now in a nursing home." Madison spoke in a thin but earnest voice. "I work as an assistant gym instructor at the University School of Continuing Education to support myself. It's important to me to be self-sufficient. I don't want to have to depend on anyone ever again. I plan to take a class or two at the U."

Angela and Brian exchanged glances. Where was this going?

"I've always known I had a real mother out there somewhere," Madison went on. "I wished, if only… But when I received your daughter's letter, I was afraid to meet you. I hadn't heard a word about you since your meeting with Lynn thirteen years ago. She told me she contacted you when she lost her job and was desperate. Said you refused to help, that you wanted nothing to do with a broken family with no father and had no respect for those who couldn't hold a steady job. I was afraid. I couldn't imagine why you would want to see me. What would you be like? And worse, how could I possibly meet your expectations?" She spoke in a soft, steady voice.

The other three regarded her speechless, taking it all in.

"This is a big surprise to us," Brian said finally.

"That's not the way it was at all, Madison!" Angela exclaimed. "Lynn lied to us. She claimed you were near death and misrepresented your family status in order to extract money from us." She eyed the girl sitting across from her, shoulders erect, eyes bent on her lap. It must have been difficult for her to come there, to face a household she believed had rejected Lynn so sanctimoniously, so cruelly, years ago. No wonder she was acting guarded.

As for her credibility, if her aims were selfish, if she primarily wanted money or connections, it would be revealed soon enough. It was possible that she truly sought the link of blood ties, that she was exactly what she appeared—a self-sufficient young woman used to surviving on her own, responding to an invitation that curiosity and optimism wouldn't let her refuse.

"I see that my arrival is jarring," Madison said. She placed her hands on her knees, revealing long, slender fingers and a small violet ring. "The last thing I want to do is disturb you." Moisture glistened in her eyes. She looked at the others, clasped her purse, and stood up. "I wanted to meet you, to see my biological mother with my own eyes. Now I can continue in peace. I have everything I need."

"But you don't have a family," Sage cried.

"I don't want to disrupt your lives," Madison began, but Brian cut her off.

"Sit down, Madison. You're not going anywhere. You were invited here, and I'm glad you came." Angela could tell he was intrigued by her story and could not let her go so easily.

"You seem to be doing well for yourself," Angela said. "I admire that." A strange buoyancy was beginning to swell in her chest.

"I'm determined not to lead the life Lynn did. She became crazy as we became poorer and poorer. She falsified documents, faked illness, did anything to get by. She relied on her boyfriends, and when that dried up, she claimed she couldn't cope on her own. I will not be like that."

Tantalizing possibilities loomed as Angela listened. Could this charming person be the daughter she had long banished from her existence? She was beset by images of her childhood and the old house on Ramsey Street, of family picnics, of festive dinners on a St. Croix pontoon boat, of buzzing conversations around a Thanksgiving table, of evenings gathered around a spitting fire, of school graduations, of home. Suddenly, all her old longings centered right here in this room, focused on the girl sitting across from her. She wanted to believe it all.

Brian laid a hand on Madison's shoulder. "You don't have to do it alone. Maybe we can help."

To their surprise, Madison burst into tears. "You're a happy family. I'm a stranger. Are you sure...?"

"I'm sure!" cried Sage. Excitement flooded her face. "And we're not a happy family, not all the time—Dad can be a dork, and Mom can't always control her temper. And you're not a stranger. Hey, we're *related*."

"You'll stay for dinner," Brian said firmly. "There's plenty of pot roast."

"Yes," said Angela, "there's an empty chair, and it's yours."

THE HOUSE PULSED WITH THE ADDITION of a tall, slim girl who liked to wear white linen shorts and a floppy straw hat. They were thrilled to have acquired a new daughter, to have an expanded family that filled the far corners of the house. A delight, just as anticipated, outgoing and bright. A real addition. The new household of four spent many afternoons in the Baja runabout, picnicked in the local park, and attended Madison's gymnastic meets.

As time wore on, cracks began to mar the shiny surface of their new family life. Madison tended to be seriously late, an unfortunate habit that she attempted unsuccessfully to break—her classes, her job, and her new friends from the Sierra camping group kept her on the run. And some nights she didn't return until the late hours, tiptoeing into the house.

A twenty-five-year-old is responsible for her own life. But it wasn't easy to watch her take precarious right and left turns and offer her good guidance without assuming a great deal of unsolicited control. Their household had rules. Where to draw the line?

Sage adored her, followed her every move. What kind of a model was Madison? Angela and Brian feared disappointment was in store for Sage, that Madison, who catered to Sage by taking her places and teaching her things, would become absorbed in adult pursuits. Or that some blow-up would cause Madison to disappear, leaving a hole that Sage could never refill.

But they were inclined to make allowances. Madison had suffered a difficult childhood and would have to deal with the traumas she had endured. And they would help, whatever it took. They would do their best to block out the past and bring her into the fold.

It wouldn't be smooth sailing. There was work to be done.

But it would be a labor of love.

# Jacqueline

**CILLA CLUTCHED HER HANDBAG** tightly under her arm. "What a madhouse! I can't believe I'm seeing this." The two women were strolling through the plaza in front of their building, Cilla in a droopy sun hat from L.L. Bean and Maeve in a loose blouse and beige support shoes. People of all ages crowded along the sidewalks, stepping off willy-nilly to crisscross the grassy median. Everywhere, dogs dressed in costume sniffed eagerly, some straining at the leash, squawking and barking excitedly, caught up in the bustle. The women maneuvered their way through a cacophony of barks, whines, commands, and squealing children, sidestepping as a terrier in a sailor jacket and matching hat brushed by. A dog trotted along in a pirate hat tightened over the ears, sword hanging around its neck, followed by a tiny poodle with a tutu twisted around its stomach and black ballet shoes on its paws.

"All these animals urinating right and left, barking and clamoring, disturbing the entire neighborhood," Cilla said, sticking close to her friend. "It's one thing to walk your pet quietly on the public sidewalks; who doesn't like a sweet, friendly dog on a leash? But this!"

"It's degrading, that's what it is!" Maeve agreed. "These dogs are treated like dolls. They deserve to be respected, not made into laughing stocks. It's a mockery of the animal world."

As usual they were in agreement. They habitually anticipated each other's reactions, especially when it came to the inadequacies and follies of society, which they uncovered with sharp discernment. They approached the end of the plaza where a dissonant clash of instruments was warming up, and a six-piece country band began to spew notes of "Muskrat Ramble" into the warm summer air. A large sign announced *SUTTER PARK DOG COSTUME CONTEST.*

Cilla groaned, "What's this circus? The serenity of a beautiful Sunday afternoon turned to craziness by dog owners who see their pets as mere toys."

"How can anyone enjoy such raucousness?" Maeve exclaimed.

Just then a figure swung across the grass toward them, violet and yellow blouse flowing gracefully around her petite frame. They recognized Jacqueline, the new resident on the third floor, recently arrived from California. No one was able to determine what brought her to Minnesota, as she avoided details of her recent departure, prompting the other residents to wonder if she was harboring some inglorious secret.

She was out of breath and smiling widely. "Hey! What a gala! Are you enjoying it?" A strand of gold bracelets jangled on her wrists. Her friendly expression radiated sunshine. "Isn't it fun?"

"Really, Jacqueline," Cilla replied. "It is too ridiculous. These poor creatures are being paraded."

"That's what it is, a parade! Everyone looks so cheerful, so happy. Why not enjoy?"

"This madhouse? And the band is ear-shattering." Cilla frowned, pressing a hand against her ear.

"One can't even think," Maeve said.

"Oh, you two are in another world. This is alive, the people love it, and the dogs adore the attention. Do you see any dogs that aren't wildly wagging their tails?" She looked around thoughtfully. "You're right, it is noisy. But that's part of the fun."

It was getting hot, and Cilla noticed small sweat beads collecting on Maeve's neck. "All that will be left tomorrow are stained lampposts, urine spots on the sidewalks, piles of poop, and litter in the fountain basin. You'll see."

Jacqueline laughed. "I'm sure it's not as bad as all that. People around here are well mannered. And there's a cleanup crew."

"There's a cleanup crew after a tornado, but that doesn't make it a welcome event," Maeve said brusquely.

"We're heading inside where it's cool," Cilla said. "Will you be joining our book club? We meet next Wednesday."

"Oh, yes, I can't wait! I love books! Here, Maeve, your arms look pink. Take my sunscreen. I have another. Keep it." With a wave she disappeared into the crowd.

"I don't believe she has ever belonged to a book club," Cilla remarked looking after her.

"She knows books as well as I know fly fishing. Best to have no expectations."

"She probably reads frothy books that are pure entertainment."

They shook their heads. Maybe she would get frustrated or bored and drop out. It was all they could hope for.

"LET'S GET STARTED." It was Cilla's turn to lead the monthly meeting. Everyone took out their books and notepads with a look of anticipation. She and Maeve had started the book club soon after moving into the Gladstone six years ago, Maeve from New York City and Cilla from Los Angeles, where she had lived all her life. The two discovered immediately they had much in common. They continually landed on the same side of every topic from politics to animal rights to their favorite opera. Occasionally they attended socials in the party room, although after an hour of cocktail chatter their supply of chit-chat was often exhausted.

Cilla pulled out her notes with a no-nonsense air. She was thin, with gray hair that hung past her shoulders and a waistline that had expanded with the years into a midline bulge. Her black turtleneck covered a spread of unseemly wrinkles. She claimed she had nothing to hide, that age was a natural progression of life, but there was no reason she couldn't touch it up a bit.

"Jacqueline, why don't you start us off," Cilla asked. Jacqueline, wearing a baby blue mohair sweater, was seated on the couch, flanked by Cilla and Bobbie. "What do you think of Kristin Hannah's novel overall?"

Jacqueline looked expectant as she scanned the faces of the other four women. "I thought *The Great Alone* was great!" She ran her hand over the hardcover on her lap. "What a great story. I loved it. And there was always something new happening; I couldn't wait to find out what was going to happen next. The poor mother and daughter. It was so sad." The rest of the group waited. "I guess that's all I have to say. I'm so glad you chose it. I really liked it."

"Okay, the book was great and sad." Cilla shot Maeve a glance. "Thank you, Jacqueline. Let's hear from someone else."

Maeve took up the slack. "The book was a regular litany of catastrophes. I was angry at just about every character. Ernst, the abusive father, made my blood boil. As for the feeble wife, she was pathetic, the way she enabled him, allowed him to beat and imprison her and their daughter. I can't like a book if I detest the characters. The entire mess was tiring. If you want to spend your time delving into miserable lives in the cruel environs of Alaska, be my guest. Not for me."

"Maeve, the fact that you reacted so strongly shows the author got through to you. You have to admit it." This from Jo, an energetic woman in her sixties still flush from her recent yoga class.

"It's no use trying to turn a negative into a positive. I did not like the book," Maeve insisted.

"I found it a real page-turner," Bobbie said eagerly. A plump blonde, at fifty-one she was the youngest in the group. Her degree in comparative literature gave her some authority, and she invariably unraveled some of the stickiest sections of a story. "The book is packed with interesting characters facing overwhelming situations and overcoming them. The fierce Alaskan environment acted as a character and played an important role in mirroring the devastation they suffered."

Jacqueline was nodding eagerly. "You're so right!" she exclaimed. "That's such good insight." She looked around. "I wish I were as educated as the rest of you. But I'm getting there."

"Of course you're getting there! You already are," Bobbie cried.

"Everyone's opinion is valuable here," Jo stated in her squeaky voice.

"You have to dig out the meaning," Cilla said. "Do more than skim the surface. It takes effort."

"You're right. I value your opinions so much." Jacqueline smiled, turning to look at each of the women pressed shoulder to shoulder on either side of her. "You're very smart."

Maeve spoke up. "Jaqueline, I had an academic upbring. My parents were college professors, and I often express myself with long words." Maeve gave her brilliant smile that belied the severity of her brisk speech. "Jo, I'd like to hear your take on the book."

Jo brought out a list of examples of the author's style that she considered beautifully crafted. After a spirited group discussion, Cilla consulted a sheaf of papers in her lap. "Now, let's see what the reviewers have to say."

As they broke up for the evening, Jacqueline slipped Bobbie her extra copy of the next assigned book.

"You have allowed me use of your spare parking stall for the winter. And now this. I don't know how I can repay you," Bobbie protested before she was caught up in a tight hug.

"It's a joy beyond belief to make others happy. I know that now more than ever." Jacqueline opened her mouth to say more but seemed to think better of it and simply smiled.

ONE BRIGHT MORNING, Maeve knocked at Cilla's door. "What are you doing? Anything important?"

"I'm identifying the human genome," Cilla retorted. "Everything I do is important. Next question."

"Nothing is more important than this," Maeve said, ignoring the flippancy. "You expressed a pining for lobster. Fresh Thyme is selling fresh lobsters by the batch, and if we want to get in on it, we'd better move. Get your coat."

"Are you crazy?" Cilla exclaimed. "I know nothing about preparing fresh lobster. I don't like things that move on the stove."

"How often do you get a chance to enjoy fresh lobster? We must hustle. My body objects to hustle, but my taste buds overrule. I have a recipe straight from Jacques Le Fond. Stick with me and you'll be in gourmet heaven."

Cilla stared at her. "Okay, you talked me into it. I'll get my coat and boots—"

"No need for boots. I'm driving and we'll park in the ramp. We won't be outside."

After long years without husbands—one divorced, one widowed—the two were in the habit of doing their own thing without the limitation of a partner and considered themselves fortunate to be free and independent. And to have found such a congenial companion with whom they commiserated on the deleterious effects of being in their seventies—forgetting the name of a newly discovered book, taking all afternoon to visit the hardware store and mail a package, once squeezed into an hour between work and dinner.

They decided to attack their advancing years head-on. This involved an exercise program that would get their muscles working while they enjoyed the invigorating abundance of nature. The exercise consisted of a routine every morning in the nearby park, where they walked past the rose garden, stopping now and then to admire an especially full yellow blossom, then settled on a park bench to take in the view of the duck pond and watch a bluebird grooming itself on a branch. Walking up the slope that led back to the Gladstone, their steps grew slower, and they paused often—no need to get hot and sweaty. They were sustained by a well-pleased feeling of duty accomplished and the anticipation of a full-course seafood lunch, the just reward of having completed a thirty-minute workout.

As they trudged up the path, they saw a figure coming toward them, arms outstretched, quick-stepping behind two bouncing Schnauzers that strained on the leash, nosing right and left with eager curiosity.

"Hello," Jacqueline cried, laughing as she stumbled toward them, hair cycloned around her head. "This is my new job. Oh, oh, stop, you demons! Oh my!" Without a pause she flew past them, arms fluttering as if she were about to take flight.

"I've been taking Holly and Pistol out every afternoon for the woman down the hall," she said returning, catching her breath, her face pink and beaming.

"Are you crazy? It looks like the dogs are walking you," Maeve exclaimed.

"Oh, the dogs are spirited, but I let them run. The exercise and fresh air are good for me, too."

"As long as you stay on your feet," Cilla said. "Looks like you've assumed more than you can handle." This petite woman with twig arms, in her sixties, what on earth was she doing taking on a job fit for an athlete?

"Hilda's ever so grateful. There's no one else—Pistol, stop!" Intent on a squirrel that shot past, the dogs tugged on the leash, and Jacqueline flew off across the grassy meadow, blouse billowing behind her.

"No rest for the mighty," she called as the trio disappeared behind a copse of lilac bushes.

"I don't know how she does it," Maeve said, shaking her head. They resumed their ramble up the steep hill. Such a frail thing, no longer young, flailing about like a sixteen-year-old!

"She's something of an airhead," Cilla said. "Why does she want to join our book club? She doesn't read literary fiction."

"Her comments tend to be shallow. She doesn't delve deeply, merely agrees with everything that's said."

"Has no ideas of her own." They jerked aside as three teens trotted by, skateboards tucked under their arms.

"She disappears for days, then shows up cheery as usual," Cilla continued. "People suspect she has some secret hidden away in the backwoods, or a clandestine lover."

"Everyone in the building likes her. She's extremely friendly and outgoing." Maeve was beginning to pant, her eyes fixed longingly at the top of the slope.

"I like her myself."

"She has a sweet manner."

"But one can't always feel outgoing and positive." Cilla was skeptical. "It's not normal to be so continually optimistic. She buries adversity with merry enthusiasm. How can she be so unauthentic? It's dishonest!"

"It's not hard if you don't think about things."

"Still, she's a favorite with the other residents." They agreed that despite her lacks, Jacqueline's charm was undeniable. One couldn't have everything.

"Look, there's Clarissa from our building." Maeve indicated a tall woman in a paisley blouse heading toward them.

"Clarissa, did you see that crazy woman fly by with the dogs?" Cilla greeted her.

Clarissa flicked a glance at the two women. "She's helping a neighbor in a pinch," she retorted brusquely as she passed by without turning her head. What the—? It was puzzling. What had they ever done to her?

And to the immediate: Where should they have lunch?

**WINTER WAS EXTENDING ITS WHITE ARTISTRY** over the neighborhood. Snow fell over the streets and covered the trees with large billowy flakes. The holiday spirit was in full sway. People swarmed in and out of the condo building loaded with Christmas packages, exchanging greetings. Many had relocated from another state, chasing jobs or family or escaping the demands of house care, choosing instead the convenience of urban living. Everyone laughed at the red-headed parrot in the lobby when it cried "Bedtime!" each time the elevator bell rang.

Up in Cilla's sixth-floor condo, the five women of the book club were settled around the glass-topped coffee table in cozy discussion, catching up on the latest holiday doings. The living room had been transformed into a fairyland of color and lights, with prancing reindeer, a tabletop Christmas tree flickering with a galaxy of tiny bulbs, and shimmering garlands tacked along the shelves. A pungent scent of pine and nutmeats, the melancholy glow of Christmas lights, and the croon of winter at the frosted windows drew a warm intimacy through the room.

The book of the evening having been thoroughly thrashed and analyzed; now they were partaking of a special holiday treat: a tray of spiced eggnog and fresh strawberries dipped in chocolate.

Bobbie noticed Jacqueline next to her, head bowed, as if lost in another world.

"Jacqueline, you've left us," she said softly. Everyone turned, conversation ceased.

Jacqueline looked up, startled, then her expression relaxed, and she wrapped her arms tight around her ribs. "Today it's been exactly six months since I moved here," she began hesitantly. "I'm feeling nostalgic. I was lost after my husband died, and it's wonderful to be living here near my son and his family." A cloud darkened her face, her eyes grew moist. "I couldn't have found a better community than this to spend my last—to spend the next years with." She bit her lip, and to everyone's amazement, two tears fell slowly down her cheeks. "I'm sorry, forgive me."

Cilla pressed her arm. "What is it?"

Jacqueline quickly wiped her cheeks with a tissue and looked at the others sadly. "Don't mind me. I'm feeling sentimental. I'm just so glad to be part of your group," Jacqueline said, her eyes moving to those around her. "I like you all so much!"

"You like everybody," said Cilla. Such lack of discernment was beyond her comprehension.

Jacqueline's face cleared. "It's easy when you have such few conflicts. I'm retired. I do what I want when I want. My husband left me well-off, and due to my medical problem—but I won't bore you—my energy is limited. I have my painting, my glorious condo overlooking the lake, an adoring family, and the friendship of you good people. I have a good life!"

The others looked at her curiously. This wasn't like Jacqueline. Everything about her appeared heartfelt and genuine, but there was a crack in her tone, a deliberation in her delivery that hinted at something missing.

"At Christmas, we all assume the good life," Bobbie exclaimed.

"We bury our sorrows in tinsel and cheer," squeaked Jo. "Jacqueline, perhaps you have managed to get rid of them altogether. Here's to you." She raised a dripping strawberry on a stick and popped it into her mouth.

Jacqueline laughed and began adjusting the bangles around her wrists.

Maeve was watching her. "You mentioned a medical problem. Do you mind if I ask you about it?"

Everyone waited, observing Jacqueline's reaction. Ever since she moved in an inscrutability hovered around her like a fog. There had been clues. She didn't drive, rarely left the building, and was picked up every Tuesday and Friday by an Uber. She would remain in her condo for days, then appear chipper and friendly as ever. People wondered, too polite to ask, but besides a pale delicacy in her movements she showed no sign of distress or illness.

Jacqueline sank back into the cushion and fixed her eyes on a Santa bear on the bookcase as if contemplating a faraway star. Her cheeks held a rosy, feverish glow. "All right, I'll tell you. I've never revealed this before, but I can tell you now. I *want* to tell you, as my friends." Squeezed on the couch between Cilla and Bobbie, her small form was like a crab hunched inside its shell. Slowly, she pulled herself forward and faced the group. When she spoke, her voice and the evenness of her gaze held a reassuring serenity. "I have cancer. Advanced."

Silence as people absorbed her words.

"It's lymphoma."

"Have you known long?" Cilla asked.

"For over a year. That's why I moved here." Her face grew animated. "It's stage three, not stage four, so in a way I'm lucky. I take seven drugs, go in for treatment twice a week, and walk thirty minutes a day. I'm supposed to eat healthy foods, but I don't. I just don't care enough, I guess." She smiled as if whatever happened was all right with her.

Cilla took Jacqueline's small white hand between her own two. Bobbie leaned closer, and Jacqueline, in the middle, seemed to relish the reassuring physical contact of the two pressed against her.

"It feels good to say it aloud," Jacqueline continued, talking freely now, eyes bright. "I just want to lead a normal life, live each precious day to the fullest for as many years as possible. I have a son, Justin, and his Anna, seeing to my every need, and the top medical care here in Minnesota. The cancer is under control and may be so forever."

"You sound positive," Bobbie said.

"They're finding cures for lymphoma every day. I keep busy with my painting—you all have one of my watercolors on your wall—my knitting, my darling cockatiel, my meditation practice. And I participate in local council meetings. I do as much as I have energy for." She looked around at the four people regarding her attentively, "In a few months I've made precious friends like you, and I'm forever grateful. You see, I'm happy as a clam."

At the darkened windows, the wind continued to whine through the cracks as the others considered how to frame a response. Jacqueline didn't seem to need reassurance, rather she seemed intent on reassuring them.

"You don't have to say anything," she told them, smiling. "Just be my friends."

This they could do, would do.

"Jacqueline, how can you be so active with all your chemotherapy?" Maeve asked. "Is it wise to do so much?"

"Oh, I'm drained for twenty-four hours after the clinical sessions. But after that I'm myself again. It's just that my active time is limited. My real problem: I don't like to eat." Her bell laugh rang out.

"My god, I wish I had that problem," cried Bobbie, leaning against Jacqueline's shoulder.

What could they do, they wanted to know, should they keep her secret?

"It's not a secret, not anymore." A benevolent smile had settled on her face. "Now I feel free—for the first time. You don't know how good it feels to share. It's liberating!"

A veil had been lifted, and no one seemed to want to break the spell. They traded stories of past ailments and challenges late into the night. At last, as the clock sounded midnight, Jacqueline pulled herself from her cocoon on the couch. Bedtime.

"We're here for you," they assured Jacqueline as they parted.

**THE CALENDAR ROLLED INTO A NEW YEAR,** and Cilla and Maeve celebrated with a long, post-holiday catch-up at Tumaini's, after which they headed to Bobbie's condo to drop off a still-hot apple crisp. As they trudged down the long hallway, suddenly Cilla stopped.

"What's the matter?"

"Look here. Number 626. Jacqueline's door. Something—Maeve, something is wrong." Swinging around, she turned a puzzled face to Maeve. "It's gone."

"What?"

"Her wreath is missing. The elaborate Christmas wreath she ordered directly from Sebastian's. You know, the brilliant circle of red berry clusters, tiny white bulbs, and pine twigs speared with silver shafts."

"Christmas is over."

"But she hasn't replaced it. Her door has never been bare. Oh, probably there's an explanation. It's just strange, that's all. And she's been closed in there for a long time. I haven't seen her for two weeks. I don't like the looks of this."

"Let's find out." Maeve knocked forcefully. No response. Knocked again.

The association manager in the office had no information, but opened a spreadsheet on her screen and punched the son's number on her cell. Justin answered, and he had much to tell them.

The death had been peaceful. The cancer had invaded her body, and a buildup of harmful chemicals was found in her blood. Her last days had passed in bleary confusion, bolstered by regular doses of morphine. Justin reported that his mother had not uttered a word of complaint, that during her few lucid periods she'd spoken only reassuring words to her family. He apologized for not contacting her friends sooner, explaining that she had not been in a state to see anyone, and he had been consumed in caring for her needs and facing the inevitability of her death.

"Even after the fatal diagnosis," Justin told them as they bent over the speaker phone in stunned amazement, "she held tenaciously to the possibility of remission. She wouldn't allow pity or gloom to dominate but threw herself into her whatever life had to offer." He seemed grateful to be conversing with his mother's friends. "Everything fascinated Mom. Recently, she was studying the annual birth of Sol Invictus, the sun god that foreshadowed Christmas. She was always trying to better herself."

Cilla and Maeve looked at each other. Cilla's feelings whirled as she tried to fit this picture of Jacqueline into her own assessment. She was unable to find anything to say besides snatches of *so sorry, we didn't know, how sad.*

"It was hard for her to leave her life in Carmel. Living at the Gladstone among those who cared about her made her last days happy ones," Justin said, his voice heavy. "Being a part of the book group was important to her."

Cilla experienced a sour taste in her throat. Evidently their frivolous friend had possessed unexpected depths. She and Maeve had disparaged the scattered turns of Jacqueline's mind, her blithe approach to life, her shallow insights, her over-the-top exuberance, her inability to sustain serious thought, and her unfounded optimism that flipped negative situations to positive without blinking. Cilla was not certain she could tell any longer what was real. Or, in the ragged state of her mind, what to think. Would she ever be able to walk past the bare door again without being stabbed with doubt?

**THE INVITATION TO THE MEMORIAL** had been slipped under their doors several days ago. "You look worried. What is it?" Maeve remarked to Cilla. They were headed down the hallway toward Jacqueline's condo.

"I've been gone all morning at a Black Lives Matter meeting, now this memorial. I hate leaving Pluto alone so long."

"Don't be ridiculous," Maeve said. "People often leave their cat all day to go to work."

"Pluto lies at the front door until I get back. Never leaves it, not even to drink water."

"How do you know he doesn't drink? You're not there."

"You think I don't know my own cat?"

"You spoil him. That animal lives like a king. Toys, constant treats, his own jungle gym. And those play dates with the cat on the second floor."

"He's happy," countered Cilla. "And safe. I don't let him out; I protect him from the real world, which contains misery and heartache. It's a jungle out there."

"You're so negative, Cilla. You always see the dark side, the side that needs correcting. You distrust everything, you challenge everything, you're hopelessly pessimistic. If you receive a delivery of flowers, you assume something bad has happened."

"According to national wisdom, a cynic has a crucial role in keeping society in shape."

"I know," Maeve responded decisively. "I've read that."

"Maeve, is there anything I can mention that you don't already know? No one can tell you anything. You pride yourself on knowing all the facts with perfect accuracy. I wish you'd ask me a question, just once."

Maeve shot her a glance. "We know each other so well," she said with a weak smile. "I'm a know-it-all and you're a doubting Thomas."

Muted voices issued from inside 626, a low hum of humanity. They stared at the bare door.

"It looks so unwelcoming without the wreath," Maeve said.

"Do we dare go in?" asked Cilla. She wasn't certain where the hesitation came from; their relations with the deceased had been amiable. Jacqueline had often brought them superfluous desserts, as well as articles on touring art exhibits and new Egyptian archaeological discoveries.

"We'll be able to meet the son she talked so much about."

They remained standing in the empty corridor, listening to the low hum of unseen voices from within. Then, taking a deep breath, Maeve knocked, the walnut door swung open, and they walked directly into a spray of luminous hallway light. People were moving in and out of the kitchen, and scattered groups in the far living room commiserated in low tones. The walls were smartly decorated with bigger-than-life collections: framed prints of Jackson Pollock, Toulouse-Lautrec, an Escher etching, and on shelves a bowl of pink ostrich eggs, a statue of Ramses II, and a row of early American crochet dolls. A collection of music boxes gleamed inside a glass cabinet.

"Jacqueline certainly had artistic taste. Me, I have as much artistic talent as a worm," Cilla said.

Maeve agreed. "This is impressive."

They searched the crowd for faces of allies, but neither Jo nor Bobbie was to be seen. Cilla spied people from the Sunday social, also Pete and Clarissa standing by a table spread with hors d'oeuvres, and Adrienne and Sarah walking to Rob by the fireplace.

The two women inched across the room, picking up snippets of conversation from the scattered groupings:

"She had a way of looking on the bright side that heartened those around her."

"She never ceased doing favors for people. Insisted on driving me to repair my Venetian blind. 'I'm retired,' she told me, 'I have time.'"

"That's just it—she knew she didn't have a lot of time. And we never caught on. What she meant was, she had plenty of time to do things for others. That her time was ours."

"Remember when she drove Harvey in unit 300 to his scoliosis surgery?"

"And did you see how she adored those dogs! Walked them every day. She might have been frail, but she had gumption!"

"...never heard her complain."

"...made me feel as if what I said was important."

"...a model of what a human being should be."

Cilla flushed down to her neck. *Damn it, she and Maeve had* not *been wrong. Jacqueline had been a scatterbrain, a flake, and there was no denying she wasn't the brightest flame on the block. How could these people be so blind? Maybe they were merely paying homage to her memory...* Her mind choked with doubt.

"What are you two doing here?"

A tall woman walked up and stood confronting them. It was Clarissa, a woman they knew from the Sunday socials.

"Cilla and Maeve, the Bobbsey twins. I'm surprised that you would show your faces. I'm well aware—as is everyone in the room—that you had nothing but ridicule for Jacqueline. Why did you come here?"

"I…" Cilla couldn't recall their ever having spoken of Jacqueline. How did this woman know this—or anything—about her? "I hardly know you," she sputtered, attempting to calm the reeling in her head. "How do you know what I think?"

"You aren't in the habit of keeping your superior opinions to yourselves. Everyone knows your low opinion of Jacqueline. She would never speak against you, would excuse your belittling comments, but it's no secret how you felt."

"You know nothing…" Maeve began, eyebrows arched, overcome by a stinging anger.

"I was walking in the hall behind you the night of the self protection lecture in the community room. I heard your demeaning remarks about Jacqueline. Others have overheard similar comments. Up to now no one has said anything, out of politeness. But I'm one to speak my mind."

Cilla's heart was pounding. She was not used to being confronted, and her mind scrambled for a response that would not instigate an all-out battle. She looked at Maeve, who was staring at the speaker in disbelief, cheeks flushed with indignation.

The chatter around them had ceased, replaced with a deadly quiet. Cilla and Maeve looked around at the faces, friends and acquaintances of Jacqueline looking on with surprise, some with alarm or avid curiosity. No one spoke in contradiction.

"You're wrong." Cilla struggled to keep her voice even. "We liked Jacqueline. She wasn't perfect, but we were her friends. Ask those women over there." Heads turned toward Bobbie and Jo standing by the window, conversing with a man in a checkered suit.

"Oh yes, the book club. I know in your group Jacqueline felt overwhelmed with inadequacy. It was a trial for her to hold her own."

"It was Jacqueline's choice to join us!" exclaimed Maeve. "She loved being there. You don't know what you're talking about."

"You two ought to be ashamed," the woman persisted, ignoring her comment. The two women standing next to her nodded.

Maeve coughed and put her hand to her throat as if pushing air out of her mouth. This abrasive woman knew nothing, except possibly what Jacqueline had told her. Sure, they had challenged her to learn, maybe a bit harshly—but Maeve was not about to banter her behavior with this swellhead. "Enough of this." Maeve slammed her punch glass on the table. "You are out of line. We're here to honor Jacqueline. This is no time or place for a confrontation. I won't participate."

With vigorous steps, she marched out of the room. Cilla, following, whispered to her, "I was about to say the same thing. Good move."

As they entered the dining room, a tall figure in a houndstooth jacket approached. "Welcome! We haven't met. Justin here." He greeted them warmly, offering his hand. "My wife pointed you out. She's seen photos of your book group. Mom was proud of being part of it, said you were the key members. I'm so glad you came. She often said how she admired you two."

Despite the man's friendly demeanor, Cilla felt speechless in the face of his deep sorrow. "I'm so sorry for your loss," she said, unable to think of anything original. She was determined not to be superficial, not to say anything she didn't mean, to be straight and above board. "Jacqueline was special," she mouthed at last. "She had a spark that drew others to her."

"There was no one like her," said Maeve, having regained her composure. "She had many talents. A very giving, generous person."

Justin regarded them evenly. "My mother knew what you thought of her," he said in a tone that was not unfriendly.

The two women stood in shocked silence. A wave of shame swelled in Cilla's throat. She was unable to detect reproof in his tone, although how he could not harbor resentment she could not imagine. *What was he getting at?*

Seeing their agitated faces, Justin reached out and encircled both with a bear hug, squeezed, let go, and regarded them earnestly. His voice was accommodating. "She said she believed you were absolutely right about her; she was all those frivolous things you thought she was. You just didn't see the whole picture. Your academic backgrounds, your super-serious approach, as she called it, were different from hers. She said you were considerate and kind to her anyway."

Maeve looked stunned, as if she had fallen into a vat of dye and emerged a different color. A lifetime of moral orientation seemed to have been turned upside down.

"We—I guess I didn't realize..." Cilla began lamely. Something in her clung to the idea that her and Maeve's view of their friend had been accurate.

"She appreciated your sharp knowledge of almost everything." Justin smiled, still holding their hands. The sympathy in his voice was unmistakable.

"I appreciate your directness," she began in the midst of her confusion, but Justin cut her off. He had to get something. With that he hurried to the next room and returned immediately holding two objects.

"My mother told me that not only did she learn a lot from you, but that after hearing of her illness, you loaned her books and brought her meals. To show her appreciation, she wanted you to have these."

He held out two carved mahogany music boxes created in Louis XVI style, each with a delicate gold fleur-de-lis inlay, the base and lid rimmed with gold. "They're from her collection. She wanted you to have something beautiful."

Maeve stood speechless. Cilla stared at her box, holding it as if it might burst into flame. They had no right—a sense of shame deepened as she held this last gesture.

Cilla protested. "Thank you, Justin. But—but I just brought her a meal when I picked up my own dinner. No trouble at all."

"And I have enough books for an army," said Maeve.

"Mother thrived on the little things," Justin said.

They left with the boxes clutched to their chests, heads bowed. The long walk down the hall was silent.

"Maeve," Cilla said as they neared the elevator. "I've been thinking."

"Yes, so have I."

"Do you think we're total shits?"

"Yes, we have a lot to answer for, Priscilla." Maeve pressed the elevator button, and a red light began blinking.

"We didn't treat her badly; we did things for her."

"But she knew! You can't disguise your attitude. She knew how we felt."

"But, Cilla, we're good people."

"Of course, but we built a façade of superiority so that we could feel good about ourselves. Jacqueline understood this. She had an instinctive grasp of human weakness."

"But we really are knowledgeable about some things!"

"Many have areas of expertise. They don't use it to justify their existence." The elevator door snapped open with a snarl.

"I'll miss her."

"Me too."

Turning over the music box, Cilla read *Beautiful Dreamer* stamped on the underside. Slowly she lifted the lid, and bell-like musical notes issued forth, the melody ringing out with clear insistence.

*Beautiful dreamer, wake unto me*
*Starlight and dewdrops are waiting for thee.*

The women smiled as the melody resonated gaily throughout the corridor.

# Jacqueline

*Sounds of the rude world heard in the day*
*Lull'd by the moonlight have all passed away.*

As the doors snapped shut and the elevator dropped down in space, they heard the slow beats, the ringing, the haunting notes vibrating along the shaft, a voice fading with a dying ring of grace.

# Going Home

**CASS ARRIVED EVERY EVENING** at the Saguaro like clockwork, shoulders slightly humped, long arms stuffed in his jean pockets, an undercurrent of annoyance blotting his face, wearing the same type of buttoned sport shirt, the same jeans, the same worn Chelsea boots. His high cheekbones and soft blue eyes verged on handsome, while his long neck and thin loose limbs gave him a gangly look. "Sweet and gentle underneath," decided Gloria. "A mean old grouch if you ask me," said Mia. "Cute for an old guy," from Bridget. Accommodation was in order.

He seated himself punctiliously at his usual corner table and extended his long legs under the rungs of the chair opposite.

"Hey there, Cass, how are you tonight?" The waitress approached wearing a blue sweater with sleeves pushed to elbows, wavy brown hair held in place with a daisy headband, the name *GLORIA* pinned to her shoulder. "Plenty of sunshine out there to warm your bones." With her sparkling brown eyes, the saucy curls peeping around her ears, and wide smile, she radiated sunshine herself.

"Too much blasted sunshine, I'd say," he responded gruffly. "Melts the tar under your feet. Sucks out your breath."

She continued to smile brightly. "Preferable to doom and gloom." She set a can of beer in front of him. No glass for him. "I brought your Heineken. That should cheer you up."

"No call to be cheerful twenty-four seven," he grumbled but began to relax. He was getting used to her relentless buoyancy, her sure optimism.

"You're looking good. The sun must be curing your asthma," she said conversationally.

"Yep, haven't used my inhaler in a week."

"The Arizona country agrees with you. Better settle here."

"Not on your life. I'm a Wyoming guy."

His plans were fixed. In five months the horse racing season would be over, and he would be ready. He grinned up at her as if he had already run the track and emerged victor. He would obtain Blue Star, and for the first time his life would be established just the way he wanted it. His spirits soared as he recalled the Zoom meeting earlier that morning with the agent and Blue Star's owners; everything had gone well, an agreement reached, the papers prepared.

Meanwhile, he waited in Tucson for the latest test results. His bronchial condition was improving. It was only a matter of time. A message that morning had informed him that a lump was found on his scan that the doctor didn't like. No doubt another false alarm. Dr. Asghar insisted on testing every molecule in his body, determined to find some dooming ailment when all he needed was to cure the inflammation in his lungs. As soon as he took care of the asthma that had drawn him to the Sunbelt, Cass would be back in Wyoming where he belonged and out of this blistering sun.

But he didn't share any of this with the staff at the Saguaro. They would make a fuss, and nothing was final.

Only his plans, which nothing could stop. He had worked for decades on a Wyoming ranch, cleaning outbuildings and caring for a stable of horses and six hogs. While the other hired hands gathered at a long table, eating and fussing noisily, Cass remained on the fringe, bent over his plate, slipping off to read by himself. He did not join the gang when they got drunk in the large barn. He was not a part of that. Too bland. Too quiet. Not a party guy. Did his job with consistency, never missing, never late. Old Sourpuss they called him. Smart, too: He could master a Rubik's cube in three minutes and get the stable's central computer working in ten. Letting two years of college education go to waste—what was his problem? They left him alone.

After retirement he set about to fulfill his goal—the dream that kept him going, gave meaning to his life. A remote ranch tucked in the shadow of the mountains where he would live with the horse he would save from destruction. The dream dominated his thoughts, his every move.

It was while volunteering at the Wyoming Downs racetrack that the crown of his life emerged. Cass spent every free moment attending to the sleek black horse named Blue Star. Arriving early each morning with a handful of carrots, he would be greeted by a welcome nicker and nibbles on his sleeve as he brushed the shiny coat and wiped the eyelashes clean. During daily exercise, he liked to gallop Blue Star to the creek, which the horse dashed into eagerly, pawing the water, creating a fan of sprays, shaking his mane, dipping his nose into the bubbling water. Cass would hum a tune of far mountains and high fences and dream of wide-open spaces, a refuge where one would be lost in the wild nothingness.

One day he heard news that sent his heart racing: Blue Star, past the peak age for racing, was to be retired. At once a thought exploded in Cass's head: a future life with Blue Star exploring the open range, filling the ranch with breath and life. He walked into the racing office hat-in-hand and requested the name of a good attorney.

When Cass had finished his bread pudding, Gloria came over and leaned with two arms on the back of a chair across from him, clearly in one of her chatty moods.

"Good news: We have a new Jack Russell puppy. Bad news: This morning he chewed up Teddy's stuffed giraffe, and Teddy shut the puppy in the refrigerator. Now how could I punish him when I couldn't stop giggling? So, I explained that the puppy almost died, and did Teddy want to have to give it a funeral? This excited him. 'Let's do it, as long as the puppy wakes up afterward.'" After further commentaries, she pulled out a photo of herself, her husband and son holding hands in front of the hummingbird exhibit at the Desert Museum, another of Teddy hanging upside down on a chair in front of a sparkling Christmas tree. Cass envisioned the family sitting around the dinner table engrossed in easy, familiar talk, telling concerns, exchanging experiences, dipping into wells of understanding. Something he'd not believed existed. But this was real. A dry emptiness lifted in his stomach.

Gloria straightened and folded her arms. "Why the faraway look? What about your family, Cass?"

Cass picked up his beer and, finding it empty, lowered it slowly to the table. Family. Almost. He had almost had a family. So, fleeting, an illusory bubble passing in the night.

"I had a wife. After eighteen months she left with our daughter. Said she found life in the sticks unbearable. Years later, my daughter came to spend the summer on the ranch where I was employed, to experience the Wyoming outback, or something like that. I could never understand her teenage whims. She worked hard, helped in the barn, but observing the field hands gathered in a tobacco-spitting contest, she declared them vulgar and backward and would have nothing to do with them. After supper she took off for town to search for what she termed *action*, which usually meant she attended the only movie theater by herself. I bought a larger TV. I taught her to ride the best horse and how to play chess. But there were no people her own age and nothing for her to do all day. Her craving for constant activity and variety wore me out. I gave her spending money and allowed her free rein, but she sat around listlessly, as if waiting for the sky to burst open. Her usual response to my efforts to tempt her was 'Whatever.'" Cass pulled at a strand of hair by his ear. "I was no good as a father or husband. From then on, I stuck to myself."

"Sounds like you gave up on people." Gloria pulled her sweater tightly around her shoulders. "Seems to me you're missing a lot."

Cass drew his long legs under his chair. "Maybe. But soon I will be living in peace in the wide outdoors, riding Blue Star, reading, listening to the wind beat around the house." He looked up. "And you? What's your dream, Gloria?"

"I have no time for such ideas. The twists and turns of family life keep me occupied, and I wouldn't give up a single minute, not even the problems." She unfolded her arms. "Right now, my object is to catch the spider I see walking toward your boot there under the table. And my dream is that his buddies won't come looking for him." Grabbing a napkin, she bent down and scooped up the insect. At a wave from a far table, she scurried off, but not before bending over his ear, "What I've got is enough."

SEVERAL WEEKS LATER, Cass trudged across the street, head bowed, his thin hair moist against his scalp, shirt and jeans loose around his six-foot-six frame. The blinding Arizona sun beat down hot and relentless, blanching the sidewalks. This miserable heat! He longed for the towering mountains of Wyoming, the sweet summers followed by autumns, snappy and purposeful. It made him unsettled and grumpy to not see a familiar face or building. The street he was on stretched arid and dusty. The bright stucco buildings dazzled in sunshine, and the signs displayed names like Juarez and Obregon. He had never felt so out of place. He might as well be in Bangladesh. And now this idiot yelling at him for crossing in the middle of the street. Get lost!

Careful not to miss his one o'clock, he increased his pace.

Once inside, the clerk behind the reception desk fastened him with a look of concern. Several nurses gathered around, and two physicians in white coats came up to him and made inquiries. What was this? Living here in the dry Arizona air, his asthma seemed to be under control. No need for such a fuss. The solicitous concern with which everyone treated him was irritating, implied he had a dire condition that led directly to the grave.

He was ushered into a large office, where Dr. Asghar greeted him warmly. "Good news first," Dr. Asghar said with a benevolent smile once they were seated in the spare, white-walled room. "The asthma is improving, although long-term it's too early to tell. A new calcilytic drug on the market looks promising. And the inflammation in your bronchial tubes has subsided." But Cass must do his part by watching his diet, eating well, getting plenty of sleep and maintaining an exercise routine—yoga highly recommended.

"And the bad news?"

"As yet undetermined. The tumor we discovered in your intestines showed signs of cancer, but the results are suspect; further tests are required. Could be a false alarm. We'll set you up with an appointment."

"Don't get up, there's more." Dr. Asghar held out a brochure. "Read this. The questionnaire indicates that you drink too much. Cutting back doesn't work. You must cease drinking altogether."

Cass nodded, with no intention of doing any such thing. The fuel of his evenings. *Not on your life.* "Don't expect miracles," he growled as he stood up.

The doctor shook his head. "We'll do our part, and you must do yours. There is no get-out-free card."

**THE FOLLOWING SATURDAY** found the Saguaro packed with weekend diners. Brent scurried back and forth at the bar, pouring drinks. The bartender struck an arresting figure in his gold collared shirt, skinny black tie that hung to his waist, and plaid newsboy cap pulled down over his thick layer of dark hair.

Cass sipped his whiskey sour and watched Brent set out a row of frosted highball glasses, wiping the bottoms and sides dry with a bar mop. A friendly guy, Brent—had a way of scrutinizing the customers, nailing their characters, and anticipating their needs. The first night Cass showed up, he slipped surreptitiously onto a barstool and sat, head bent, elbows clamped against his ribs, like a crab burrowed deep in its shell, as if fearing something would be demanded of him that he could not possibly live up to. He avoided looking Brent in the eye. When their glances met briefly, he flinched as if in pain. But with his wide grin and attentive gaze, Brent soon had Cass talking about the mountains of Wyoming and the routines of the Wyoming Downs stables.

Suddenly, a tall, willowy figure burst through the front door, crashing it loudly against the wall. The girl, somewhere in her twenties, was dressed in a long red skirt and oversized peach t-shirt reaching past her hips. Lifting one arm in an easy arc, she swept off her Panama hat, shook her long hair, and snapped the hat back on her head. Something about her air of confident exuberance as she strode past the tables drew attention. As she approached the bar, two men sitting next to Cass left their stools, and she perched on the farthest, leaving an empty stool between them. Looking around, she crossed one leg over the other with a careless, impish air.

She ordered a gin and tonic, and when Brent set it on the counter, she picked up her glass and waved it at Cass. Cass swallowed a long drag of whiskey sour before raising his glass in response.

"This is a cozy place," the girl said, addressing Cass. "I had to get out of the house, away from the suffocating apartment. My parents insisted that I accompany them to their friends' home for dinner where they will sit and talk about me and my future and what I am going to make of it. Ugh!"

Cass regarded her. Why did this young pretty female want to talk to him? His jeans were stained, his sport shirt wrinkled. He didn't dress up for Saturday night, no point in that, he'd be hanged before he'd partake in such frivolity.

"You're a queer bird," she remarked. "The way you slouch like that, looking like you'd bite anyone who approaches. This is a nice place, why do you dress like a backwoods field hand?"

Cass chuckled. "You sure are blunt. Maybe I don't care about fancy clothes."

"He is staying in a nice apartment," put in Brent, who had been listening. "He eats here every night, a regular."

"I don't cook." Cass raised his glass to his lips and felt the fire swarm through his limbs, then quaffed another. He felt his muscles soften as he confronted this bigger-than-life, aggressive female who seemed ready to pounce.

"Neither do I, but I can't imagine going to the same place day after day. How terribly boring!"

"I'm easy." He reached over and grabbed peanuts from a pewter dish as if they were ammunition. This girl was not going to let up.

"Let me guess," she said, looking him up and down. "You have trouble managing to live alone. You don't have any friends."

"Humph. I've managed on my own all my life. I don't like to cook. What's hard to understand about that?"

The girl laughed. "I guess you're telling me to mind my own business. I'm pretty outspoken. Some don't care for that."

She tilted her hat back, and he looked into her eyes for the first time. "You're direct. That's good," he said. "And outgoing. Something I've never been." He leaned back against the stool, cheeks flushed. "People say I'm something of a loner," he said unexpectedly.

The girl removed her hat and placed it on the stool between them. "I'm a loner too." She regarded him thoughtfully. "I chat incessantly, but my friends think I'm too serious, that I tear everything apart. Well, you know, that I'm no fun."

"I get that, too. People find me dull. I guess I am. It's *their* problem." Cass leaned back against the stool. "I don't see why you have to be fun."

"But I am fun! And my name is Samantha. Sam if you're a friend."

Cass took a sip of his third drink. "Look," he said, "don't expect to spend an entertaining evening with me. A young girl like you should be with your own kind, your own age."

"Hey, you know nothing about me. I find people my age unbearable."

Brent swept up. "Ready for another, young lady?"

"I'll let you know when I'm ready!"

"This here is Cass," Brent said, ignoring the snap in her voice. "Come all the way from Wyoming."

"Well, if the sun don't shine on those in luck! I'm from Wyoming too, so we have something in common. But don't let it go to your head, you old codger." She kicked Cass's protruding leg with her shoe. "You're in my space."

"Be welcoming," Brent said, "He's new here."

Cass was tempted to tell Brent to mind his own business; he could handle this uppity young lady. Maybe he couldn't manage a wife, but that was years ago, and gradually their memory had faded into a permanent mode of low expectation. From then on, he had avoided female entanglements.

"Fricking heat!" the girl exclaimed. "I planned to go hiking this afternoon, but it's too hot. I'm sick of the damn sunshine. Never varies. Hot, hot, hot."

"One finds plenty of shade if one knows where to look," Cass said.

"That's no help. Sickening heat never lets up."

"We have an invention these days. It's called air conditioning."

The girl swung to face Cass. "Aren't you the snarly one." She tapped her fingers on the counter impatiently. "Why don't you relax and enjoy yourself?"

"I'm as relaxed as I want to be. You don't seem very happy. What's a young girl like you doing alone in a place like this anyways? You're very good looking."

"If you're interested in me, an old codger like you, forget it."

"Don't flatter yourself." You knew where you stood with this one. No cagey games here. Cass liked that.

233

"Samantha, Cass is a regular here," Brent broke in. "I can vouch for him."

"Nothing that's regular holds the slightest interest for me," Samantha said. "I'm stuck here in Tucson for the summer with my parents. They're about as regular as you can get."

"Excuse me." A stocky man with a dark beard and thick black eyebrows slipped onto the empty stool between them, leaned his arms against the counter, and ordered a Scotch and soda. His presence blocked further conversation, and as if aware of his intrusion he looked from one to the other and asked, "You guys watch the D-backs yesterday?"

"Don't do baseball," Samantha said. "Too slow."

"Missed that one." Cass finished his drink. His face and neck were flushed with a rosy tinge. "Tied up yesterday with important dates and requests for my autograph. Never a moment to myself."

The stranger guffawed, pulled out a handkerchief, and blew his nose.

"Me too, nothing but requests and invitations right and left," Samantha exclaimed. "I'm so sought after I have to lose myself in this far-out bar."

A lively conversation ensued between Brent and the three at the bar, covering the medically beneficial cacti found in Arizona, the types of boots best suited to arid dust, and the identity of the sports figures mounted in frames behind the counter. Followed by a lengthy account of the horse Blue Star and how he beat the odds three races in a row. By closing time, the stranger had consumed several rounds. When Brent passed out their tabs, the stranger stood up shakily and pulled a one-dollar bill from his wallet. Looking perplexed, he dug his fingers frantically into each of his pockets.

Brent watched him carefully. "Problem?"

"Er, I don't seem to have enough cash." A dark blush spread across the stranger's cheeks.

"A credit card will do."

"Ain't got one of those." He coughed, grabbed his jacket from the back of the stool. "Guess I'll have to go home and get some money. Yah, well, I'll be back."

Brent bent over the bar. "Can't let you do that unless you leave collateral."

"Don't have anything like that." The stranger looked down at his feet and began shuffling back and forth.

Slipping off his stool, Cass pulled out his wallet. "I've got it."

The others stared at him. "You don't have to do this," Brent said. "We have ways…"

"The bill isn't that large." Cass had made up his mind. "You live pretty far off, Buddy. Can't have you driving all the way to Tanque Verde and back." He fumbled in his wallet and drew out his credit card.

"I don't know how—" The stranger looked incredulous.

"Pay me back when you see me. I was once stuck after a long night at the racetrack bar and a fellow I didn't know from Adam took care of it. Said I could pay him back or not. I was flummoxed." He stuffed his long arms in his pockets and looked at Sam and Brent with a twinkle. "Learned that word today from my landlady. Said the other residents gave her nothing but grief and she was flummoxed."

The others laughed.

"Never saw the fellow again. So I guess I'll pass it on to you."

The stranger nodded, then he was gone. He would try to be back— but don't wait up, was all he said.

Cass paid for his drinks and, stuffing his wallet in his back pocket, prepared to leave. "I can't make out that Cass," he heard Sam say as he headed toward the door. "What a cantankerous old guy. What's with him, anyway? The way he drinks, transforming from a shy, unassuming recluse to a friendly companion. And he continually goes on about horses and life on the ranch, and that Blue Star." Brent nodded sympathetically. "But something about him is—is real." It was the last thing he heard as he moved out the door and melted into the night.

**LATE ONE AFTERNOON BRENT EMERGED** from the back room carrying a crate of liquor bottles. Setting the box on the counter, he began replacing the empties on the shelves one by one, first wiping the new bottles carefully. Then, flinging a fresh towel over his shoulder, he turned to Cass and Sam, who were seated silently at the bar.

"Okay, you two, no need to be glum. The sky is blue, the birds are singing, there's summer in the air. It's happy time."

"You'd find perfume in a garbage dump," Cass countered, drawing in his chin.

"What kind of sappy nonsense is that?" Sam said.

"Hey!" Brent said cheerfully. "What's wrong with you two? Cass here must have gotten up on the wrong side of the bed. And Samantha, it's not natural for a smart young lady like yourself to be so crabby."

Cass and Samantha exchanged looks. *This guy is insufferable. This Pollyanna must be silenced.*

"Why don't you get real?!"

"Go jump in a bottomless lake!"

To their mutual surprise, all three giggled. The next drinks were on the house, Brent declared, now that they had landed on the right foot. Cass regarded the fresh whiskey placed in front of him. He could hardly refuse, despite what he had promised Dr. Asghar. He had recently taken to limiting himself to one drink, which he had just finished. Well, one more…

Samantha studied her glass. "This morning my parents laid down the law: I'm to pick myself up and find a job. I've bummed around for a couple of years, and I guess they feel it's about time I became something other than a pain in the ass. If I can get a scholarship I can go to the University of Arizona. It would make sense. I'm smart. But I absolutely refuse to go to UA. I don't need to attend a party school and waste away with frivolous co-eds."

"I'd say college would be a good way to find out what you can do," Cass said. He had been filled with pride when his grandkids Hunter and Rock graduated from the University of Vermont; he hardly knew anyone with a college degree.

"But I hate it here. The land is bare and parched, and there's nothing to do. Well, except for horseback riding."

"You ride?" Cass asked, alert.

"Oh, I adore riding out in the open full throttle. Not those slow group rides up a mountain trail on a lazy horse—boooring."

Boring appeared to be her reaction to almost everything.

"So what are you looking for, Sam?"

"Freedom. To do something creative, interesting, powerful. Maybe I'll pursue oil painting, I received A's in art. As long as I'm as far away from home as the moon. My dad wants me to work at the dry-cleaning shop he built with his own hands, like Mother does, and learn the business. Or go to school, then settle down and work at the shop. They want me to have a steady life—their life. Nothing is going to force me into a mold!" Tugging the edges of her Panama hat down around her ears, she scrunched her face into a frown.

"If you want freedom," Cass suggested, "it might help to have some skills to back you."

"Your parents will support you in getting an education," Brent said.

"But it's on their terms. They'll only be happy if I go to UA, and that ain't happening."

Cass felt suddenly old. At seventy-six he might not have much to offer, but he had finally emerged from his rut, chosen his future, made it happen. It pained him to see her mirroring his stubborn resistance, the way he refused all assistance. This girl rejected advice or direction, trusting the world to recognize her unique skills. Of which as yet there were none to be seen.

"I want to do something unique. You may not believe me, but I know what I'm doing," Samantha said.

Cass and Brent looked doubtful.

"You family is guiding you out of love," Cass said. "Don't hate them for supporting you and wanting you nearby."

"Maybe I want to be like you, on a ranch somewhere in Wyoming surrounded by horses."

"It's a lonely life for someone with your spirit."

She sighed, studied her fingers dubiously, then turned brightly to Cass. "Enough about me. So, what do you do with yourself all day, Cass?"

"Not much. Watch TV. Feed the birds. Read John Grisham and Arthur Conan Doyle. I don't go out except to come here. Nowhere to go anyway. I don't know anyone."

"You might make an effort."

"No point. I'm only here until this asthma clears up. I've lived all my life in Wyoming. Wouldn't live anywhere else."

"Really, you're such a stick-in-the-mud. But if you want to be alone and do nothing that's your business." She swiped a french fry from the plate and popped it into her mouth. Then another two in quick succession.

"I've always been a stick-in-the mud. At this point, I'm just waiting for my horse." Cass described running across Blue Star while working at Wyoming Downs, cleaning stalls and sweeping the grandstand, currying, brushing, bandaging, bathing the racehorses, cleaning gear, checking hooves.

"The groomers liked having me around. I would do anything. I know how to anticipate horse injuries. A horse needs to run. A horse who spends twenty to twenty-three hours a day shut in the stall can become feisty. Their pent-up energy results in leaping, squealing, biting, kicking."

When he first learned that Blue Star was to be euthanized because he was considered past his racing prime, Cass made up his mind. "When

I get my ranch, Blue Star will be able to range to his heart's content after years cooped up in a stall. We'll spend our last years together."

"How about another?" Brent had been following this with interest.

"Can't do. One is my limit. I'm trying to cut down."

"But you've already had two," Samantha exclaimed.

"You can't take such a serious step in one swoop. I'm working up to it."

"Who are you trying to kid?"

"You want to take away my one small pleasure. I wish you'd mind your own business!"

"Well, Mr. Snarly, suit yourself. I swear, If your missing mother showed up out of the blue dripping on your doorstep, you'd complain about the puddles."

"What's there to cheer about? You take what you get, and most of the time it doesn't amount to much." Cass could feel the warmth from his last drink expanding in his chest. "Look here." From his billfold he pulled a photo of a sleek black creature that stood tall and proud, looking directly into the camera. "With proper care, a horse can live thirty years. But Blue Star here is eight and slated to be shot."

Samantha took the photo from his outstretched arm, held it aloft.

"A racehorse has a hard existence," he explained. "Horses' thin legs are almost too fragile to hold their large bodies, and they don't heal, so if they break a limb they must be killed. They are pack animals who travel continually on the road, separated from other horses, always at risk of being injured on the track. And when they no longer bring in millions for their owners, they are most often put down."

He watched her study the image, tilting it to the light. "He's beautiful," she said, a smile spreading across her face. "Cass, I love Wyoming too. I spent many summers there with my widowed grandfather. Maybe I'll even settle there in my old age." She straightened, slapped on her straw hat and continued brightly. "Cass... I have a favor to ask, but it will keep.

Now I'm off for a boring dinner to perform my filial duties. Pray to the Buddha for me."

**IT WAS A BRIGHT MORNING,** the day outside filling with sunshine. Cass stood at the window, watching a swarm of goldfinches dipping into the mealworms he had poured into the food tray. He gazed for some time as they danced for position, pushing each other aside, flapping their wings. Then he moved into the kitchen, swallowed some pills from a date-organized pill box, drained the last of his coffee, and entered the bathroom. A razor, a jar of shaving cream, a bristle brush, an electric toothbrush, and various pill jars littered the marble counter.

He stared at his image in the mirror: a sullen face, although he felt rather pleasant now after observing the birds. His default expression was glum, no getting around it. If he appeared grouchy it was just the way his mouth angled naturally and his habit of concentrating on the task at hand. He ran a hairbrush through his thinning hair. He was not bad looking, the girls used to say, with his even features and what his wife had called a sensuous mouth, although she had not succumbed for long to its charm. Not that his looks had ever done him any good. Let's see, how many women had chased him, anxious for his attention? None. And he did not reach out. Too risky; things might go wrong. He didn't like to feel fluttery, like the birds at his window anxiously fretting for a place at the feeder.

He put down his hairbrush and, turning from the mirror, went to gaze out the kitchen window. The birds had quieted, and the leaves across the lawn hung still. A dreamy smile spread over his face as he envisioned riding Blue Star over long stretches of wild prairie grasses.

It would be enough.

The cellphone rang, and Cass pressed *accept.*

"Hi, Cass. Happy birthday."

"Oh, yeah, thanks." His heart pounding, he sank onto a kitchen stool, clutching a steaming coffee cup in one hand. He'd had rare communication with his daughter since the teenage summer she had spent on the ranch all those years ago that ended with her fleeing back to Vermont to a life beyond his reach. Over the years he had received scattered announcements of the birth of her two sons, Christmas cards picturing the family of four, and a brochure announcing the launch of their new ski shop near Mount Snow. His ex-wife had long ago evaporated into the past.

"It's me, Eleanor. So how are you?" Her voice hearty. "I tried to call you earlier."

"My message machine was off."

"Well, that's a fine attitude. Don't you want to talk to your family, your friends?"

"I don't have much of either."

A rustle, possibly a sigh on the other end. "So, what are you doing on your big day?"

"I'm having dinner at a restaurant. That's about it."

"By yourself? Don't you have friends?"

"Nope."

"Not much of a talker, are you? Trouble with you, you hole up on your own too much." A pause. Then a muffled voice: "No, no, I want the blue jacket with the belt. I'll be there in a second." Louder: "Sorry. So, what are you doing this afternoon?"

"Nothing. Watching TV." His life was boring. If there was anything Eleanor did not abide, it was boring. Nothing mediocre or stale would satisfy her standards.

"Are you getting better, Cass? Will you return to Wyoming soon? Do you need anything?"

There, she had gotten all concerns out of the way in one swoop. Ready to move on to whatever was enticing her from the other room.

"Yes, yes, and no," he replied. "I aim to return to Wyoming when the latest test is completed. Whenever that is. There's been some vague talk about a tumor."

"Oh, really?"

"Damn fool doctor won't tell me a thing."

"Try not to be so cranky. You turn people off."

"If people want happy happy, they can go elsewhere."

He didn't see how she could know what he was like. She had spent little time in his company over the years. Her life was far removed from his, surrounded by a nurturing family, a close-knit society that consumed her.

"Good of you to call every year on my birthday, Eleanor. Say hello to the boys and—"

"I'll get it!" she yelled. "Cass, I have to go. Happy Birthday."

"Yes, yes. Goodbye Eleanor."

**THAT EVENING AT THE SAGUARO** was hell as far as Cass was concerned. He had been served a full-course steak and lobster dinner and presented with a large musical birthday card that chirped greetings from a pop-out Donald Duck. He sat, hands clasped in frozen discomfort, while Gloria, Mia, and Bridget led an embarrassing round of "Happy Birthday" with the entire restaurant whooping and clapping. At the conclusion he nodded, bowed, even raised his fist in appreciation, longing for the moment when he could escape to the bar.

Brent was sympathetic. "They had a great time even if you didn't," he commiserated. "How about a Black Russian, birthday boy? I just opened a bottle of Kahlúa. I'll even break code and have one myself to celebrate." He poured the dark liquor into the highball glass, threw in a shot of vodka and slivers of cracked ice, stirred briskly.

"I could use one. Just one." Cass picked up the glass and took a deep swig, feeling warmth flow down to his stomach and out to his limbs, like silk. To hell with Dr. Asghar. If his friends wanted to drink to his big day, the least he could do was go along.

"The docs have done what they can. One more test, then it's back to Wyoming," he announced.

"I suppose you'll return to your old job in Jackson?" Pulling his plaid cap down over his forehead, Brent lowered himself on a stool and leaned on the counter.

"Not on your life!" He lowered his voice. "Brent, I have $800,000 saved up, penny by penny." It felt good to reveal it at last, his nest egg, the one thing that he had to show for his seventy-odd years.

"Hey, that's a mighty sum!"

"I've scraped, lived in meager rooms, eaten cheap foods, never took a vacation. These savings will allow me to purchase a ranch with a wrap-around porch and a view of the mountains. And I'll own the finest thoroughbred that ever lived." He smiled as he recalled the ranch he had located, a low rustic one-story with a brick fireplace and a noisy stream snaking through the trees, winding behind the house and past an old barn streaked with mountain wind.

"Sounds great, Cass."

Cass drew his long legs from under the adjoining stool. He'd had three beers with dinner, which he didn't count as real liquor. And then the Kahlúa. Okay, now he would stop.

At sudden commotion at the other end of the bar, Brent stepped off the stool and hurried over to investigate. A man in a ridiculously large cowboy hat with sweeping sides sat running his index finger hypnotically around the rims of three shot classes lined up in front of him. A bright red-and-yellow polka-dot bandana hung loosely around his neck. On the stool next to him lay a leather briefcase, which two women in jodhpurs were screaming for him to remove, something he steadfastly refused to do. "I have priority here," he claimed, ignoring them. Their complaints grew louder. When Brent approached, the man looked up, revealing dark bean-like eyes and a smooth pale complexion that looked like it had never felt the sun. Smiling amiably at Brent, the man grabbed the briefcase and slipped it under the counter.

The women, appeased, took their seats, and the hum of voices along the counter resumed. Before long Cass noticed the man staring at him, then again, no mistake, and when Cass turned, the man nodded to him. Cass regarded the outsized hat, obviously expensive, the bright red shirt that looked like it had just come out of the box, and his pale complexion that seemed like it belonged in an office. He looked like an Easterner's idea of a cowboy. With his calculated air of deliberation, his squinty eyes, the sly way he surveyed the room, he appeared to be a man on a mission. What was he up to?

Cass quizzed Brent at length, but the bartender could tell him nothing. "Never seen that guy before," he said. "How about another drink?"

"Had my limit."

"One more, Cass. It's early."

"*I'll* have another!" The man in the cowboy hat perched himself next to Cass, setting his smart leather briefcase on the floor. "A martini."

"Oh, what the hell." Cass exclaimed. He really had no place else to go. He'd get on the wagon tomorrow, cold. Tomorrow he would eliminate the first one and he'd be fine.

"My name is Jarvis Lloyd," the stranger said smiling. He reached out his hand. "Just arrived this morning from Wyoming."

Brent pulled a gin bottle from the shelf.

"Fell in love with Arizona right off the bat," the cowboy said. "What mountains! What sunshine! What fine open country! Real dude land. And I hear the best riding horses this side of the Rockies."

Cass shifted uneasily as the man's gaze lingered on him. "You're interested in horses? You a rancher?"

"Not me, I'm a city guy. Let's say I have a strong business involvement. I have some material here that will interest you. But first I'm seeking advice on entertainment here in Tucson. I'd sure like to dig up a golf partner."

Cass eyed him narrowly. "So, what's your interest in horses?"

The cowboy pressed his mouth together. "All right boys, I don't mind telling you. I can see by the way your eyes light up that you're horse lovers.

Now I'm not a horse guy. Never been on a horse in my life. But I know a great deal about the business. I speculate on racehorses. I match promising prospects with wealthy buyers."

Cass stiffened.

"My latest is a beauty due for retirement, but my client can work him for two more years and make a handsome profit. A unique horse, a top national winner, you see, and my client is determined to have him. My search has led me all the way from California to Wyoming to Tucson—in fact, to this very restaurant."

Cass quivered in every muscle, blood draining from his face. This meeting could not be a coincidence; the man was looking for a specific horse and had something professional on his mind. Something that involved him, Cass.

Cass stood up and from his looming height stared down at the man, who looked as if he had not seen a day of manual labor in his life. *Damn Kahlúa!* He tried to think straight. Dread surged through him, and he determined not to reveal anything that would give the man an edge. The man wanted something, wanted it badly enough travel across country to a town he'd never been to before.

"He's a magnificent animal, a top two-percent winner," the cowboy continued. "This prize horse's owners don't appear open to a deal. Evidently, there is a competitive buyer. But my client is determined to have him." He regarded his listeners with arched confidence.

Cass absently downed another Kahlúa. He ached all over. The rest of the evening played out in an inebriated fog.

The cowboy regarded Cass. "I understand you have worked at the Wyoming racetracks. I would appreciate any lead on this other buyer." He handed Cass a business card stamped *JARVIS LLOYD, R&H MANAGEMENT*. Cass stuffed it impatiently in his pocket. This was clearly not the end. But if this blowhard figured he was an easy target, he got it wrong. He would never give in.

"I don't know what you think I can do, but not interested in your schemes."

"All right, straight to the chase." Lloyd pulled the briefcase to his lap. "I'm an investigative attorney. You're a regular here, you live alone, you've no close family, and you plan to return to Wyoming." He ignored the drink Brent set in front of him. "I have a sweet offer for you."

"You've been checking up on me?"

"I think you're the man I'm looking for. That you aim to own this horse, Blue Star. The one my client is determined to have. To that end, we have a proposition."

"You're wasting your time." Cass's breath slowed, his chest barely moving. Thank heavens a legal contract held his prize in an ironclad grip.

"Maybe you have a contract, but that contract is not binding until paid in full. My client is prepared to make you an offer that will more than compensate you. Here is my card if you care to know the details."

Cass stuffed the card mechanically in his shirt pocket and, mind racing, calculated his options. He was a nobody with only one thing going for him: He would fight to the death. But iron determination would not be sufficient. *How could Blue Star's owners refuse the offer of a client with an enormous bank account?* On the other hand, he and the owners—who had bred, raised, and trained the horse—were linked in a mutual desire to give him the best home possible. They liked Cass, supported his plan.

But the cowboy had legal and financial clout.

The man regarded Cass steadily. "You'd better think hard. We aim to buy out your contract one way or the other. My clients have made up their minds."

"You're barking up the wrong tree."

"Understand, Blue Star will still be active." the cowboy said in a soothing manner. "He's past his prime, but we plan to race him for two more years. We think he still has it in him to make money."

"And," Cass said slowly, "what would you do with him after two years?"

"Well, Mr. Broughan, you know how it works. These horses are not fit for breeding, and too expensive to keep when no longer racing."

A guffaw from Cass. "That horse must not be put down. Blue Star deserves to live out his remaining years fully and in peace."

"I see my suspicions confirmed." The cowboy slapped his briefcase. "I have the papers right here. It's a good offer. Think it over."

Cass drove home along the darkened streets lost in thought. He had already spent a hunk of his nest egg on medical bills, legal fees, and travel. The $800,000, which had seemed so colossal a sum, had dwindled. Too careless—a big mistake. He still needed thousands for the ranch, and to pay off on Blue Star. He would have to be careful. The cowboy could weasel a deal behind his back.

It looked like he had a way to go.

**"MY GOSH, YOU'RE TALL."** Sam stood on the threshold looking up at him.

"I guess you're busy." Cass had expected more of a welcome. He took a step backward. He shouldn't have come. He hadn't known this girl long, although the evenings they spent together at the bar drew him as close as he'd been in a long time to knowing someone. He enjoyed her fascinating and often bizarre spurts of imagination. She was light as a bird in flight, whizzing joyfully through the air, then alighting in a sudden halt to throw out a serious question. So young, innocent, boisterous, so sure of herself. A child.

"Why are you here, Cass?"

Cass hesitated. He avoided confrontation that pulled him out of his usual comfort zone, insulated by his unswerving live-and-let-live stance. Off in his own orbit, people mostly left him alone.

"You haven't been to the restaurant for three days. Brent tells me you were there last night crying between swallows of beer, talking to no one. He didn't want to reveal what you told him, said it didn't make sense anyway. I had to do something." He stuffed his hands in his pockets and shrugged. "I remembered you gave me your address so that I could take a look at your new Mexican tile murals from Tubac, and I thought I'd…that is, I wanted to see you. Maybe I can help."

"Okay, come in." Her expression was serious. "My parents are visiting Aunt Sadie at the hospital, so I'm alone. I'm not in a good place and would like to talk to you. Don't just stand there."

He followed her into the marble-topped kitchen, the corner breakfast table strewn with a large sketchpad, several boxes of colored pencils and charcoal, an open package of figs, and a hardcover book with a ripped cover. Cass picked up the book and thumbed through it.

"That's Somerset Maugham. The main character in *Razor's Edge* sets off in search of transcendent meaning in life. That's what I aim to do."

She poured coffee from a Cuisinart pot into a tall mug and handed it to him. He stood leaning against the counter, feeling the liquid slowly warming his insides.

"I've been waiting to hear you say that. You're twenty-two, Sam. I wondered when you were going to get started."

"You mean, what have I been doing since high school? Nothing. Trying to figure things out. I don't want to live in a small town with a main street that goes nowhere. My parents are determined that I remain in Winslow, a nice, quiet Arizona town where people know each other's affairs and keep them in line. Where things are steady and predictable. My dad insists I learn his dry-cleaning business. Expects me to work my way up. Except, you see, there's not far to go. It's a stalemate; my parents pull one way, I pull another. I want out."

She ran her fingers through her hair and tucked a loose strand behind one ear. "Let's take our coffee outside and talk."

She seemed to have something on her mind.

Cass followed her through the living room to a tiled patio that opened onto a central courtyard with a turquoise pool at one end. The horseshoe-shaped apartment building enclosed the courtyard, except where it faced the street on the open end. Most of the windows were open, from which soft strains of pop music drifted. The chairs lined around the pool were empty, although with the sun getting hotter, they would not be for long. People not heading for the mountains or out shopping would be showing up to tan or soak in the warm water. Most of the units were inhabited by transients whose stay in Tucson was too long for a hotel—tourists, visitors with family in the area.

Flopping in a chair, Sam folded her legs under her and adjusted the straps of her peach camisole.

Cass seated himself across from her. A splash of coffee landed on his arm; he swiped it off on his jeans. Then he waited.

"Okay. It's dumb." She pulled herself up to a lotus position. "My boyfriend found someone else. Broke it off on the phone: one call, two sentences. I guess he got tired of my craziness." A fly flew across her cheek, and she watched it land on her bare knee. "I haven't told any-one. I could have had any boy, but I had to pick the handsome quar-terback, the hard-to-get jock that every girl wanted. And he bailed." She lowered her head with an expression of hopelessness. "I'm through with men."

Cass squirmed. "What can I do?" He regarded her anxiously—if only this could be handled without too much drama.

"I'll make it on my own, Cass." The tears fell slowly down her cheeks, wetting her fingers. He'd never seen her like this, her voice thin, as if there was nothing holding it, as if a framework had collapsed. If only he knew what to say, how to reassure her. He repressed an urge to put a hand on her bent shoulder, remained in his chair and regarded her helplessly.

"Hey, gorgeous!" They turned to see a figure at a third-story window across the pool smiling and waving energetically. "When are you coming over to see my etchings?" he yelled. "You're wearing out that chair. Why waste a beautiful afternoon?"

Slowly Sam turned her head. "Don't you ever leave that window?" The old sass had seeped into her voice. "Can't you see I have company?"

"Grandma's gone in for her nap. There's nothing to do over here." With that he lifted his arm and began bouncing a paddle ball back and forth. "Look what I found in Grandma's closet. Ever seen one of these?"

"That's Wayne," Sam explained in a low voice. "He's barely out of high school. Thinks we're rich, but we're not. Doesn't know that Aunt Sadie is paying for this fancy apartment while she's recuperating at the hospital. He wants to take me to lunch. I'd rather spend time with you."

"I'm coming over. What's your apartment number?" the boy yelled across the courtyard.

"No, you're not!" Sam yelled back. "We don't have a number. We occupy the entire floor."

They heard a "ha ha ha" and a window slam.

She swirled back to Cass. "I've seen three different girls lolling at that window. Not for me." She drew up her legs and rested her chin on her knees with a wry smile, tears evidently forgotten. "He *is* cute. I wonder if he can handle a thoroughbred horse."

"I thought you were…" Cass had a strange feeling that he was in alien territory. He had never been able to fathom how women operated. First, she says she's through with men, then she's ready to take on this brazen fellow.

"Don't worry, Cass, I'll get over the breakup," she said with a resurgence of determination. "Good riddance. But no more relationships. At least with someone who is not going in the same direction I am. Not for me the tract house, the squalling kids. My parents don't get it."

Without warning, she reached over and clutched his arm. "That's what I want to talk to you about. I'm going out of my mind. I want to paint. I want to ride Queenie at my aunt's ranch, the horse she gave to me on my fourteenth birthday. Someday I want to explore the world and discover what's really important."

Releasing his arm, she looked directly at him. "I'll tell you my secret wish." Her eyes flashed. "First I want to go to Sarah Lawrence to study art. I've kept a catalogue in my top desk drawer since I was seventeen. We can't afford such a college, of course. My parents have a different dream for me. But I will follow *my* dream! I will!"

A wistful look came over her face. "My parents don't care about me. That is, *me*, who I am." She dropped her head for a moment, then looked up at him earnestly. "Did your parents care about you?" Her voice barely a whisper.

Cass wiped his hands on his jeans and crossed his arms. "I don't know. We didn't talk about those things."

"But you knew they did."

"No. It didn't seem to be a problem. To be there was enough."

"But did they push you, try to get you to be something?"

"No. They didn't care what I was."

Sam scrunched her face thoughtfully. "So. We both come from the same root, grown into different trees."

"I don't know what that means, Sam." A splashing from the pool, where three youngsters in blue-and-white bathing suits leapt gleefully into the water. He watched as a striped ball sailed back and forth, back and forth over the sprays.

It slowly dawned on him—it appeared that parents who were overbearing and controlling or and parents who were negligent and dismissive were equally difficult to withstand. Where did she get this? The girl had more depth than he realized.

She dropped back in her chair. "I'm sick and tired of control freaks who try to run my life. You understand."

"No, I don't understand!" The unaccustomed introspection had drawn him to a pitch of anxiety. "Your parents want to help and are doing everything they know how. You feel smothered, sure, okay, but you reject your family, friends, everything. Yet you live at home doing nothing. Why aren't you working, training, going somewhere? You are beautiful and smart. What's the matter with you?" He was shouting now. "I bet your parents are doing what they believe will make you happy, and you do nothing but criticize and complain and think of yourself. You act like a spoiled brat."

"Oh, really? What have *you* ever accomplished? You're alone in the world. You do nothing, you go nowhere. You have no life. Who are you to talk!"

He flushed uncomfortably.

"You don't care about people. You go around in unpressed shirts and grubby jackets that have never seen the laundry. You look like a bum."

"No one cares what I look like," he retorted defensively. "I don't care."

"You should. How long has it been since you've had a haircut? Don't you want to be accepted? Your only friends here are the hired help." Samantha's words poured out in a rampage. "The servers at the restaurant take pity on you as they pocket your generous tips. And no wonder! You have the worst disposition of anyone I've ever met. All you do is grouch and make yourself disagreeable. Nothing is to your liking. You're an old sourpuss. So don't tell me to shape up!"

Cass stared at her. What did he have to show for himself at that? A life without place or family or friends, lacking brightness or charm or cleverness or attainment. He raised his arms, dropped them heavily. "You're probably right."

He lifted his eyes as an explosion of sunlight covered the patio. A breakthrough in the clouds had brightened everything around him: the green-and-orange Mexican tiles, the black-eyed Susans, yellow marigolds, and orange lilies blooming along the walls, the turquoise pool, and farther, looming over the roof of the white stucco apartment building, the bold outline of distant mountains carved into the sky.

Yes, of course she was right. He had always thought only of himself. Why hadn't he seen it before? Sam was fighting for her future. Fighting!

And he'd not lifted a finger, simply slipped out of the way of whatever came down the path. Isn't that what he'd always done to get through the days, to make his own way? Never stood up for anything. Until the last few months and his plan.

Sam needed someone. She needed guidance. But he was a fool to think he could help her. How could he be so arrogant?

He needed time to think. "Maybe I'd better go so you can see your friend." Cass looked at the window across the way, now empty.

"I want no part of that idiot. He refers to girls as *chicks*. Don't you listen?"

"Sam, do you have to be so snappy? I'm always willing to listen." His blood was running fast. Too many draining thoughts; he was running on pure energy.

"Sorry, sorry. Oh, I can be bitchy." A child's laughter reached them from the pool. "I wanted to live with Aunt Sadie on the farm, but my parents refused, said I wouldn't meet anyone eligible isolated out there. I guess that's why I'm so testy, or maybe it's just a lousy disposition. Gosh, Cass, what's the matter with me? My friends are deep into college or marriage, and I'm left to my dreams. I want so much to *be somebody*, and here I am dangling like a fly on a string. I don't know what to do or where to go, or what I'm good for. I feel lost. People think my paintings are fabulous, but they'd be nothing out in the real world. If only I could fly away!"

"Look here, I have my dream too, my hopes for obtaining Blue Star. That cowboy fellow at the bar outbid me but now has offered to sell the horse back to me at the original cost after running it profitably for two more years. Sure, maybe I can wait two years. But I trust that fellow like a fox in a rabbit den. He was friendly and smooth on the phone. But those fancy lawyers can twist anything to suit them, can find exceptions and loopholes. I have to decide what to do. Everything I want in the world is tied up in this." But this wasn't about him. He lifted his gaze. "How about you? What is it you want, Sam?"

She swung from her chair, stomped to the edge of the patio, and stood looking out at a little girl skipping across the yard holding a yellow balloon aloft. Several children followed her as she circled, clapping their hands, following the arc of the balloon as it bounced on puffs of air. Then the girl let go of the string, crying, "Free! Free!" and they all laughed as the balloon floated upward and away into the vast sky.

Suddenly Sam whirled and grabbed Cass's shirt with one hand. "Cass, let me go to Wyoming with you!" He stared at her in surprise. "I want to get out of here. I can't bear it anymore. I know horses; I've had my own for years. I love being on my aunt's ranch, helping in the barn, and I can even cook—really, I can make an awesome chimichanga. I can help. I'm a hard worker. I can get a job." Dropping her hands, she flung herself in a chair. "I know it's asking a lot," she said more evenly. "It's just until I can work out plans. I don't require a lot of maintenance. And I can do anything I set my mind to. I will save up enough to attend college—that's a promise."

Something softened in him, an unfamiliar tenderness. Such a child, she could be his granddaughter, the family he never had. He could rescue her. But to take responsibility for a disgruntled twenty-two-year-old—he had no talent for the management of another human being. He had never taken care of anyone. He didn't know how he would even go about such a thing. It wouldn't work. He would fail her.

"Sorry, I can't do it, Sam." He braced himself against the emotions that swelled inside him. "I don't mix well with others. You're right, I have no friends, except a few stable hands I schmooze with at the track bar. No life for a beautiful young woman like you."

She focused her eyes on her fingernails. "You're afraid people will get the wrong idea."

"I don't give a rip what people think. I don't believe I could handle it." Her parents would blame him, and then Sam could change her mind, her expectations disappointed. For starters. She might be ready to strike her own path, but life on a ranch with a crotchety old hand was not the answer.

Yet he hesitated. Sam deserved to be supported. There must be a way. The thought filled him with a strange power. He could accommodate her. All he had to do was follow his heart. It would add a new dimension to his plan, to his life, a deeper purpose. To be needed, is that so different from being loved?

But he wouldn't. He couldn't be responsible. He had no right to interfere with this young girl and her family. Even if it filled an open space within him, it would be the wrong thing to do.

She mustn't count on him.

"I can't do it," he repeated. "You'd better check your options."

Sam turned her head away. "You're hopeless with people," she said at last, tossing a crunched Kleenex on the table. "And stubborn as a mule. We're kind of alike there. Maybe that's why I like you so much."

He went over and lay his hand on the back of her head. He had accomplished something today. He had learned things, as much about himself as about Sam. He had learned how much he had to learn. Sam mirrored a picture of himself he hadn't seen before. He wasn't sure he liked what he saw.

"OH, CASS, I'M SO GLAD YOU PICKED UP! How are you? Are your tests back? Ronald and the boys have been pestering me for an update. From now on, I want you to phone as soon as you know something."

His daughter sounded strange. Not like herself.

"You didn't have to call."

"Of course I did. You're my father. What kind of a person would I be if I didn't keep track of you?"

"You have a busy life. A family. You don't have to worry about me." No point in laying obligations on her. That she phoned once in a blue moon was enough. He hadn't contributed to her life. As an absent father, he had no rights on this front.

"I need to know how you're doing, what you're up to. Have you purchased that ranch yet?"

"Not yet. But I have plans."

"Tell me more!"

"Nothing to tell. Just a pipe dream, a wild thought." He knew exactly the ranch. It would be on the market soon, and when he returned to Jackson he would make it happen.

"Remember, I'm your daughter," Eleanor was saying. "I have a right to know things. I want to make sure you are all right, that you don't need anything. That the medics are doing their job."

What? She'd never questioned it. He waited suspiciously for her next words.

"So, what's the latest diagnosis?"

"The CT showed a new suspicious area," he began cautiously.

Outside the kitchen window a dog started barking furiously at the bird feeder. At the sound, the tiny bodies scattered, chirping loudly. Cass pounded loudly on the window. *Bam, bam! Quiet!* The barking ceased, and the dog stared upward, jaw open.

"What's going on there, Cass? You're busy. I'll get to the point. The ski shop has gone into receivership. We're so dependent out here on the weather and the economy. And we've been saddled with unlucky investments. It would be a loan, of course."

Cass was speechless. How did she know he had money? Maybe he had bragged about his $800,000 stash on one of their calls, let it slip. How he was set.

"Eleanor, I have medical expenses." In truth, he didn't know how much of his funds remained. "I probably have just enough to pay for the ranch. If that."

"What are you saying?" The connection went silent. After a few moments of static, her voice continued, this time with more vigor. "You've never given me an ounce of care or guidance. Never contributed a cent for Hunter and

Rock's college. You only care about horses and hanging out at the racetrack. You think only of yourself. It was a mistake to ask you for anything."

"I don't think…"

"Never mind, Cass. You're hopeless."

He froze, clutching his phone so hard his knuckles turned white.

He couldn't deny it. He had been a failure. He had never made an effort to know his daughter during her brief summer on the ranch. Had expected the novelty of the Wyoming farm to be enough, no need for him to do anything. If only—

The cell went black in his hand.

Gone then, the final link to his short marriage, a core family unit that for eighteen months had briefly defined him. A feeling of inadequacy and loss drew him to a chair where he slumped helplessly. He had failed her, deserved her rancor. There was nothing he could do.

**CASS AND SAMANTHA ENTERED** an office at the end of the hall marked *Executive Suite*. There, surrounded by floor-to-ceiling windows, plush carpet, and a mahogany bar cabinet along one wall, the figure of Jarvis Lloyd smiled at them from behind an oversized desk. He was dressed in a light blue seersucker suit and tie, hair slicked around his ears, manicured nails folded on the desk in front of him. The oversized hat was nowhere to be seen.

"Delighted to receive your call. I'm glad you've come around at last." Rising, he stretched his hand over the desk with a flattering smile. "Cass, Samantha."

"We're here to close the negotiations for good," Cass began, ignoring courtesies.

"Please sit down. How about a drink? Business is better conducted with a bit of lubrication."

"Let's get to the point. The horse, Blue Star, is not for sale." Cass's face grew hot. So much depended on this meeting. That it took place in the territory of his opponent, who sat behind a fortified desk in an imposing office, was intimidating. But he had right on his side, his motives were clean. "We have a contract. We think the owners will honor it."

Samantha pulled a manila envelope from her oversized tote bag and slapped it on the desk. "Here is a copy. You might as well give up the case," she declared.

The cowboy, ignoring the envelope, reseated himself with a congenial air. "Due to a contingency clause, that contract is not final until the end of the year."

Cass started. How did he know that?

"To the point. We understand this horse means a lot to you. That it's personal. My associates have agreed to compensate you for your loss with a hefty $50,000 to release your contract agreement."

"I will not let Blue Star go," Cass countered. "How do we know the horse will receive humane treatment? The number of retired racehorses that wind up being mistreated, drugged, injured, or neglected is well known. We can't accept your deal."

"Let me assure you, Mr. Broughan, that the pot has been sweetened. We have added incentives you can hardly ignore." Pressing a button, the cowboy spoke into the speaker. "Hilda, bring in the Broughan case." He leaned forward with a confident smile and placed both hands flat on the desk. "My client is prepared to reimburse you for the costs you have incurred, including all legal fees, and to cover what we understand are your extensive medical bills. It's a very generous offer."

"There is no offer I will take." What good would a pile of money sitting in the bank do him? Besides, he disliked this slippery man who was reaching all the way from Wyoming to string a legal noose around his neck.

The door opened, and a woman in a navy suit entered and laid a folder on the desk.

Mr. Lloyd went to the window and stared at the concrete office building across the street. "The papers are prepared and ready for you to sign. If you refuse, you'll get nothing." He turned, every sign of conciliation gone.

"Our funds are extensive, beyond the scope of an individual like you, and the owners have indicated that they are considering our offer, which is above the asking price."

"I'd like to know," put in Samantha, "why you are so determined to get this particular horse? There are plenty of other horses out there."

Mr. Lloyd reseated himself behind the desk. His voice was measured. "Blue Star is being retired, but we think he still has plenty of vigor. A little less of the top performer is still a lot more than most. This is the horse my client wants," he said. "My client gets what he wants."

"Over my dead body."

"Think it over. You'll never get a better deal."

But Cass and Samantha were already heading for the door, and it snapped closed behind them.

"Fuck that asshole," Samantha said as Cass pulled the car away from the curb. She leaned one arm on the window frame. "Maybe you should get legal advice. The cowboy is out to get you, and he won't stop."

"Think I don't know that? I already have an attorney working on it. He's negotiating with Blue Star's owners."

Cass headed past a line of pottery and millinery shops toward Sam's apartment. She had insisted on accompanying him to the meeting. He liked having her as a backup. She had spunk, that girl.

His cell rang. No need to answer; no one called him except the clinic with wacky requests.

"I'm in this with you, Cass," Sam said as they pulled up to her building. Getting out, she leaned into the open window and addressed Cass in the driver's seat. "You've filled me in on the ins and outs of this battle of yours, and I've studied the legal issues. I'm smart. I can help."

As she walked off, Cass smiled. She was really into this. He pulled out his cell phone—a message. The voice was unfamiliar. Not Dr. Asghar. Not Millie the associate. The tone was solemn. "We have been unable to reach you. Dr. Asghar and the auxiliary physicians' team have the latest diagnostic reports on your cancer and want to talk to you in person. Please contact our office as soon as possible."

**AS SOON AS SAMANTHA ENTERED THE RESTAURANT,** she sensed something was wrong. Gloria scurried over and without a word led her to Cass's regular table in the corner. There, propped between the cactus-shaped salt and pepper shakers, lay an envelope with Sam's name on it in block letters. Samantha scanned the room curiously. Several of the staff, including Mia and Bridget, stood looking on from the sidelines. Brent, hanging clean stem glasses on an overhead rack at the bar, moved over and stood next to them. *What did they know that she didn't?* She picked up the envelope.

> *Dear Sam,*
>
> *I have intestinal cancer. It has taken charge of my body and is inoperable. It works slowly, but I have things to do, and this is a blessing. I'm going home, back to where the bison once roamed. I have notified Blue Star's owners that I am out of the running, and they have promised to find a good home for him and make sure he doesn't land in the hands of greedy investors. Then it will be my turn to close shop. Forgive me for not saying goodbye; I don't need any weepy farewells or regrets. What I do need, and want with all my being, is for you to go to college, someplace where you can stake out your true path. I never did. I have drifted rudderless—up till now. Now, for the first time, I have taken a stand that makes sense, that is bigger than me, something that will endure after I'm gone. It will be soon. I have made up my mind. With you—well, with you it will be different. You have much to offer.*
>
> *My attorney will phone you soon. He will make the arrangements and set up the needed funds. I hope you will do this for me—and yourself.*
>
> *Say goodbye to the others. You are my family. Tell them. Cass*

Sam clamped the letter to her chest and sank slowly into a chair. Impossible! She might never lay eyes on him again—and he had done this for her! Her mind swirled. She looked desperately up at the others, who were watching her intently. "When was he here? Did you know?"

Gloria explained. Cass had come in that morning with the news and told them not to worry about him. He had taken control, was going off to fulfill his destiny in a way that made sense. He acted as if he had discovered a new continent, going around the room shaking hands, acting strangely animated and alive. It was all in his letter, he said. Said he had no time to talk.

Sam raised the sheet of paper. "Listen, you'd better hear what he says." She began reading.

**CASS SET HIS SUITCASE ON THE BED,** opened the top, rummaged around for the dark brown bottle, and set it on the table. The flight to Evanston, skimming through the high reaches of the planet, cut off from the searing earth, had instilled in him a strange calmness. He'd often stayed here at the Elsinore Hotel during his racetrack days. Home. It didn't exist. He had no more concerns.

All was in order.

He had arranged to leave Eleanor a handsome amount in his will. Sam had enrolled in an eastern college and flown off on her own journey. With what remained of his nest egg, he established a trust to cover her educational expenses. If anyone could grasp the world by the tail, it was Sam. The knowledge that he would have an impact on her future was worth any earthly pleasure he could imagine. Now that he no longer had plans for the ranch, his funds were enough to match the cowboy's offer for Blue Star. The owners, who were pleased at the turn of events, had located a sympathetic rancher who would adapt him to train youthful riders, and the horse would be sheltered until his life reached its natural end. The final documents had been signed. The bills were paid, his car donated to a neighbor's teenage son, his sparse furnishings dragged to Goodwill. He was leaving Arizona tidy and clear. The frantic medical problems, the endless tests, the severe treatments, the not knowing—all that ended.

The physicians, pouring over the records, vowed to use every skill in their power to save him. It could happen, they assured him. He could have years. Of course, he didn't buy this for a second. Nor did he approve of their blind adherence to the fruitless prolongation of life at all costs. Far better to enjoy an enriched shorter life than endure a prolonged empty one.

He had made up his mind. He had in his possession a brown package of maximum strength bromethalin. Rogue kids used it to kill cats and watch them die. The pharmacist had assured him it was strong enough to kill a bull.

He drew on his slippers; might as well be comfortable. There was no hurry. Time had become abstract, with no meaning other than determining whether it was day or night. He just might check out old acquaintances—the boys at the Shifty Dog would be glad to see him, and he would look up John at the track, his cohort for so many years. Many things he thought of doing.

But no, the journey had been long, and he was tired. His back hurt. Even though part of him longed to revisit the old haunts, now he wanted nothing more than to sink into quietness. Sitting on the bed, his body relaxed into fuzziness, a lack of focus that smooths the release into surrender. An almost spiritual sense of completion invaded his body, and he smiled to himself. He had done right, had provided for Sam, for Blue Star, and had been filled with satisfaction beyond his imagination. What else was there? He felt light, as if floating on an unseen current.

No point in waiting.

Moving to the sink, he filled a plastic glass with tap water and gulped down three glasses before he filled it with darkened liquid and swallowed it slowly, breathing deeply with each gulp. Then, letting go of his breath, he lay down on the bed.

Minutes pass. Leaving the door unlocked, he walks six miles to the racetrack where he has spent so many years. How good they look, the buildings so familiar—the large storage barn, freshly stained, the track headquarters with electric signage mounted above the roof, the paddock where thousands of his footsteps have marked the soil. Few are about; only one or two workers with keys hanging from their belts drift like shadows around the buildings.

Leaning against the railing, Cass surveys the deserted track, listening for the pounding of hooves. He can smell the sweet odor of sweat swirling in the air above the flat dirt; he can see Blue Star, speeding around the curves, wild, focused, unbeatable.

A voice sounds in his ear, a reverberation of his old supervisor. "Hey, long time no see. Where've you been, Cass?" The fellow stands next to him, grinning with a friendly nod of his head. "Ain't looking for work, are ya? Could use an extra hand."

Cass shakes his head slowly. His working days are over. He says this with relief. It feels good to let go, to let go of it all. Life, with its insecurities, its rejections, its unpredictable turns, its enigmas, its stark disappointments. Not to be crushed with regret, shame, guilt, not to have to face the failures that swarm and drown the hopes of those caught in the past. He feels a quiet lowering in his stomach, feels the warmth spread through his system with surprising force. He draws a deep breath, and his limbs stretch out as if drawn by puppet strings.

A man in a leather cap approaches, one hand on his hip, as if to admonish Cass for being in a closed area, but he glides on speechless, like a ghost.

The air on the track is still. It had evidently been sprayed that day, as its surface sparkles with moisture. He imagines himself stepping onto the cool surface, running evenly around the track, gaining speed, taking the curves with ease in a breathtaking streak of strength, flying smoothly, easily, his feet barely touching the ground, the cool air caressing his face until he lifts off and loses awareness of where he is going.

# Gray Skies

**THERE'S ONLY ONE THING TO DO** when one reaches the age of no return—throw a party. That's exactly what Maggie intended to do, pulling out a fresh invitation and checking off the next name on her list. The mere thought drew her out of the funk she'd been in all day, waking up in bed alone, stumbling into her slippers to go out and face another day at Serene Harbor. The very name riled her; serene was not what she was after, yet here she was, sequestered in this old-age hideaway. Her two sons had insisted after she burned a casserole, a charred mass that hit the garbage pail with a thump. Could have happened to anyone. She certainly couldn't smell it from the bedroom, although they claimed the house reeked of burnt charcoal.

What did they know? Fuss budgets, her two sons, especially Barrett. He hovered over her like an old hen. The idea of her eighty-nine years staggered them both. She represented a century, a generational span that covered an age without television, jet planes, transistors, Skype, spaceships, central air, or the pill. When yellow streetcars cruised the streets, people traveled the Atlantic by steamer, divorce was scandalous, and family closets were packed with skeletons of dysfunctional layaways. Amazing times. Amazed that she had experienced such extreme cultural change, as if she had each foot planted in a different century. Amazed that so much had come and gone during her lifetime. Amazed that she still lived.

"It's only because we love you," her sons Barrett and Jimmy told her as they closed the door to her old apartment for the last time. Oh, yes, they loved her: a non-contestable rationale for trying to stop her from doing what she wanted, from challenging herself and getting some oomph from life. For years the word *love* had not intruded in their lives. The assumption was that the care and devotion between them as a family displayed ample love right there in process, no need for fussing. Now that she was old, it had become her sons' favorite four-letter word, every push and coax coated with love, feelings that she suspected served as a palliative for them as well as her.

In the twelve months since she'd moved into Serene Harbor, she had learned to navigate a slower system, among the canes and walkers and ubiquitous side railings. Everything in the place seemed old, including her. Yes, the slightest bump popped her skin with purple bruises, it took her forever to dig in her purse and locate the tiny tube of sunscreen, and she moved with a slower gait. But she had vigor. She could drive in daylight. She could tend to an apartment, her own apartment where she belonged. It wasn't too late. She still challenged fate; she still grew new cells each day. She was rechargeable. She could still go back!

It hadn't been easy. At her last checkup, the nurse practitioner had asked her to remember the words *pear, antelope*, and *machine* for three minutes. Then he asked her if she knew what day it was. "Judgment day," she shouted. He had no sense of humor.

She fought the repressive limits and constraints every step of the way. No, no, not for me. I don't want assisted anything. I may be eighty-nine, but I'm still functional, still kicking, thank you very much. But you *are* an old lady—this came from Barrett, who had long disapproved of her living alone in her spacious apartment in Linden Hills. Since her husband Keith died three years ago in the flush of health, collapsed from a stroke as he mowed the steep hill behind Jimmy's three-story colonial, she had gotten along just fine. At first, she had to deal with the shock of an empty house and a tremendous feeling of loss as she navigated a couple-less world. She set herself to resurrecting some sort of life in her newfound independence.

Then along came her two fussing sons, who maneuvered her into submission with alternate bouts of persuasion, temptation, and ultimatum. They cited her deteriorating eyesight and diminished memory. Along with her arthritis, her weaving, forgetting to show up for a lunch date—not like her at all.

She needed care.

Her sons wanted her to be safe and comfortable. It was for them that she was here, overlooking a wide backyard strewn with speckled oak trees and beyond the woods a shimmering lake with a pontoon boat tethered against the dock. Barrett was the worst, insisting that she slow down and desist. To him, anyone over eighty had nine toes in the grave. Fiddlesticks and damnation! She wasn't ready to be stashed away. And yet here she was, at her desk, staring out the window at the grand old oak not much older than she was.

It was a flourishing July day, with eager bulbs and flowers opening their buds to the sky. Maggie leaned back in her chair, squinting to take in the plot of pink arcadia beyond her window, the rich green grass, the pink honeysuckle bushes, the prairie grass flowing along a brick wall. The leaves of the tall oak tree fluttered protectively over the lawn, sifting out the hot rays of the overhead sun. It stood like a familiar presence, one that never doubted her strength or persuaded her to move from a comfortable apartment to a den of tottering old folk on the brink of extinction.

How had it happened? Barrett had engineered the move, got his wife Edith to plead, with Jimmy echoing in the background. They signed her up for an independent apartment with a balcony, close to her friend Agnes, and when the time came that she needed routine care, the assisted living unit was right next door. Two months later she moved in with a smattering of necessities and a few beloved furnishings. Her life had become small, and so had she. To her family she had diminished, not only physically, but her shrunken life had little to show—no ups and downs of raising a family, with continual commotion and interesting twists. Just a predictable routine: meals, Sunday jaunts on the pontoon, three workouts a week, canasta on Wednesdays, and chess with Clive once a week. Little to interest those who relished an occasional challenge to keep the flesh alive. It was for her own good, they insisted. Her importance in the cycle of life had diminished, and she would have to acquiesce.

But not quite yet! She bent over the pile of invitations in front of her, picked up a pen and arranged the papers and stamps on the desktop. Energy still flowed in her veins, fueled by a fierce determination. There was still life to be lived, and she would not be cheated out of an ounce that remained. This would be her final statement, a declaration of purpose. She would fly, make the leap, and land among them in one grand thrilling affirmation of life before blowing out the candle. Fly or die, she said, describing what she had planned for her birthday, and her listeners regarded her with lifted eyebrows.

Rolling her shoulders to shake out the arthritis, she tightened the blue angora sweater around her neck and bent over the list, checking off the names of the guests. An oversized magnifying glass lay next to the desk lamp, a constant aid since macular degeneration had set in. The party would be simple. Hamburgers with all the trimmings, set outdoors next to the airfield where she would blow out her birthday candles and bask in the thrill of the challenge. She felt light, almost weightless. At last, something real, tangible to look forward to. She hadn't felt this stimulated since the squirrelly days of her youth when she cruised the Pacific rim from the Marquesas to Tahiti in a thirty-foot sailboat.

The trouble with birthdays: They were all about age. Everyone would exult that she had reached eighty-nine, as if it were an abnormality—as if she had just joined a freak show. "Age is no gauge" was her motto. "You're as young as you feel. And I feel fifty." That put a stop to the continual "you are amazing," "it must be hard," "you're going to set a record," "you look so young"—which meant *how could you look so young and be so old?* Helping her sit down, get up, put on her hat, locate the stairs since she must be blind or daffy. If one more person repeated, "Here, let me do it for you," she would boot them in a place where the sun don't shine!

Recrossing her ankles, she folded another rose-petal-edged invitation and inscribed the next name, Janette Langdorff, on the envelope in neat serif letters. Let's see, Emma Dunbar. Well, scratch that one off, long dead. And Maribel Caster, carried off by ovarian cancer. Checking down the list now—Harriet Brandson moved to Scottsdale to be near her children, the last Maggie heard, she was locked in a memory care unit. Few of her old friends were left, even fewer were ambulatory.

She looked up when the door knocker sounded. "Come!" An elderly man with scruffy grey hair peeked in hesitantly, then rambled over to the desk and stood like a hovering bear, all six-feet-one of him, beaming down at her. Maggie set down the gel pen and smiled up at him. It always cheered her to witness Clive's round, roseate face, open and welcoming, as if he didn't have a care in the world, meeting each moment with an indomitable air of good humor despite his bad knee, crippled with arthritis, and the rash of dermatitis spread along his arms and one side of his neck.

"What are you up to?" Clive asked. His soft blue eyes met hers with a shadowy twinkle that caused her to smile.

"You'll never guess." She straightened her shoulders. "My upcoming birthday party. You're invited. You and Agnes."

"I'm honored. You'll have to reveal your age—it will be the highlight of the day."

"Oh no, it won't. My jump will be the topic." She shot him a mischievous look. "Besides, I don't hide my age. It's not necessary in this refuge for the aged. People always forget."

"I haven't forgotten, Maggie."

"That's because you're partial to me. Since we first met here, I've told you the story of my life, and you remember everything about me. Even how I felt when I got my first kiss."

"I no longer remember things like that about myself. Sweet romance, never to be seen again. Long ago and far away." He screwed his eyebrows into bushy question marks, as he often did when he wanted to emphasize a point.

"Oh, I don't know. You still hold a masculine appeal beneath that thin skin of yours." She reached out and touched his hand. "You're still warm, Clive."

"I have no idea what you mean. Come on, Mag, let's go to lunch."

"You go ahead. I want to finish these invitations."

"Well, I'll save you a place. Wait…what jump?"

"See you later. Ta-ta."

**THERE! THE ENVELOPES WERE DONE,** small beige squares with her address printed in the upper left corner. She would stuff them later. One arm on the desk, she stood, wavered briefly, then padded into the bathroom, grabbing onto the edge of the marble counter to steady herself. Funny how quickly the muscles lock up when you take a rest; they insist on being active. With a slight kick she shook out her right leg, coaxing it awake. Ah, back to normal.

The bathroom was padded with every accoutrement known to civilization: a support bar next to a raised toilet; a hinge opening on the bathtub; a pull cord alongside the mirror; a rubber non-slip rug; a Mickey Mouse night-light; and a row of Tylenol, milk of magnesia, and Aleve on the shelf. She stared in the mirror at her hair, once a luxurious chestnut bouffant framing her face, now a thin mat that showed glimpses of her scalp. Using an eyebrow brush, she tamed the hairs of her eyebrows that stuck out like bug legs in all directions and smoothed the stubborn ones down with Vaseline. One of the many parts of her that were becoming less controllable, less defined. She grimaced into the mirror, showing a row of teeth that had caused little Celeste to remark more than once, "Why do you have such yellow teeth, Grandma?" Thank heavens her value didn't reside in her looks, not at her age. She brushed her hair to a neat wave along her face and, leaning close to the mirror, carefully applied ruby-red gloss to her lips. In the image that stared back at her she detected a faint remnant of prettiness that had animated her youthful days. But the bags under her eyes were prominent. As were the wrinkles that squeezed around her eyes and mouth like drawstrings. Her shoulders sagged; she hadn't realized how tired she was, operating on empty. Typically, a long lie-down was in order to get through the day.

She shuffled to the jewelry box on the chest of drawers. Let's see, the turquoise pendant would perk up her outfit nicely. Drawing out a gold chain, she crossed her hands behind her neck and, pressing the clasp open, attempted to attach it to the ring on the other end. She tugged and pulled repeatedly until her fingers grew sore. Damnation! Why did they make the openings so tiny nowadays? Finally, she gave up and slipped a plain copper chain over her head.

Gathering the key fob from the front table, she slipped out and shut the door after her with a snap. As she entered the main lobby, she spied a familiar figure emerging through the front door: a tall, limber man who strode athletically into the center of the room, caught her eye, and hurried over. Maggie found herself clasped in a pair of lanky arms and heard a breathless "Hello, Mother."

"My heavens," Maggie exclaimed. "What a treat!" She gazed into his face, taking in his curly blond hair, the soft curve of his chin, the squint with which he looked out at the world as if in a minute he would understand what it was all about.

This was the younger son who always wanted to please, wanted everyone to be happy. It was Jimmy who covered for her when she spoke too abruptly, who dropped everything to drive her to the airport to attend her seventieth college reunion in Evanston, who always supported her without preconceived ideas or judgment.

"You're just in time for lunch. I'm sure they can squeeze you in. What a treat. It's been a while."

"I can't stay, Mother. I must get back to the office. Barrett wanted me to bring over these papers for you to sign. Giving him power of attorney, remember?"

"Surely you have to eat lunch?"

"Well…"

It had always been impossible for him to say no, and now he struggled. She took pity on him. "Of course, you're busy. There's a desk. I'll sign it now." He breathed a sigh of relief and shot her a quick, vanilla smile. Giving her elder son Barrett power of attorney would facilitate the settlement of her estate should anything happen to her and relieve his persistent apprehension about her ability to manage.

"By the way," she said as he slid the signed pages into a manila envelope, "did you know your brother is not speaking to me?"

"Well, yes," he said, turning his head away. "He said something…"

"I'd like to know why."

"Well, it was the canoe outing. Barrett didn't think it was a good idea. Of course, you meant no harm."

"You mean because I took Celeste riding in the canoe? Celeste wanted to go out on the lake—she begged me. We had such fun. She did ballerina arcs with the paddle and laughed at a turtle sunbathing on a rock. It was a rare time alone with my great-granddaughter. I am not allowed to babysit; Barrett and Edith don't approve of sitters. A bit smothering, if you ask me."

"But she doesn't swim. Barrett thinks it was far too dangerous. You know how overprotective he is of his only grandchild, especially since he and Edith became Celeste's legal guardians after the death of her parents."

"We were wearing life jackets, for Pete's sake."

"Oh, Mother, you know how tippy canoes are. Just the two of you, and you—you unsure on your feet. He thinks you took a big risk."

"He knows I'm an experienced river canoer and know how to stroke a paddle. He's being ridiculous."

"I'm just telling you what he said. I'm sure you had everything under control. I tried to reassure him."

"Oh, Jimmy. You're such a comfort. I'd die if I couldn't see Celeste again."

"I'm afraid—well, maybe it will blow over." With a quick kiss and a smile, he marched off stiffly, envelope clutched under his arm.

The lobby was crowded with folks heading for the midday meal. A few snailed their way deliberately, crossing the room in baby steps. Maggie pressed through the bodies amid the tapping of canes, the scrape of walkers, and the low rumble of chitchat. A few visitors were lined up at the marble reception desk waiting to sign in.

Two women in knit sweaters sat curled in a corner settee, walkers nearby, stringing colored paper cutouts on string that hung across their laps. Maggie recognized Mildred, a housewife from Circle Pines whose husband had shot himself when he learned his stage four cancer had metastasized. There she was smiling happily; what force carried her through it all? Perhaps dementia had its compensation, if one were ready to opt out. Although when her turn came she wouldn't flinch, would prefer to face it straight and clearheaded.

Maggie approached the flight of stairs and grasped the side handrail—not that she needed support, she told herself, but the occasions when she swung off balance and brushed against a wall or tipped to one side rounding a corner were too numerous to ignore.

A parade of silent diners had formed a lunch line. Maggie detected the odor of stale urine and perspiration, along with a whiff of chili powder and onions. Not chili again!

She searched the room for Clive. Better get to him and claim her spot before a swarm of females took advantage of a single male seated at a table alone, a rare commodity in this female-prevalent community. Men, she was convinced, with their macho refusal to acknowledge weakness or pain, tended to die early.

Spying Clive seated next to a potted yucca plant, Maggie scooted onto the bench next to him. He slid over, leaving her plenty of space. He always gave her the space she needed.

"Hey. Chili's excellent today," he said, lifting his thick blonde eyebrows. He wore a rich green mohair sweater and the usual gold Rolex watch. She liked his substantial body and his general deportment: casual, warm, approachable. A former commercial banker who had established sixteen branches and traveled the globe, she quickly detected behind his businesslike manner an easygoing disposition. As hall neighbors, they had dealt with many twists and turns of the residence together. She knew he would do anything for her.

"I feel so close to you," she once told him in a moment of sentimentality.

He had squeezed his eyebrows. "Of course, you live next door." She detected a hint of avoidance behind his teasing tone. They both laughed.

"You know, you're quite huggable, Clive." She felt an urge to keep on a personal level.

"I know I'm overweight…"

"You're comfortable. I feel warmth when you're near me."

"A high-powered metabolism. Don't be fooled," Clive exclaimed.

She had stared at him. Hopeless, like trying to steer a mule into a cage.

His voice drew her back to the present. "Are you going to tell me?" He adjusted the silverware on either side of his plate, smiled up at her. It was the smile that did it—that and the warm fuzzy sweater.

She scooted closer, lowered her voice. "I'm throwing a party. At Winsted Airfield west of here. Just a few close friends and family. There will be brats, hamburgers, beans, and wine. No frills. To celebrate my life on this earth, which I will gaze at from a new, higher perspective."

"You don't mean it," Clive said severely, but his eyes glistened.

"Is it ever too late to fulfill a dream?" she asked.

He regarded her quizzically.

"It's all arranged." Maggie glanced at the next table and lowered her voice. "I'm sending out the invitations today. I will be tandem skydiving from an airplane." Her eyes lit up as she watched her companion's face for his reaction. "They aren't concerned about my age; all they require is a free spirit, a medical clearance, and a $500 deposit."

"Now Maggie, you know I support you in anything, but this sounds very dangerous." He bent forward, towering over her. "The world will lose a shining light if anything happens to you. I—I don't want to lose you. Why take such a risk at your age?"

"It's exactly my age that makes sense. What have I got to lose except a few more years in this—well, it's lovely, but in this columbarium for the aged?"

"But to leap from a plane, to land on your legs…"

"It's a tandem jump. We'll have four legs. Plenty."

"Very funny. I'll visit you in the hospital."

"Clive, I can no longer ride the Tower of Terror roller-coaster or ski down Death Run, but I can do this. To fly through the air in total freedom, looking down at a tiny, insignificant world"—she leaned forward, fingers clutching the folds of her linen slacks—"and all weight drops away and you float light as a feather, cares absorbed into the cosmos. It will be total liberation!"

"You're in dreamland! Oh, dear Maggie, do rethink this!"

"You'll be there?"

"Of course. I wouldn't miss it. I will watch you fall through space and head for the hard earth in the arms of a slingshot instructor. I just hope the atmosphere clears your mind of any more crazy ideas." He didn't look down as the plate of steaming chili was slipped in front of him. "I will be there with an ambulance and a psychiatrist and a bank loan to cover your medical expenses."

"Clive, why can't you understand? I seek to prove that I'm still here, I still exist. When I look in the mirror, I see a face I hardly recognize, some weary rendition of me that age has concocted to warn me that time is short. It's a way of projecting myself, of displaying what remains intact— my self-determination."

"Maggie, you could philosophize away the clouds in the sky. All right, I'll applaud your courage and the satisfaction it gives you."

"But don't tell Barrett yet. He'll try to stop me."

She grabbed his hand. It felt comforting, like the feel of warm soup in your stomach after an icy tramp in the woods.

A crash cut through the hum of voices, the shatter of breaking glass, a whelp of distress. All heads turned as clicking feet scurried across the room. "Take me to Maggie," cried a meek voice.

Maggie and Clive watched as a limp figure in a pink pantsuit was carried by two black-shirted waiters to their table and gently lowered onto the empty chair. "Oh, dear!" With a weak sigh the figure gazed up at the two waiters. "I broke the vase. I'm so sorry. No, I'm fine." She waved them away, then looked up with a watery smile at her two astonished companions. "Silly me. Hello, Maggie."

"Agnes, what happened?" Maggie reached out and took one of her friend's hands. It lay in hers like a limp flipper.

"I fell. Silly me."

"Are you all right?"

Agnes looked down at her legs. "I guess so."

"How about something to eat? Are you hungry?"

"I don't know."

"Have you eaten?"

"I—I think so."

"She finished half of her egg salad sandwich and the cherry pie, didn't you, Agnes?" the waiter offered. "I think she's done." Smiling, he backed away, responding to a call at another table.

Agnes sat in a forlorn heap, her pink jacket twisted under her, a tuft of bobbed hair protruding from one ear. Maggie regarded her sadly. She and Agnes had grown up together, lived two blocks apart in a secluded neighborhood without children. Each of them an only child, they spent every free moment together, got so they could read each other without a word being spoken. It pained Maggie to see her friend like this, out of touch, barely navigating the exigencies of everyday existence. Closeted in her own narrow little world, Agnes had been losing *bodily strength,* her circle of activity receding in a dimming awareness. Eating, sleeping, and getting about the apartment was all she could manage.

Agnes lived two doors down from Maggie, one apartment past Clive's. Occasionally, after dinner, Agnes joined Maggie and Clive in Clive's apartment to watch a film of Basil Rathbone portraying an invincible Sherlock Holmes. Agnes would walk in, watch the flickering images on the screen, evidently caught up in the glitter of the action, then get up and walk back to her apartment without a word.

The three neighbors looked out for each other: Clive with his deliberate manner, making certain everything unfolded properly; Agnes, whose disposition never darkened as her world shrank; and Maggie, always seeking something to do.

"Let's take a moonlight ride on the pontoon boat," Maggie would suggest, but Clive objected.

"We can't take it out by ourselves—it's against the rules. How about catching the van's next trip and treating ourselves to a Dairy Queen at the mall?"

"Ugh," Maggie protested. "And take three hours to accomplish what an individual could do in one?"

"Maybe we could walk."

"It's five miles away!"

As they helped Agnes into her chair at the lunch table, she raised her head to her two friends. "I'm so sorry. I'm such a klutz," she murmured. "I'm always breaking things."

Maggie patted her friend's arm. "It's all right, Agnes. Come, let's watch some television. Clive, box my dinner for me, and I'll help Agnes upstairs to the theater." Maggie often took Agnes to Serene Harbor's TV theater. It was one of the few things they could do together, given Agnes's dementia. Agnes grasped very little of the story line, but she would watch contentedly until the show ended, a look of enjoyment on her face.

Maggie was determined to not allow her deteriorating vision to prevent her from watching her favorite detective shows. She managed to circumvent the macular degeneration by using eccentric viewing techniques to clarify images. This involved looking slightly away from the subject to view it peripherally with another area of her viewing field. A technique at which, after coaching by an eye specialist, she had become proficient.

They were quite a pair, Maggie thought, as they sat of an evening watching the screen. Each blind in her own fashion.

Entering the TV theater, they saw a man in a twill jacket and leather slippers seated in the lineup of recliners. He was bald except for a horseshoe strip of brown hair that circled around the back of his head. Agnes smiled at him. "I've just had the nicest lunch with my friends, Maggie and Clive," she told him, looking pleased, as if she had just left a delightful party.

The man growled, "I'm watching a program. Quiet!"

Still smiling, Agnes followed Maggie and sat in the leather chair next to her. Three women in similar short-sleeved pullovers sat close together in the row behind them, watching the screen, mouths open.

"Do you know that unpleasant fellow?" Maggie turned to ask the one with the daisy scarf around her neck.

"Who? Oh, him? That's Henry. He's here all the time. Keeps yelling at everyone." She didn't appear disturbed but riveted her attention immediately on the flickering seventy-inch screen as if she'd forgotten his existence.

Maggie vaguely recalled seeing the man here and there about the residence, looking dour and alone, reading in a corner or crunched on a bench peering into his iPhone. A real sourpuss.

After a while Maggie had enough of the clamorous car chase flashing in front of her eyes. "Next choice is ours, Henry," she called. Best to let him know that he did not rule the roost and that Agnes had friends to fend for her.

The man gave a brief nod and resumed watching.

A commercial flashed on the screen, and Maggie heard whispers behind her.

"It was Barbara's dog—no, her daughter's dog. I leaned over to pet him." Three women in the back row had their heads together. The one in the middle, shorter than the rest, reached up to touch a bandage that covered one side of her face. A rhinestone bracelet slipped down her wrist.

"He wet on you? Oh, my goodness." One of the women next to her cupped her cheeks with both hands.

"No, I was PETTING him. I kissed him on the nose and he off and bit me. Required six stitches."

The other two gasped.

"How dreadful. What kind of dog was it?" asked the woman on her other side.

"Ah—I don't remember. But a man ran out and started pounding on the mutt with a baseball bat, which was even scarier."

"You say it was a terrier?"

"What are you saying? Speak up." The woman on her left raised her voice, as if she were the problem.

"I said I don't REMEMBER."

"I CAN'T HEAR WHAT YOU'RE SAYING," the other shouted.

Henry turned abruptly in his seat. "Quiet back there, you gasbags!" His voice rang through the room. "Maybe you can't hear, but the rest of the world can."

There was no response from the back of the room. Without exchanging a word, the three women pulled themselves from their chairs, shuffled across the room, and, not looking back, filed out the door, shutting it carefully behind them.

For some time, there was silence. On the screen two men chased a bare-chested man into a train tunnel, dodging bullets from a sniper with a military rifle who emerged from the bridge above. The gunshots resumed, and a car squealed into action. Out of the corner of her eye, Maggie noticed Agnes fingering the remote she'd found on her chair. Without warning, the skidding sound of raw tires stopped, and Renata Tebaldi's voice sent a lilting aria into the room.

"Excuse me!" The man called Henry glared at Agnes. "That's not a plaything." He lifted his own remote, and with a flick of his finger the channel returned to the car chase.

Agnes watched silently for a while. Then, seeming to forget Henry's existence, she clicked again, and the indignant face of Joan Crawford filled the screen.

Henry swiveled around in fury. "You have got to stop coming in here and interfering with my program. You wait your turn." He darted a fierce look at Maggie, as if she should take better charge of her rogue friend.

"Oh." Agnes regarded him with innocent surprise. "I'm so sorry."

"I'll thank you to watch your tongue, you cranky old man. You should be whipped for attacking this poor woman who can't defend herself," Maggie yelled.

He kept his face turned to the TV screen. "She shouldn't be allowed to run amuck like that," he growled. "Now quiet, I'm watching the show."

Agnes tugged at Maggie's sleeve. "Never mind. He's so alone over there…"

"He's rude and obnoxious!"

Agnes couldn't leave the remote in her lap alone. Maggie looked on with trepidation as she fumbled with the buttons and arrows. She kissed

Agnes on the cheek and slipped the remote from her hand. "Time to go home."

Agnes smiled and stood up, hands hanging at her side. Sweet, easy-going Agnes. Maggie had hardly noticed as her companion aged over the years, but recently the changes had accelerated. She watched her good nature slowly merge into total compliance, her gentle humor gradually turn to passive acceptance, grateful that enough remained to hang on to, enough to recognize, to love, to care for. Although the give-and-take friendship no longer existed, Maggie would always be there, tending to the precious remnants of her dear friend.

There could be no doubt: Her friend was on a downhill slide, and nothing could be done to stop it. After Agnes's last medical checkup, she had reseated herself in the lobby, forgetting the appointment had already taken place. They took her keys, turned off her stove, and put her on the waiting list for the memory-care unit in the adjoining building. Maggie hoped there would be a long wait so that she could keep Agnes near and watch out for her.

She watched Agnes switch on the light in her apartment and, bidding her good night, pulled the door shut.

**THE FOLLOWING MORNING,** Maggie plugged in the Keurig and carried a dish of strawberries and an almond bruschetta to the kitchen table. The previous night's dream still raged through her mind: them lying together in the boat, adrift, his arms closing around her. She felt the warmth of his body beneath his green sweater, felt the rhythmic swell of the lake pulling them forward. The face was hidden, but the lemon scent was familiar, and she felt safe, attached, enveloped in a timeless zone of no return. Nothing else mattered.

What did it mean? She couldn't tell. The dream persisted, the images recurring vividly as she went about getting breakfast. How warm and tender she felt! She wanted to crawl back into bed and let the pillow carry her back to dreamland.

Her thoughts swept back to her marriage. She missed the nights in bed with Keith, the touching, the reassuring feel of human proximity. She missed Keith's adoring presence. They were known by friends as the couple who had not fallen out of love and into accommodation, unlike most marriages, everyone agreed. They reveled in long sojourns together to the Swiss Alps, the Alhambra of Spain, the Buddhist temples of Indonesia.

Since her husband's death, romance no longer held a place in her life. It had faded along with a host of other expectations. She lived in an environment where breathing and mobility were prime concerns. Captured in this prison for the infirm, she valued above all her self-sufficiency; it made her feel competent, bolstered her strength. She had no need for romance.

Still, if a warm male body shared her bed at night, when the day had played out and all the little struggles ceased, she wouldn't mind. She smiled at the thought of Clive. What was he doing at this moment? She was struck by a wild desire to see him—maybe they could try Chez Colette, the new restaurant over on Lyndale. If only he'd suggest it. But she'd have to reach out; he'd never make a move.

She lifted the coffee mug to her lips and felt the hot liquid flow down her throat and into her stomach. The clock on the bare wall reminded her that the Friday Silver Sneaker class would start in the fitness center in twelve minutes. Time to put herself together, pull on her exercise garb. Yes, a workout was in order, something to bring her back to earth.

Working out three days a week kept her agile. After the stretching class, she positioned herself on the leg-press machine and began pumping—in, out, in, out. Then the leg curl, the calf stretch, the bicep curl, then onto the mat for ab lifts and a thirty-second plank. She returned puffing to her apartment and stretched out on the couch for a lie-down. Only for an hour, maybe two. She was determined to complete the invitations, which, along with showering and chopping the fresh tomatoes, cucumbers, and gold peppers for a salad, would consume the entire day.

**THAT EVENING AT SEVEN ON THE DOT** she arrived, knocked perfunctorily, and entered the apartment. Clive was relaxed comfortably on the couch reading the *Tribune,* wearing his green sweater and brown fleece slippers.

"I'm fed up with the Body Works class," she cried, without bothering to greet him.

Clive lowered the paper, his face brightening as he regarded her.

"They pulled me off the BOSU. Afraid I would fall. Evidently my advanced state of deterioration makes them uneasy. Said I was too macho, and they didn't want the responsibility."

"You do tend to overdo it, Maggie. When you climbed that aluminum ladder yesterday to pose for the camera my heart nearly stopped…"

"Clive! You know the ladder was perfectly secure. I've climbed ladders all my life. I painted our first house singlehandedly—I lived on ladders. Jimmy wanted a photo of me standing on the third rung, something original, catchy. You'll see. It will be on my Christmas card." Maggie laughed merrily, seating herself at the table. "Don't look so stern. Clive, you're such a stick-in-the-mud."

"And you, Maggie, are going to fall off the end of the world one of these days." His eyebrows lifted a notch. "My wife used to lapse into nervous fits when things went wrong, and I would tell her to get a grip. I say the same to you, if you don't stop defying your age." He looked directly at her, and she saw the warmth in his eyes.

"I'm fond of you, too, my dear friend. Except…" His plump body looked relaxed, peaceful, with his easy posture, head of silvery white hair, gentle eyes that were too small for his face. "You're so damned cerebral," she said, "there isn't a romantic bone in your body, you poor beast."

"At my age! I'm afraid my organs don't function as they used to."

"Oh, you men, all you can think of is sex. There's more to bonding than that." Should she tell him of her dream in the depths of the night, of being wrapped in a man's arms as they drifted on the lake in sweet silence? No, she wouldn't speak of it; he might think he was the man she was embracing.

"Don't you miss the intimacy you had with your wife? It's been eight years."

"I miss it, but it's too risky. There are all those expectations, and what if it fails? Then there's my painful gout…" Clive stood and moved to the dining table. "Come on, it's time to get out the chess game."

"Okay, handsome, whatever you say."

Going into the kitchen, Clive pulled two Heinekens from the fridge, grabbed two coasters from the shelf, and seated himself across from her. Then he bent over the chess board and set out the pieces on the squares with his long, plump fingers.

She moved her knight three squares. Clive fingered his chin, contemplating the board.

"Don't you even get the urge for a female partner?" she said into the silence.

He looked up. "What are you driving at?"

"Oh, nothing."

"I have you."

*My friend might be brilliant, but he certainly possesses a blind side.* "Me? Why, you could have anyone, with your looks and charm. There's a slew of women in this building to choose from."

"I chose you. Now let me think."

"While you plan your move, I'll get some snacks."

She started toward the kitchen to fill some popcorn bowls when the door knocker sounded.

The figure standing in the hallway looked expectant, as if she were the one answering the door. She clutched a bouquet of yellow roses against her breast.

"Agnes! Is something wrong?" Maggie exclaimed.

Agnes struggled. "I don't know. I came to see you for something, but I can't remember what."

"I live next door, not here, but no matter. You look terrible. What have you been doing?"

"I don't know, but it must have been something, because I'm exhausted." Not only did Agnes appear ready to weep but looked so befuddled that Maggie slipped an arm around her.

"What are the flowers for, Agnes?" she asked softly.

"My son sent them. I don't know. Maybe it's my birthday. I'm going to give them to Henry. He has nobody."

"Old Sourpuss, the TV crank? You don't know where he lives, do you?"

"I guess not."

A sickening feeling clutched Maggie's stomach. Her friend's unbalanced swings were becoming more unpredictable, and she feared Agnes was losing her last threads to life. A feeling of loss pervaded her, the sad, empty feeling that the world as she knew it was disappearing and before long every trace of familiar life would be gone.

"We'd better get you home," she whispered in Agnes's ear. "Everything's fine now. I'll see that Sourpuss gets the roses." When would the memory-care unit be available? It looked like Agnes needed a locked environment.

Clive resumed studying his next move. Kind, agreeable Clive. Blockhead Clive. As for her, she would be making her own move in September. She could hardly wait.

MAGGIE WAS SLEEPING PEACEFULLY, head sunk into her Tempur-Pedic pillow, when she heard tapping, repeated in little jerks. Dragging herself from bed, she staggered to the living room and pulled open the front door. There stood Agnes, hands clasped over her stomach.

"Couldn't sleep, dear?"

Agnes usually had no trouble sleeping—with minimal memory, she was unburdened by a nagging conscience or persistent anxieties. What was she doing here at two a.m.?

The overhead ceiling light revealed Agnes's wide blue eyes, usually clouded with a soft amiability, now filled with panic. The head of thinning white curls pulled back from her face gave her a pixie look despite the wrinkles that wove across her face. Her mouth trembled as she spoke. "Pot's gone! I can't find him!" Agnes thought the name catchy, perfect for a sleek black cat with yellow roving eyes.

"We'll figure out what to do." Slipping an arm around Agnes, Maggie kicked the door shut with her foot and drew her inside.

Agnes began to weep quietly. "When I woke up to go to the bathroom, he wasn't there in bed next to me. I couldn't find him anywhere. Maybe I forgot to let him in. Oh, Maggie, we have to find him!"

"You let him outside?"

"Yes, he begged and begged. He likes to lie on the stoop and listen to the forest noises." Agnes must have snuck him out the emergency door at the end of the hall, although animals were strictly confined to the owner's apartment.

"We'd better go look for him."

Agnes perked up. "Yes, yes. But he's never out for more than a little while. He'll be scared."

"When he hears your call, he'll come running," Maggie assured her. She drew on her slacks over her nightie, a nylon jacket, and an old pair of Adidas. Grabbing a light coat for Agnes—her leather scuffs would have to suffice—she took Agnes's arm and guided her down the hallway to the side door. Maggie gave a thrust on the perpendicular latch bar, and at last it opened reluctantly. Why did she have to push so hard? Really, they were making the doors heavier these days. What a nuisance.

"Pot! Pot!" Agnes walked next to Maggie, holding onto her sleeve, calling out in a thin silvery voice. Deathly silence. They padded across the grass and into the black curtain of woods. The possibility of finding the cat in the darkness was remote, but Agnes was determined. They trudged on gingerly. With her limited vision, Maggie squinted to make out the path, barely visible in the thin flickers of moonlight that pierced through the upper branches. Luckily, she had often taken the path to pontoon boat outings. Soon she detected the weedy odor of the lake up ahead. Thank heavens!

"Pot! Pot!" Finally, under a heightened yellow moon that glimmered on the water, they sighted the pontoon boat tied alongside the dock. Maggie inched her way along the dim planks, stepping carefully. Suddenly, a foot flew out from under her so quickly that without stumbling she slammed onto the dock and lay face down. Catching her breath, she breathed in the musty odor of lake vegetation just under the dock, which was somehow reassuring. She lifted her head. Her surroundings were a vague array of shadowy forms, one barely distinguishable from the next. If only she could see! If only she could get up! After several strained efforts to stand, to get her feeble, spongy legs to obey, she lay quiet, chained by a feeling of helplessness. Her body was abandoning her. In all this rich verdure there was no sign of life. She was at the end of her resources, for once drained of all volition. She felt utterly alone.

When she finally dragged herself to her feet, Agnes was gone. Wandering about the woods, no doubt, where if left on her own she could wander in circles until dawn. Maggie stumbled weakly into the woods and attempted the piercing whistle she'd been famous for as a girl, but her lips wouldn't vibrate. Nothing came out. She noticed her arms were trembling. What was with her? She seemed to be falling apart.

A cry rang out. "Pot! Pot!" Agnes reappeared out of the darkness, dragging her jacket by one hand. "Ohhhh, it's so black! Pot!" she yelled in a cracked voice. "Oh, my poor kitty! Oh, there you are Maggie. I'm scared." She scurried up and grabbed her friend's shoulder. "Maggie, what can we do? He'll never survive out here. It's all my fault!"

Before Maggie could respond, Agnes bolted, running crazily onto the dock. "There! I hear her! I'd know her cry anywhere. Pot, baby! She's on the pontoon! I'm coming!"

Maggie watched as Agnes's shadowy figure climbed on the boat and swayed out over the water. "He's gone! I saw him go under! There, out there, I saw him. Here I come! Oh Pot, I'm coming with you!"

Maggie heard a splash, followed by sputtering, and without thinking stepped into the water until she reached the struggling Agnes. There was no sign of the cat, no sound or cry. "If he's here, he'll swim to shore," Maggie reassured her friend, clutching her arm. They thrashed their way together to the bank.

An ambulance shrieked into the driveway. Shouts of paramedics rang out, members of the home staff rushed back and forth through the parking lot, the yard was alive with blinking lights. Agnes's inert form on a stretcher was carried into the back of the van, and Maggie, assisted by two paramedics, climbed in beside her and grabbed her hand as the ambulance sped off into the night.

Later, unable to reconstruct exactly what had happened, the episode drifted around Maggie's head in a blur. Glimpses of Agnes hurling out over the water with a deafening shriek, a cry almost of joy that echoed up to the sky, followed by a thunderous splash. Maggie squinting to make out movement in the blackness. Then the feel of the cold water, making their way to shore, staggering back for help, the immediate alarm, flashing lights, medical apparatuses, official reports.

Everyone claimed Maggie had saved her friend's life. The way Maggie saw it, she had barely saved her own. Never had she felt so feeble, so help-less, so unable to control the basic functioning of her body.

Agnes lay in a daze. When questioned she merely stared down at her fingers. Her body was covered with bruises and open wounds along her back, indicating that she had hit obstacles when she dropped off the boat, and hit them hard. A nasty slice in her skull and a layer of crusty material in her hair suggested bleeding of the brain, confirmed by later tests.

Agnes kept calling out Pot's name. No one had the heart to tell her that Pot had been discovered sprawled on the edge of the driveway, tire track marks running across his chest.

**AFTER THIS EXPERIENCE AGNES CHANGED.** She still responded to suggestions with her usual sweet demeanor, but nothing drew her interest. She made no demands and met everyone with her usual compliance, but now she followed her own agenda. She met requests—to take medications, to turn over, to raise a limb—with fixed silence. She responded to being transferred to the locked memory-care unit with nonchalance, as if beyond such concerns. Her son Dennis, her only relative, flew in from South Dakota, but he couldn't convince her to consume the dishes—especially selected to tempt her—that appeared regularly on her swivel tray, nor could the attorney, nor her faithful caregivers, Anne and Hilda. She refused to eat or leave her room.

Even Maggie and Clive were unable to reason with her. At each suggestion she would shake her head stubbornly. Dennis returned to his home duties. Her dear Pot was gone. She appeared to be lost in a world without definition, laying immobile on her back, staring at the ceiling with empty eyes. As if her will followed a single path: She would check out, no regrets. The staff, forced to follow her explicit health care directive, was unable to circumvent her refusal to take food or drink.

"Do something! It's just a piece of paper." Maggie let loose her frustration at the rotation of physicians and nurses who breezed in and out of Agnes's room. She balanced on the edge of the bed, holding her friend's hand in her own two. "Agnes, listen to me. You can get better. Your wounds can heal. Don't give up."

The figure in the bed turned her head slowly toward the speaker. "Maggie. My best friend. Maggie, I'm glad you're here."

It was the first time Agnes had spoken in two days. Maggie was encouraged. "Why are you…" But it was no use. Agnes didn't respond to why questions. She preferred simple thoughts that didn't require analysis. Maggie paused. "I love you, Agnes."

"Love… Good. Yes. And sleep." Agnes sank her head into the pillow and closed her eyes, an ethereal smile spread across her face.

A HANDFUL OF PEOPLE attended the funeral: Agnes's son Dennis; a college friend from Madison; the pretty blonde caregiver from Serene Harbor; Maggie; Clive; Agnes's friend Clarissa, a cat-lover from the residence; and surprisingly, Henry, the TV junkie who had battled with her in the television lounge every chance he got. The last to arrive was the attorney named as executor of her will, who explained that she hadn't wanted her money to be squandered on useless health care, which she considered money down the drain.

To Maggie and Clive it was devastating that Agnes would slip out of the world without regret, would give up a life that, though shallow, allowed her a pleasant, harmonious existence. And that they would have to do without her. As they sipped tea on the patio, shielded from the July sun under a flowered umbrella, Maggie twisted the obsidian ring on her finger back and forth, gazing at the black stone as if looking into a crystal ball.

"Taking your own life is an act of aggression. Not like Agnes at all," said Maggie. She glanced at Clive, hoping to hear an explanation from him. "She was so easygoing. She took things in stride."

"Maybe it's because she couldn't remember she had problems." Clive recrossed his legs in front of him.

"Still, it took will to brave such a step. To end one's life—it takes guts."

"All she had to do was let go and stop eating. What could be more passive than that?" He considered. "But why did she do it? She wasn't suffering. I can't imagine dying merely out of lassitude. It's normal to cling to life, no matter what."

"Maybe not if you have nothing holding you here, Clive. She had been shrinking for a long time. And her body was damaged badly in the accident. It takes quite an effort to go on as living becomes more and more arduous. There was no reason for her to continue the necessities of remaining alive. She had no ties or purpose that required her existence."

"She had us!"

"That she did. I guess it wasn't enough."

Maggie cradled her teacup in both hands. "Agnes is now at peace. It's we who suffer. Maybe there is method in her madness."

She stared at the pool of water outside the parlor window, clutched by intense sadness. The surface blazed with blinding sunlight, stirring up images from the past, her childhood with Agnes: playing marbles during recess; sneaking out at night to go skinny-dipping at Cedar Point beach; dropping water bombs from the girls' lavatory on the heads of the boys that popped out of the window below.

How she missed her! The comfort of being with someone who knew and understood her, who needed her—how could she replace that?

But she was being selfish. Agnes didn't want to live wrapped in a cocoon of blankness. Maybe it was too lonely.

Now she had only Clive, who interacted on a polite, superficial level, whose friendship grazed the surface without penetrating the depths. There he was, sipping his tea. She had never felt so alone.

"I wonder if I could be brave enough to act as Agnes did, should it come to that," she said. "If I could decide that existing in an empty space was not worth the struggle of getting up to spend the day fussing with things and dragging a weak, unresponsive body from one room to the next. Would I be able to undertake the final, definitive step?"

"You'll probably do what you have to," Clive said.

The thought of her birthday party coming up in September gave her a momentary lift. The invitations had been mailed, responses had been swift and incredulous. Only two months away.

FOR SEVERAL WEEKS AFTER Agnes's death, Maggie remained in her apartment, reading on the couch until her eyes gave out, napping, cooking frozen meals in the microwave, and retrieving responses to her birthday invitations, which she threw unopened on the desk. A heavy sadness weighed on her. Agnes was gone. She should never have involved her in the risky undertaking to find Pot. Her husband Keith was gone. Every year her small circle of friendships dwindled, lost to the grave, like the dying flowers that had stood in a row on Agnes's windowsill, plucked off one by one, day by day. As her life decelerated, the activities that had filled the hours diminished. The days moved at a slower and slower pace as if edging toward a final halt. An entire day with nothing scheduled, nothing to define it, and she flowed along, one day blending into the next, occupied with pulling on clothes, making a sandwich, polishing the marble counter, watching dull TV shows.

She floated in empty space.

In such a manner the days slipped by like pages of a precious book ruffled in one gesture through your fingers or clouds blown by breathless winds.

**WHEN ONE NEEDS REFUGE** one generally turns to family, but for Maggie this was not an option. She had no right to burden her children's hectic lives with her problems, with Barrett balancing wife and child and career, and unmarried Jimmy roaming over the country training thoroughbred horses, impossible to pin down.

One late July afternoon, Maggie stepped down the hall and knocked on Clive's door. She had not seen Clive since Agnes's funeral, had not answered his phone calls nor responded to his familiar taps at her door. He had finally given up and no longer buzzed her when she didn't show up for meals.

At the sight of her he was all smiles, sat her down, thrust a glass of iced tea in her hand, and resumed his comfortable seat on the couch. The room looked homey, with plump couch cushions, newspapers, an unopened bag of trail mix, and boxes of board games spread over the tables. From the kitchen drifted a faint scent of roast coffee and raspberries. Clive looked substantial and good-natured, with his shirt hung loosely over his round shoulders, his ample bear-hug arms, his face glowing with warm geniality, and the remains of a once-handsome mane curled behind his ears. She'd never seen him look so—look so good.

"So, you've emerged from limbo. What have you been up to?" he asked, sinking back into the oversized brocade pillow. He regarded her as he bit into a half-eaten apple.

"I've been moping. Agnes dead, most of my friends gone, not one invites me anywhere. At my age I'm allowed."

"Not when I'm around. None of that." He placed the apple on the table. "I hope you don't blame yourself for Agnes's suicide."

"I did lead her to the dock—"

"You rescued her from the lake and spent every minute afterward holding her hand. You couldn't have done more."

Clive would not let her wallow in blame. An untidy conscience was not for him. He didn't mess up his mind with introspection or cling to regret. "That's what I admire about you. You don't dwell on things. Easy come, easy go, that's you," she said.

"I don't dwell on things. No point in it."

"We're opposites, Clive. I maintain order around me, but my brain won't stop assessing and predicting and worrying. You're a slob. Look at this room. Every surface is strewn with papers; here's an apple core on the table; the chairs are filled with sweaters; the kitchen sink is stacked with dirty dishes. Yet your head is clear as a bell. No mess, no frills. I love that about you."

"Well, I'm glad you overlook my grave faults," he said, pursing his mouth. "I keep my mind occupied with safe things." He gestured to the chess set on the shelf.

"I love the way you accept my craziness," she told him. "The way you don't gripe. You embrace the world as long as you don't have to put yourself out too much. I can count on your stability. It means a lot to me."

"In other words, I'm predictable and boring as hell." Clive arched his eyebrows into a question mark.

"I mean you never seem to suffer. I've never seen you unhinged, not in a big way. You take things as they come. You've recovered from the loss of your wife, you are perfectly content being alone—never once have you asked for my help or needed my encouragement. It's incomprehensible."

Clive laughed. "I just don't dwell. That's all there is to it."

"Of course, that's not all there is to it, you idiot! It's not that easy."

"Look." He remained sunk back in the couch, his long legs stretched out in front of him, displaying a pair of soft yellow-and-black socks. "Life is suffering. That's the basic truth. Accommodation follows that."

"Oh, so now you're a Buddhist?"

"No, I'm nothing. Really, Maggie, I'm just a plain guy." She threw him a dissenting look. "What do you want from me?"

She left her chair and slipped next to him on the couch. "You're my friend. My good friend." She stopped, lifting her gaze from his yellow shirt to the gentle smile on his mouth. "Clive, hold me."

He turned to look directly at her, eyebrows twitching above his blue eyes. "Well, sure…" He made no move.

She leaned back against the couch, her shoulder against his. The touch sent a warm shiver down her side, and she smiled up at him. "Do you want to?"

"Well, sure…"

"In that case, you can kiss me as well."

He turned to her, looking for a second like a turkey before the axe, then his expression changed to wary, amused, interested.

She chuckled, stood up. "I'm teasing you," she said, picking up her cardigan.

She'd made a mistake. What had come over her? Now to make a graceful retreat. She forced a smile and summoned up a blithe goodbye—if her retreat was convincing, the scene would be patched over. They would laugh; he would forget.

Before she knew it, he had sprung from the couch and drew her to him in a bear embrace. For once, she was speechless. She felt the press of his warm, ample body, the contour of his chest and stomach and thighs, his cheek pressed into her hair. Her entire body melted with a sense of well-being. They stood for a long moment while the stillness of the room, with its warm scent of honeysuckle from the window, wrapped around them.

"That's all I can manage for now," he said softly, drawing his head back and looking at her. "The kiss will have to wait."

She understood by the flush across his face and the awkward movements of his arms that this was a big step for him. Avoiding conflict, keeping himself remote and secure—that was his modus operandi. She had broken the mold, challenged his serenity.

"Clive, the truth. Did you like that?"

"Yes and no. Yes. But Maggie, I'm not used to this sort of thing. Where will it lead?"

"What about the kiss?"

"I'd like that, but why ruin a good thing? We're so close, and we understand each other so well. Our relationship is so easy, so convenient. Why look a gift horse in the mouth?"

"That's the stupidest saying I ever heard! Clive Jones, you might as well be dead!"

With that, she grabbed her cardigan and slammed out the front door.

Seconds later, the door opened a crack, and she leaned her head in. "I didn't mean that. See you at dinner."

But he had the last word. "*I'll* invite you places!"

The door clicked shut.

"WELCOME EVERYONE. You've heard the ground rules. Now, who wants to begin?" A good-looking man in his forties, wearing a burgundy sweatshirt and horn-rimmed glasses, looked around and took a hefty gulp of black coffee. He exuded an air of easy authority. The people circled in chairs around him looked around with curiosity. The large basement room was hung with paintings depicting Mary and the Child and the Ascent to Calvary. From an adjoining kitchenette the sound of percolating coffee could be heard.

Maggie wasn't at all sure she wanted to be there, but she was tired of waking up each morning with a sick feeling of loss. She had to do something.

"What do you want us to say?" A young fellow with a black-and-red checkered scarf around his neck spoke up. "We're here because we're in pain and there's nothing we can do about it."

"We're here to share," piped up the woman seated next to him. "To tell our stories."

"What's the point?" insisted the young fellow. "We've all lost someone. I'm here to listen to solutions, not bare my soul."

"Well, if you don't have anything to say, I do," Maggie exclaimed. "I'm here because my husband and my best friend died, and I'm having a hard time adjusting." She twisted her hands in her lap, aware that her palms were wet.

All eyes turned to Maggie.

"My husband died out of the blue three years ago. Much as I've tried to add zip to my life, I can't shake this deep depression. With Keith gone, I sometimes feel helpless. I find myself turning to men for help. If I ask one of the women in the residence, they wave their arms helplessly. Takes a man to do that!" At this, she heard a couple of coughs, possibly a note of dissent, but the female listeners were paying rapt attention.

"Recently my best friend of fifty years died. My sons have put me into a home. My poor body is going downhill fast. I need a knee replacement, but I'm too old for the operation. They won't let me drive, I can't partake in outdoor sports, I can't ride a bike, I trip on my cane, every hour of activity requires three hours of rest, and, well, it never ends."

She sucked in her lower lip. "I feel my life narrowing down until it's crushing me. Lately I seem to have given up trying." She went on more slowly. "I'm not sure I want to do this anymore."

"Can you say more?" The group leader regarded her closely.

"My entire life, I've been looking for the next adventure, but verging on ninety, it seems I'm not able to have those now. I've always had people, though. My husband and my best friend, they needed me." She shot a glance at the leader. "And I needed them. And now they're gone."

"I know what you mean. I live in a nursing home," cried a woman with a maroon shawl covering her shoulders. "I hate it. You're serviced like a sick horse. The food stinks. The help is either not available or full of sickening cheer. But"—tears rose to her eyes—"I have nowhere else to live." The woman next to her laid a hand on her shoulder.

"Let's face it," said a middle-aged man in a striped shirt, a gold chain around his neck, "there's a lot of pain in life. And it's beyond our individual knowledge. We're specks in the universe. There's no way we can see the big picture."

At this point, a door flew open, and everyone looked up as a tall figure in a slim-cut suit and beige tie walked in. "Excuse me, I'm looking for Maggie Dahl."

What in the world?

The man stood by the doorway searching the room. "There you are. Maggie, I need to speak to you."

Maggie stared at him. What was Barrett doing here?

The leader looked over his shoulder. "This is a closed meeting, but if you wait outside we'll be done soon."

"You'll have to excuse Maggie. This is important."

"Really! Someone better have died," Maggie exclaimed when she and Barrett were by themselves in the next room.

"What are you doing in a place like this, Maggie? You've never been able to tolerate these kumbaya huggers and their sad lives."

"That was then. This is now."

Barrett frowned. "Celeste has a soccer game in twenty minutes. Edith had an emergency trip to the ophthalmologist, and I had to leave the office and take over. I'm sorry, but we must leave. My car's outside."

"What's happened? What is it?" Her stomach tightening, she quick-stepped as best she could after him.

**"I CAME TO DRIVE YOU HOME.** And you neglected to take the driver test I set up for you. Maggie, you can't drive. Your vision is too poor. I'll return later to pick up your car."

They descended the steps and made their way across the parking lot.

"How did you find me?"

"The clerk at your residence. I stopped by to drop off your new cell phone, and what do I find? You've gone off in a car that you're not supposed to drive. You love to break the rules, and when you were young and prancing, we let you do as you liked, but now…" He set his mouth in a rigid pencil line. "You leave me no choice. For your own safety as well as others. How would you feel if you ran into someone? Killed someone?"

"The same as you would." Her back stiffened. "I only drive to the corner strip mall and places I can find blindfolded."

"What about the time you ran into the *ROAD CLOSED* sign and ended up in the ditch?"

"That could happen to anyone. Could I help it if the unmarked exit ramp was hidden around a corner?"

"From now on, no driving. We want you to live as long as possible."

"*I* will judge what this old body can and can't do," she exclaimed, her face flushing crimson.

"In your stubbornness you just can't admit that you're not the person you used to be."

"I am aware of that," she said, jerking open the car door. A tart response came to her, but she swallowed it. She couldn't deny it, she was willful, and here was Barrett missing work, driving all that way to attend to her.

Barrett slipped into the driver's seat. "I've downloaded the Uber app to your cell phone. You can go anywhere."

"I will do no such—" Again she stopped. An ache in her chest reminded her that she didn't feel at all well. There were no easy answers. As she looked at Barrett's worried face, something in her mellowed, and she felt a swell of compliance surge through her. She could give in—like Agnes.

"I'm not returning to the grief group."

Barrett stared at her.

"I went to be fixed, but I'm beginning to realize, listening to the frantic struggles of those poor souls, that I'm past the stage of revelation, have moved into that of inertia. No more efforts to improve things, to change. Maybe it's better to submit and ease gently into that good night." She leaned back in the seat. "All right, son. I'll take the test."

"And abide by the results?"

"Promise."

For a moment Barrett stared out the front windshield. Evidently, he had more on his mind. "There's something else, Mother."

Maggie, next to him, waited.

He drove across the lot and turned onto the street. "You must drop this crazy idea of jumping out of an airplane. Don't glare at me. Two women at the front desk asked me about it. They agree that this 'celebration' you're planning is madness. Jimmy and I feel it is our duty to dissuade you."

So, Jimmy has joined the Barrett police force. She tightened her lips. Over her dead body! She wouldn't give up this one last thing.

"With your bad joints, macular degeneration, and judgment problem, it would be far too dangerous." He smoothed a lock of stray hair against his temple.

"Judgment problem! Judgment problem?" Every time she had to deal with a health issue, no matter how slight, Barrett and Edith rushed to put on the brakes, restrict this and restrict that. "Barrett, it's my life, my decision."

"Mother, please do what you are told."

As if he owned her territory and everything in it. She felt her blood rise, and buzzed the window open with her finger. It would be a long ride back to the residence, and he would be trying to curtail her every foot of the way. Barrett was boss at the office and boss at home, which suited his wife Edith, as long as he didn't interfere with her rigid schedule of school, soccer, yoga, Junior League, cooking, and shopping.

"You know as well as I do that you mistake distances," he went on. "Last week at Celeste's soccer game you fell on the bleachers."

"Barrett, you're a broken record. Stop telling me what to do. I love you, but stop treating me as a has-been. Use it or lose it—you've heard that? Well, I intend to keep using it as long as I can. When I have to stop, I'll stop."

"But you won't. That's just it!"

She couldn't argue with that. Maybe he was right. She did have a tendency to go over the edge.

"Barrett, I admit I like to show off, to impress with my daring, to make a splash. This jump will prove I can still do it, that am jolly well alive and intact. That I matter."

"Of course you matter."

She hardly heard Barrett's words drifting from his side of the car. All avenues were blocked. She had to face it. Her brain was fragmenting into pieces, with no sense of direction. Her sense of time vanished. When the car stopped at the entrance to her residence, she was unable to move.

"Remember what I've told you. Edith and I have nothing but your well-being at heart."

Her muscles gathered, gained strength. "I know you do, son. I know you worry about me." She opened the car door. "I'll take the test. Goodbye, Barrett."

**THE DEAFENING DRONE OF ENGINES** rang in Maggie's ears, drowning out the wild beating of her heart. She had watched the Cessna 182 unload its pack of novice jumpers twice and simulated the drop over and over in her mind. Sitting next to Nash on the long bench in the fuselage, her mind raced. Was this really a good idea? Nothing to fear but fear itself, she thought crazily. Get a grip. She hadn't worried up to now, nothing more than a scintillating shakiness. She'd resisted the many efforts to dissuade her, convinced that she had to share this one last adventure with friends and family in the last birthday she would celebrate in high style—a testament to her life. The skydive managers had obtained medical records and the assurance that she was healthy enough to make the jump and that she had full charge of her faculties. She had won. People had protested, pleaded, but all planned to attend, unable to stay away after all.

Isn't this what she wanted? To show the world she could do it? To get the accolades, the recognition?

But sitting on the bench shaking, she was no longer certain what she wanted. Her life had been moving in slow motion, closing tighter on all sides, leaving a cramped space that held her in its grip. No longer could she ignore her failing body or pretend that her physical body matched the mental picture she had of herself. Her diabetes, high blood pressure, and osteoporosis had to be managed, and the polyps discovered in her large intestine regulated with a new medicine just on the market. The pills she was taking sucked up her energy. Now the arthritis had twisted her left foot so out of shape that she found it difficult to walk.

Maybe it was time to let go. Yes, and she would be ready.

She sat upright, stomach fluttering. Her occasional gasps for breath were drowned out by the thundering roar of the plane, a loud, grinding noise that pressed against her ears insistently. The cockpit had a stifling odor of gas and upholstery cleanser. She stole a look at the rigid back of the pilot, who faced a glittering spread of operating instruments, huge earphones clamped over his head. With a sudden jerk, the plane tilted downward; one wing tipped, then righted itself. The calm look on Nash's face indicated it was nothing, a minor adjustment. As her instructor, he had coached her on deep breathing and landing techniques, assured her all she needed to prepare was a good night's sleep. Across from her, the windowless sliding door blocked the exit that would be opened for action. Outside lay the cool fresh air, where she would soon be free-falling into unknown space.

Nash laid his hand on her arm. "You're shaking all over." He regarded her figure slumped against the wall of the fuselage, neck arched. "Are you okay?"

Maggie pressed her trembling fingers in her lap. "I'm not scared, that's not it. I shake all the time. It's an involuntary tremor. I can make the jump."

"You don't have to do this," he said, leaning toward her and speaking loudly over the loud drone of the plane.

"But I do," she cried. "It's my final blowout. I need to do this. I will give it my all. Then I'm done."

The Cessna droned on toward the drop point. It was happening!

She recalled that earlier that afternoon she had been full of anticipation, seated beside Jimmy as they drove to the airfield in his new Prius. Having long given up trying to dissuade her, he launched into a litany of encouragement: what bravery she showed, how everyone was rooting for her, how he had checked and double-checked the reputations of the sky-dive company and the tandem instructor, Nash, who would be Maggie's Siamese twin and bundle her through the air to safety.

"I know you have to do this. You'll be in good hands." Jimmy threw her a beseeching look. "Nash Barnes has twelve years of experience and has made thousands of drops. Just be sure—"

"I'm very sure. Oh, Jimmy, you're so sympathetic. You always stick up for me."

"Of course, I'm with you, Mom. I know you can do it. You know how anxious I get—I like things simple and orderly and peaceful. Sometimes you're a real challenge."

Maggie laughed. "I love you so much. Barrett as well. Don't ever forget that my love for you is and always has been unshakable."

"Wow, Mom, I've never seen you so sentimental."

"Age mellows you. I want to go out with a shout. This is my last hurrah; then I intend to be quiet as a lamb."

"That'll be the day."

Maggie was jiggled by a sudden lurch of the plane, reminding her she was speeding at high altitude. Feeling Nash next to her, attentive and supportive, she was beginning to feel less wary. The arrangements were in place, the food had been set out on picnic tables on the grassy meadow, along with bottles of French wine and six-packs of beer. And the spectators would be there. Waiting at the airfield for her to land.

As the plane approached the drop point, she glimpsed, peering down from the window, the distant spread of low outbuildings on an expanse of bare earth and meadow, set in the middle of a flat empty countryside. Although the sky below was cloudless, the scene appeared to be veiled in a thin mist, reducing the objects to vague outlines. She shook her head and looked again. There was a cluster of picnic tables spread on one side of the meadow, along with chairs, a protective tarpaulin, and a row of binocular stands facing the sky. Tiny ant figures had gathered, some still arriving, cars lined up beside the rows of plain rectangular hangars, people getting out, greeting each other. Squinting, she focused on a red speck that stood out through the fog—could that be Barrett's red denim blazer?

And between them, nothing but miles of empty, gaping space.

Nash's steady voice roused her. "Time for final preparations."

She stood up. Nash snapped on her helmet and adjusted the parachute equipment, tightening straps around her body, between her legs, across her back, under her arms, testing the buckles and straps with a brisk air of efficiency. Soon they were bound together into a single package. He held her reassuringly, his tall figure at full alert. "You'll be great. Remember, you're in good hands." He spoke with confidence. "Leave everything to me. You don't need to do a thing."

*That's what you think! I have to leave this plane and fall through empty space.* Looking down at the gigantic void into which she would have to throw herself, she felt the veins in her neck tighten. Maybe she couldn't do this after all. Nash rechecked the automatic activation device and with a reassuring grin pointed out her red reserve pull line and the yellow pilot line designed to unleash the main chute that would lower them safely to earth.

Maggie looked out at the soft bank of clouds drifting in a variegated blue sky beyond the now-open hatch. They stood at the very edge. Above, the streaks of blue and white trailing far into the distance suggested a comprehensive universe that extended to the ends of time. Strapped in on all sides, cradled in the contours of her companion, her heart resumed beating naturally. She could do this! She sucked in a deep pocket of air and let it out slowly, easily, feeling her nervousness ease. Past and future, young and old, accepting the status quo or fighting to the last release of breath: It no longer mattered. The air rushed past her, swept against her hair. She had entered a core zone, completely caught up in the stir of the moment.

"NOW!"

She gasped as Nash sprang off the ledge and she felt the two of them launch into space. The air grabbed them like a hungry beast, and they dropped like stones, plunged in a sixty-second free fall that sent her adrenaline racing. Below, the earth spread in every direction. She was able to make out a veiled labyrinth of mountains and valleys and superstructures outlined vaguely as if underwater. She felt herself caught in the rush of air brushing by her, and her body became weightless, timeless, defined by the pull of gravity. Lifting her arm, she adjusted the helmet that partially covered her eyes and beheld web patterns of stray sunlight, the distant trails of white clouds, the cluster of silver-blue stars blinking on the dark horizon with lightening sharpness. She thought she detected the cosmic sparkle of interplanetary space that reached beyond time. The world seemed to have exploded and realigned, freeing her, and she felt past regrets, desires, intentions, contentions absorbed into the stark reality of the cool air on her skin.

Totally alive, with nothing subtracted, nothing added.

The pilot chute opened with a jerk, then they slowed, and her brain shifted into gear. She was aware of Nash at her back, felt him holding her, holding the sky as they plunged through space.

The scene below was minuscule, the blurred hangers and outbuildings no more than 3D blocks, people mere pebbles bobbing about on a distant earth. How removed she felt! What did all that have to do with her?

And then she knew. Knew what she would do. This would be a final closing, a fit end to her waffling deliberations and endless efforts to hold back the inevitable.

She could see a narrow stretch of moving objects below, small and insignificant. The images grew larger as they fell, and she was able to make out the outlines of the buildings and two airplanes on the tarmac, next to them a field of parked cars lined up like dominos. One of them looked like her old neighbor Annabel's yellow sports car. She thought she recognized—it must be—mounted on the central table like a royal icon, the birthday cake that Edith had decorated the day before, adorned with bright red candles and topped with the bold number 90, and in capital letters: WE LOVE YOU.

As the ground advanced, she made out her family grouped by a row of wine boxes. That must be Edith in an orange sweater and Barrett in his red blazer and cap; the tall one had to be Jimmy. People grouped around the picnic tables and spread out into the meadow, heads tilted to the sky. A group from the residence wearing yellow arm bands clustered together. She spotted Doris and Jeanine and several others, and some old neighbors from their Linden Hills years; and gracious, there was Reverend Courtland from the Unitarian Church. She hadn't seen him for years, not since Mary Ann Olson's funeral. There was little Celeste, running out into the landing field, waving her arms excitedly, Edith close behind, catching her skirt. And oh my, standing over by the hangar door it was Clive, staring up at the sky as if seeking a lost star. A solitary figure stood at the edge of the grass, bathed in sunlight—to her surprise she recognized Sourpuss from the television lounge. Since Agnes had gifted him with the yellow roses, Henry's expression had changed from belligerent to merely grouchy. Now his figure looked lonely standing off to the side, as though he had not a friend in the world—something like herself. She felt all annoyance with him vanish, absorbed in the radiance of the sky.

So familiar they all were—and so distant! Remnants of a life lived.

She shifted her attention to the vastness surrounding her, to the rich gold and aqua blues dotting the sky in a million variations, beheld the effervescent dancing on the edge of space that foreshadowed an endless universe. Lifting her arm, she adjusted the helmet that partially covered her eyes, expanding her vision, and felt the past absorbed into the stark reality of the cool air on her skin.

And then she knew. Knew what she would do. This would be a final closing, a fit end to her waffling deliberations and endless efforts to hold back the inevitable. For the first time she felt whole, no longer split into two levels of consciousness, no longer fragmented by past and future. Never had she felt so free, so sure, there in an expanding, weightless universe, mind flushed of debris, aloft in a weightless world. Not possible to speculate or think but totally immersed, totally alive with nothing subtracted, nothing added. An otherworld thrill claimed her, a sense of sheer elation. She felt that destiny had brought her to exactly where she was supposed to be and what she needed to be doing. The end, far from being fearful, lifted her into a brilliance that came to meet her.

**SHE RECALLED THE GOLDEN SUMMERS** as a child, when she raced over the meadow at full speed, breathless, absorbed, aware only of the wind on her cheeks and the sun on her back, her body at full strength. When she was certain she could face or do anything. It was the same thrill, only now she was drifting, drifting into a realm where she no longer had needs or desires, absorbed into the eternal mind.

Past regrets and desires that hammered her mind swept off the face of the earth into cleansing space, leaving her clear and free. An emptiness filled for a split second with glorious relief.

# About the Author

**JUDY MCCONNELL** was born in Charleston, West Virginia. At age five, she moved with her family to Minneapolis, Minnesota, where she grew up and now resides. She wrote short stories and poetry during her youthful years and holds a BA degree in Comparative Literature from the University of Southern California and a master's in Education from the University of Minnesota.

But it wasn't until retirement from a career as a secondary school teacher and training specialist that she took up writing full time. *The Night Owl Sings* is her fourth published book, and her first book of short stories. She likes to induldge in bridge, hiking, the theater, entertaining at her lake cabin, singing in a community chorale, and most of all, writing down the bones. And top of the line: spending time with her two children and five grandchildren.

www.ingramcontent.com/pod-product-compliance
Lightning Source LLC
Chambersburg PA
CBHW020157070125
20016CB00027B/540